GOD'S GOLDEN ACRE

The inspirational story of one woman's fight
for some of the world's most vulnerable AIDS orphans

A biography of
Heather Reynolds
by **Dale le Vack**

MONARCH
BOOKS

Oxford, UK, and Grand Rapids, Michigan, USA

First published in the UK in 2005 by Monarch Books
(a publishing imprint of Lion Hudson plc),
Mayfield House, 256 Banbury Road, Oxford OX2 7DH
Tel: +44 (0) 1865 302750   Fax: +44 (0) 1865 302757
Email: monarch@lionhudson.com
www.lionhudson.com

Distributed by:
UK: Marston Book Services Ltd, PO Box 269,
Abingdon, Oxon OX14 4YN
USA: Kregel Publications, PO Box 2607,
Grand Rapids, Michigan 49501

ISBN 1 85424 706 9 (UK)
ISBN 0 8254 6085 9 (USA)

British Library Cataloguing Data
A catalogue record for this book is available
from the British Library.

Book design and production for the publishers by Lion Hudson plc.
Printed in the United States.

AUTHOR'S ACKNOWLEDGEMENTS

The idea for a biography of Heather Reynolds was first discussed not in South Africa, but thousands of miles away in Stratford-upon-Avon, England, one summer evening in June 2002. Heather and the Young Zulu Warriors were on a UK tour and we met at the Croft Preparatory School where both the children and adults were staying before their one-night performance in the town.

I was on an assignment for the Stratford Herald to report on both the visit and concert of this unusual party of adults and children from South Africa. They were travelling the country in an old school bus and delighting audiences with their blend of traditional Zulu song and dance. We reckoned in the newsroom at the Herald that the performance of the Young Zulu Warriors would certainly be a change for Stratford audiences from the world of William Shakespeare at the Royal Shakespeare Theatre.

Heather appeared in the garden of the school as the dancers were being lined up in Zulu costume for a photograph. I listened in astonishment as this plump and loquacious woman told me about her life and extraordinary adventures among the thousands of AIDS orphans in the Valley of a Thousand Hills, KwaZulu-Natal. She described how she and her husband Patrick had risked bankruptcy – sacrificing their business and virtually all their worldly material possessions and savings – to bring some form of sanctuary to thousands of needy children. Death and danger had stalked them at every step for more than ten years.

Heather did not consider her story to be of interest to the world and made it clear she would never have the time to write her autobiography. Having just heard a brief account of her life I realised it was certainly a story that should be told, and also one that could help to finance God's Golden Acre and its vital work, as the AIDS pandemic continued to demolish the foundations of rural Zulu society.

"You should find a journalist, a writer, in South Africa and get to work on your story," I told her. A reflective expression came over her face and she beamed the warm smile that is her hallmark. A few days later, after reading my report about the Young Zulu Warriors in the newspaper, she asked me over the telephone to write her life story.

I did not consider the proposition to be practical because of the great distance that separated us. However, a number of factors came into play over the next two years that made our project possible.

Heather and Patrick enjoy coming to England and Europe at least twice a year to recharge their batteries and also to talk to the God's Golden Acre funding organisations and people who run them. Their favourite haunt during these times is Marriage Hill Farm in the Warwickshire village of Bidford-on-Avon.

This is the home of Ann and Brian Smith who are members of a Warwickshire family that has dedicated itself to the cause of God's Golden Acre. In addition to Ann and Brian, prominent among the family are their daughter Angela Foster, granddaughter Lucy Foster, Brian's sister Angela Hands and his brother-in-law Jeff Hands. All have served God's Golden Acre in some way, both in KwaZulu-Natal and in the United Kingdom, and one of them, Rebecca Hands, is currently general manager of God's Golden Acre on a two-year assignment at Cato Ridge with her partner Tom Ward-Jackson.

Over a period of two years Heather and I recorded many hours of conversation at Marriage Hill Farm about her life. Once the early drafts were written, having culminated in a visit by myself to God's Golden Acre at Christmas 2003, Ann Smith played a key support role in helping me to bring the project to fruition. The book could not have been written without that support.

The other great support of the project was literary agent Robert Dudley who expressed great enthusiasm for the proposed book from an early stage and whose wise counsel ensured it emerged as an acceptable piece of work for our publisher, Monarch Books of Oxford, to consider. I must thank my old school friend Andrew Trotman for the introduction to Robert.

Many contributors to the book have enhanced its perspective – both of Heather, and of her inspirational work as founder of God's Golden Acre. Paramount among these is Susan Balfour. Her journals have been quoted in this book and have added perception and sensitivity to the manuscript. Susan Balfour was an early volunteer at God's Golden Acre at Cato Ridge and her vivid accounts of life there through the eyes of a volunteer nurse have been complemented by those from Hugh Evans, Lucy Foster, Vibeke Blaker, Marianne Jenum, Sophie Wong, Helen Beresford and Esther Perenyi. I should also like to thank Orin Wilson for his original thoughts about Heather and her family, and Gael Tremaux for a long conversation about God's Golden Acre that extended into the early hours of one morning while on a game park weekend with the children.

Others who have helped to provide a deep and personal insight into Heather and her work as a leading humanitarian include her husband Patrick Reynolds, daughter Bronwen Reynolds, and Heather's sister Myrtle Venter.

Outside the family Alan McCarthy, the chairman of God's Golden Acre, and Dr Gerrit Ter Haar, the deputy chairman, also made meaningful contributions, as did the benefactors Gerrit and Anneke Mons. On the staff at God's Golden Acre, Mary Van der Leeuw, Rosetta Heunis, Cheryl Harris and Alta Collins all went out of their way to help me collect background information about how things are run under Heather's management of the children's sanctuary and the rural outreach projects.

A highly readable account of his visit to God's Golden Acre was provided by my former colleague, BBC producer Bill Hamilton, and I am also grateful to Oprah Winfrey, Heather's great friend, in allowing me to use extracts from her published works on her altruistic and humanitarian work in South Africa, and in particular her visits to God's Golden Acre where she is "mother" to a number of children.

Among Heather's African "children" I owe thanks to Zanele Jila. She is a young woman of great beauty and intelligence who I believe will be among the first whose childhood spent at God's Golden Acre, and also higher education, will be repaid through a lifetime of achievement and dedication among her Zulu people.

From the valley, Nkosi Mlaba of KwaXimba was most generous in the help he gave me in providing vital information about Zulu culture, and the political and economic structure of rural life in KwaZulu-Natal. I should also like to thank an old friend, Clive Bromilow of Howick, for his hospitality and introductions to the farming communities in the region – and also for allowing me to draw information from his book, *Problem Plants of South Africa*, published by Bayer. Another old friend, Martin Edwards, President of Manchester United, was tireless in helping Heather to have the ear of other very important men in the world of professional football. These include Dave Richards, chairman of the Premier League, who has become one of Heather's major advocates, and David Davies, Executive Director of the Football Association. Finally, my thanks to Chris Towner, Editor of the Stratford Herald, for his support during the two demanding years when the book was in its gestation period.

Dale le Vack
March 2005

CONTENTS

Introduction   9

Part One   15
1. Easter 1965   16
2. Many Years Later… a Miracle at Mpolweni   21
3. Football, Funerals, Miracles – *Over the Rainbow*   26
4. Christmas Week   35
5. Christmas Eve   49
6. Christmas Morning   55

Part Two   61
7. Life on the Trading Station   62
8. Children in the Wilderness   65
9. The Family History   71
10. The Odd One Out   77
11. Love at First Sight   84
12. Betrayal and Divorce   89
13. A Foolish Decision   96
14. A New Life with Patrick   110
15. Heather Returns to God   116
16. The Deep Valley Years   124
17. A Life-changing Journey   141

Part Three   151

18. The Establishment of God's Golden Acre   152
19. The Horrors of the Valley   165
20. Local Hostility to God's Golden Acre   173
21. The Norwegian Volunteers Arrive   179
22. Bankruptcy Looms   184
23. The Street Protest   188
24. Heather's Desperate Gamble   199
25. Hatred and Resentment Grows   203
26. Buying McPherson Farm   207
27. A Man She Could do Business with   213
28. More Miracles Follow   220
29. More Volunteers Arrive   226
30. The Death of Thulani and the Inspiration of Ellie   233
31. Volunteers and Visitors in the Valley   235
32. Practical Hands Arrive... and More Miracles   243
33. The Young Zulu Warriors Tour the UK   247
34. Oprah Winfrey Comes to God's Golden Acre   254
35. The Children of God's Golden Acre   263
36. Symbols of Reconciliation   269
37. "I Feel Like Crying till I Die... "   278
38. A Treat for the Orphans   287
39. The Little Boy from Uppington   292
40. A Prophet in Her Own Land   296
41. Over the Rainbow   301
42. The Football Miracle   308
43. The Parable of the Good Samaritan   315

INTRODUCTION

In 1993 on a trip to Uganda, South African Heather Reynolds turned a corner that would change her life for ever. Heather was visiting a remote part of the country, and she encountered by chance the human and social devastation the AIDS pandemic leaves in its wake. She came face to face with the worst scourge to afflict humankind since the medieval plagues, and one that has destroyed the lives of millions of children. As she got out of her car at a small settlement to get water from a spring, she met a group of children, the orphaned victims of AIDS. Here she witnessed their misery and terror as they awaited death by starvation, uncared for by adults.

Some years before that day, Heather Reynolds had given her life to God but was waiting for the call to serve him. At that moment she knew this was his call. Slowly, she knelt down in the native hut and looked upon a little boy covered by a dirty sack. His parents had either abandoned him, or they themselves had died. He was spending his last hours alone and uncared for. The African child and the white woman could not communicate because of the barrier of language. The boy lay still, waiting for death, and the look in his eyes stills haunts Heather, even though, in later years, she has encountered many more young AIDS victims, some of whom have died in her arms.

She promised God she would live, for the rest of her life if necessary, by serving him in the cause of caring for, and nursing, babies and children orphaned by the AIDS pandemic. Heather decided she would use her life savings to provide shelter for orphaned children. Earlier, she had taken in pregnant girls to work in her pottery in the 1980s, and also provided sanctuary for youngsters left homeless as a result of the civil disorder in KwaZulu-Natal during the decade of transition to majority rule in 1994.

Now, believing they were answering God's call, Heather and her husband Patrick Reynolds, a well-known sculptor, filled their home at Wartburg, in KwaZulu-Natal, with sick and abandoned children. They called their little community "God's Golden Acre". From there, in 1999, God's Golden Acre moved on to become a cluster of foster homes at Cato Ridge, a few miles away. Built on the top of a hill, it is near to the Valley of a Thousand Hills, a vast rural area between Durban and Pietermaritzburg. Approximately 95 children, between the ages of a few months and 16 years, live in the community.

Most of Heather's children are healthy. Many HIV-positive babies die before their first birthday; few make it beyond their fourth. God's Golden Acre is designed as a sanctuary to allow this small minority to die with dignity in a loving environment, and as a family home for the surviving children, who are well fed, cheerful, confident, and attend the best local state schools. Then there is a series of rural outreach programmes for thousands of orphans who are living in extended families in the Valley of a Thousand Hills. Heather's teams of staff and volunteers distribute basic food supplies to the *ad hoc* families she has helped to create, many headed by an elderly "granny" figure, or a teenage girl. The teams supply rice, salt, mealie-meal, samp beans, and other basic foodstuffs.

Each day they rub shoulders with death, gaze upon the expressionless faces of the abused, and sometimes encounter both hostility and resentment. Heather drives her familiar

Land Rover alone into remote countryside to visit the sick and dying, offering comfort and prayer, and rescuing children. To many of the Zulus in the Valley of a Thousand Hills, Heather has become known as Mawethu, which means "our mother", or Gogo, our "gran".

Within the whole of Southern Africa, KwaZulu-Natal has the greatest number of HIV/AIDS cases. In 2000, 36 percent of its people were recorded as infected, eight percent higher than in the capital province of Gauteng. Among TB cases in KwaZulu-Natal, 55 percent were infected with HIV/AIDS, as were 37 percent of its pregnant women, and 80 percent of its prostitutes.

Many believe this tragic situation is an appalling legacy from the country's advanced motorway network – unique in Africa – that opened up the vast rural hinterland 30 years ago. Initially these new road networks brought greater prosperity to a land blessed with natural resources and a diversity of climates for producing food and wine. Later they became the arteries through which the virus multiplied itself. The drivers of the great juggernauts, away from home sometimes for weeks, travelling into and out of South Africa, use the services of the army of sex workers who can be found waiting for them at gas stations or walking along the verges of the highways. The men become infected with the HIV virus and then bring it home with them to the rural areas – with deadly consequences.

Similarly, young men from areas such as the Valley of a Thousand Hills can only find work in the towns and cities, and migrate there – returning occasionally to infect those that they love. It is an endless cycle fuelled by ignorance, and sometimes indifference. In these stricken lands of the AIDS pandemic, where murder, hijack and robbery are common, it is mostly grandmothers and older siblings who are left to cope with the responsibility of bringing up the family's children. Their own deceased offspring, the working adult generation, have disappeared, victims of the virus.

These extended families are impoverished, and the *gogos* (grandmothers) who run them find it increasingly difficult to provide for their young ones. Only a few have piped water to their home, electricity, fuel or opportunities for employment – factors which make it more difficult for the small groups to survive. Failing health and almost non-existent medical facilities further add to the seriousness of the situation. Adolescent girls are vulnerable to rape and abuse by adults. The South African state is making grants available to the needy child-led families in the valleys, but the bureaucracy that supports their distribution to genuine claimants tries in vain to process a huge backlog. In the end the grants seem inaccessible to the largely uneducated people in the remote areas.

Much of the help the children receive is dependent upon individuals like Heather, working with the support of other non-government organizations and a patchwork of charities that include the Rockefeller Brothers Foundation, Rotary clubs, HopeHIV and a London-based network of South Africans called Starfish, founded by Anthony Farr, who spent nine months at God's Golden Acre. His charity draws on the donations of expatriates working in London, who are being paid in sterling. Many Dutch charitable foundations have also been extremely supportive of God's Golden Acre.

However, until recently Heather has been alone in her task. It is only because of her total commitment to her work that she has been able to establish sufficient trust and respect within these desperate communities to bring relief to the needy. As she has continued walking her lonely path in the Valley of a Thousand Hills, it is the world that has come to find her. Heather has received growing news media coverage in all of South Africa's major papers, in British newspapers like the *Guardian*, and in television broadcasts in South Africa and on the BBC, ABC, CNN and Norwegian TV news.

The scale of what Heather has achieved over a number of years has come to the attention of both Nelson Mandela and

Archbishop Desmond Tutu. The international press is now becoming aware of the significance of Heather's work. She is a mother figure to thousands of children. In 2002 the American broadcasting star Oprah Winfrey visited God's Golden Acre and brought film crews to the valley. Deeply moved by what she found, Oprah Winfrey arranged for her private Foundation to fund projects, at God's Golden Acre and a rural outreach project.

Lucy Foster was one of the first European volunteer workers to arrive at God's Golden Acre in 2000 when she was 19 years old. She writes:

You will find 97 happy children – Heather is responsible for most of them being alive and for them being well-adjusted children with strong hopes for the future. Many of the orphans now go to very good schools thanks to sponsorship. In the valley there are thousands more people whose lives have been touched by her through the rural outreach programmes.

Heather now has pilot projects – such as the Strategic National Action Plan (SNAP) and the Child Sponsorship Programme – that could make a major contribution to fighting the effects of the AIDS pandemic in South Africa. We all pray that those who have the power politically will help her to make it happen, and that the general public in all countries will get to hear about what she is doing, and give her support.

Her faith in God, and her journey through the years with him, is part of the story of an amazing life that will surely appeal to people of all religions throughout the world, whether Muslim, Jew, Hindu or Buddhist. She is the personification, in our era, of the Good Samaritan.

Alan McCarthy, chairman of God's Golden Acre, shares Heather's strength of faith, conviction and belief in miracles: "I know many people who walk closely with God – and wonderful miracles happen because God can use them as a channel. It's not their own power, and they will be the first to say that. So they are not performing the miracles. Heather is no better or worse than most average people – but she is allowing God to use her, trying to let God guide her. When she prays she allows God's power to flow into the situation – so it's not Heather, it's God."

On a special episode of "The Oprah Winfrey Show" that highlighted her ChristmasKindness South Africa 2002 initiative and also included information on the AIDS pandemic in South Africa, Oprah Winfrey pledged to devote the rest of her life to the cause and interests of its orphans. The influential American TV talk show host, whose programme is distributed to more than 100 countries, told millions of her viewers that a child is orphaned through AIDS in South Africa every fourteen seconds – during the hour-long programme 257 children would be orphaned. She said: "Many of us are really just not aware of the challenges so many children face… My life was changed when I saw firsthand the devastation that AIDS is having on the lives of children and families in South Africa, as well as other parts of the world. [The] AIDS [pandemic] has become, as my friend Bono says, the defining moral issue of our time. For children, many of them already devastatingly poor, who are now left motherless, there is no question, no question at all, that we have to help them right now. We are human beings sharing the planet with other human beings, and we cannot continue to ignore one of the greatest crises facing humanity in our lifetime."

Part One

1
EASTER 1965

For years afterwards, the Xhosa herdsman talked about the night he saw the ghost truck in the hills on the Flagstaff road to the Wild Coast. It made him famous locally and he would take pleasure from terrifying his children with the story. By the time the herdsman's children had their own offspring, the tale had passed into local legend. To this day the Xhosa regard it as a haunted stretch of road.

It was Easter 1965. The fog was thick and the herdsman could hear the noise of an approaching truck. Then he could see headlights, yellow eyes in a wall of mist. It did not sound normal and he felt fear gripping him. The labouring engine was rising and then falling back, as the accelerator was applied and then released.

The apparition approached at a slow speed – not much greater than the jogging pace of a man. As the Xhosa stepped aside, a horse that had been hidden in the mist reared in fright and the cream-coloured Dodge truck swerved to avoid it. The herdsman peered through the windscreen and muttered an oath, his heart beating faster, his feet welded to the spot. He wanted to run away.

The truck had no driver. All he could see was a small pair of white hands gripping the steering wheel. The man's gasp of alarm went unheeded in the wilderness. He ran terrified to his kraal. The Xhosa had witnessed the supernatural, and this was not a good omen for his family.

What the Xhosa didn't see at the wheel of the Dodge was a diminutive girl of less than five feet, in her early teens with cropped blonde hair, wearing yellow shorts, and a hand-me-down white T-shirt belonging to an older brother. She was slightly chubby with sad brown eyes, and a determined jaw. Fourteen-year-old Heather McLellan had never driven any vehicle in her life, but she was at the wheel of one now, on one of the Transkei's most dangerous roads. It connects Kokstad with Flagstaff in Pondoland and has claimed the lives of many people over the years with its sheer drops and unguarded sharp bends. Its worst hazard, the 5,285-feet Brooks Nek Pass, is well known.

Heather could hardly reach the pedals of the truck from the driving position; her head was level with the bottom of the windscreen. After the Flagstaff turning to the Wild Coast, the road becomes a dust track and is much narrower. There are hairpin bends and sloping drops. Untended cattle, horses, donkeys, wander the mountain passes at night, creating further sudden hazards for the unprepared. As she drove, Heather prayed for guidance and protection. She was praying when the horse reared as she passed the Xhosa, but never noticed his presence. Her eyes were fixed on the dangers ahead. Beside her, asleep on the seat, was eleven-year-old Basil. Next to him sprawled John McLellan, drunk and oblivious to anything going on around him. The constant pleading of the engine for release into a higher gear filled Heather's ears.

Twelve hours earlier, the two youngsters had broken up for their Easter holidays from Kokstad High School, where they were boarders. They should have been home hours before. For years the McLellan children had dreaded the end of term. They feared it because their father regarded the occasion as an opportunity to meet up with his old comrades at the bars of various hotels. By the time he arrived at the school he was more boisterous – and much louder – than the sober adults who had also come to collect their children.

The McLellans were never teased about their father, but his behaviour was an embarrassment to his daughter. It had always been the same at the end of term over a period of seven years. In daylight it should have been a two-hour journey. The route would take the truck about fifteen miles through the tarmac mountain road from Kokstad, a further 22 miles after turning left at the Flagstaff turn onto the dirt road towards the Wild Coast, and then a further 16 miles along a narrow track to a dead end at the remote trading post at Madada.

Under normal circumstances, the youngsters should have been eagerly anticipating the delights of home and a welcome cuddle from Mum. But it never turned out like that. Once John McLellan had driven away from the school in late afternoon, he never had any intention of getting back home as soon as he could. Without exception the war veteran would want to play snooker with his old comrades – usually winning round after round. He would find old pals in the hotel bars of Kokstad, then he'd insist upon driving to another small town called Mt Ayliffe, and there join a second group of snooker-playing veterans to drink until one or two in the morning. He would leave the depressed children in the front cabin of the Dodge to await his drunken return, returning only occasionally with some money to send them to a tea room, or enable them to buy a glass of lemonade and a packet of chips.

The problem at Easter 1965 was that Heather's older brother and sister, who had usually shared her misery and long hours of waiting, and who always took over the responsibility of driving home, had now left the school. This time Heather was shouldering the responsibility for getting young Basil and herself safely back to the Madada trading post. Her father had promised their mother he would not go drinking, but he had forgotten that promise many hours before the Xhosa herdsman saw them. After drinking until eleven o'clock that night in Kokstad, he was drunk but wanted more.

"Please, Dad, let's go home. Please, Dad, please, Dad, don't drink any more," Heather pleaded – but he ignored the Flagstaff turn and began the long and dangerous ascent through the mountains to Mt Ayliffe. The children waited outside the small town hotel for a further two hours while their father drank with the other customers inside. At one stage a young policeman wandered out of the hotel and stood on the veranda, looking with interest at the teenager in the Dodge. For a moment the girl thought she could ask him to help her extract her father from the bar. Perhaps he might issue a stiff warning to him about the dangers of drinking and driving.

"Hey, could you tell Uncle Mac we want to go home now?" she asked him. However, as he sauntered back towards the bar with a grin on his face, Heather was old enough to sense that the policeman's motives had more to do with sexual opportunism than the call of duty. She became more frightened as he pestered her on several occasions. "Just go away and leave us alone, please," she eventually snapped. He lost interest and wandered back to the bar.

At last, John McLellan staggered out of the hotel. He slumped inside the cabin of the Dodge, stupefied by alcohol, and was soon losing consciousness. Heather shunted the big man to the edge of the bench and got behind the wheel herself. She knew where the pedals were, and what they were for, but couldn't reach them. She was too small to shift the gears in a normal way. The girl at length managed to start the vehicle and moved off, lurching forward in second gear, where the truck stayed for the rest of the journey.

At five o'clock in the morning, after more than four hours at the wheel of the Dodge, Heather finally arrived back at Madada trading station. Brenda McLellan was waiting by the gate as it pulled up. She opened the door and gasped with astonishment when she saw her daughter at the wheel. "Good

God!" she said. "We're going to have to give you some driving lessons! I think we'll start tomorrow."

The children walked with their mother into the house. John McLellan was left to snore the rest of his night out in the Dodge. The following day he didn't ask how he'd got home, and the subject was never mentioned afterwards.

2
MANY YEARS LATER...
A MIRACLE AT
MPOLWENI

Patrick Reynolds sat in silence in his studio and pondered over what he had heard from his wife at breakfast. It had not pleased him. He never intervened in Heather's pastoral work, but he objected strongly when she told him she wanted to go to Mpolweni to find out what she could do to help distressed people living there. Heather Reynolds has never been renowned for taking the advice of others – and that morning she had chosen not to heed her husband.

"Why do you *have* to go Mpolweni? It is not safe for white people. You will be taking an unacceptable risk. Don't do it. There are so many people that need you in the valley areas where you are a familiar figure," he warned her. But Heather decided to go anyway.

Mpolweni is an informal settlement, 20 miles from Pietermaritzburg, where the Church of Scotland once established a mission. Several thousand Zulus live there. Many of the Africans living there still had a deep hatred for anyone connected with the former white government. White people did not go there alone unless they had to. A popular slogan among the Zulus in Mpolweni in the 1990s was "One bullet, one Boer".

Heather had been working without serious mishap in Swayimane and the neighbouring Trust Feed, but for several years she had been too scared to venture into Mpolweni, with its network of narrow tracks that seemed to lead nowhere. This day, however, she felt the call that she must go there – despite the risk, and regardless of Patrick's advice. She recalls: "First I drove over to a minister who lived close to, but not actually in Mpolweni, and asked him if he would help me to find where the *nkosi* (chief) actually lived. It was Zulu proto-col for me to first ask the *nkosi* if he would give permission for me to help the people of Mpolweni. The *nkosi* would then con-sult with his councillors and headmen before committing himself. The minister agreed to help me. I had brought with me some of my own little children from God's Golden Acre, and he said some of his children could also ride with us.

"So we drove into Mpolweni, but I soon got confused. This was unfamiliar territory without tarmac roads and signposts – and we got horribly, horribly lost. Then my truck got stuck in a ditch as I tried to do a U-turn on a narrow track. A Zulu boy of about 16 who said his name was Eric Zondi came walking past and offered to help. I was grateful for the offer from this lad and sent him with a small group of the older girls up the road to ask local people to come and help push us out.

"Suddenly I heard my girls screaming – some were as young as eight years old – and I raced up the track to find that a group of drunken men were accosting them. For a moment it looked as if they would assault me too. Fortunately, Eric had the presence of mind to tell the drunks: 'She's going to see the *nkosi*. She is a friend of the *nkosi*.' It worked. The men released the girls, backed off, and went away. With Eric's help we man-aged to release the truck, but we spent the rest of the after-noon going this way, and that way, in confusion and mounting anxiety as Eric asked people if they knew where the *nkosi* lived. It was dusk when we eventually arrived at his house.

"Then I remembered that I should not be asking for a meet-ing with the *nkosi* at this time of day. In Zulu culture you never visit a family at dusk – for this is the time when both good and bad spirits move around. People often sweep their houses just before dusk to ward off evil spirits. However, having taken so long to get there, I decided to take the risk and asked a woman at the house if I could speak to the *nkosi*. She told us to wait, went inside the house, and consulted with him. When she returned some time later she said: 'Yes, Nkosi Mgadi will see you but he is not feeling well, so you will have to wait for him.'

"We stayed outside the house probably for about an hour and by now it was pitch-dark. Night had descended. So there we were, in the night, in an area where many Africans hated white people – and I was alone with my children. I had no idea how we would find our way out of Mpolweni and it scared me. Eventually we were asked to go into the house, and as I led the children up the steps and into the living room, they sang a Zulu song.

"I gasped inwardly when I saw the *nkosi* sitting in a chair against the wall. He was very sick, and I thought, *This man is dying. He can hardly breathe. Everything about him looks bad – the pallor, the sweating, the gasping for breath, the high fever. He is dreadfully ill.* I apologized for coming without invitation so late in the day and when he was unwell, and explained I had tried to telephone him several times but the lines were not working. Then I told him briefly who we were, why we had come, and what we wanted. There was a silence as he scrutinized me and fought for breath, his fever mounting. Then he nodded to indicate that he would consult with his headmen and let me know the outcome. He seemed positive about me, despite his condition.

"The meeting was over, but I heard myself asking him if he wanted me to pray for him. I could see from the way he was breathing and sweating that he was very, very ill. It was a dilemma for me – if I prayed for the *nkosi* and he died, or didn't survive, they would probably say I had brought a bad spirit with me, pointing to the fact that I had come in the dark. They might also say that I was not a good minister, that my power was weak. This could have negative consequences for God's Golden Acre.

"As I stood before him with my little children, a voice within me was warning that I should not pray for him. For a moment I had doubts about the power of prayer. I knew that I would not be praying for someone who was sick, but for someone who was dying. The tiny voice, from deep within, whispered, *What if God does not heal him?* but I knew I had to do it. Then, as I began to pray, my faith came flooding back. I realized that I could not walk away from this *nkosi*. I remembered what Jesus said about faith, the mustard seed, and the mountain: 'With the faith of a mustard seed you can move a mountain; what you ask in my name will be done; these things you will do and greater things.'

"When somebody is really sick, it is beholden upon us – as Christians – to pray. So I prayed with fervour and intensity – a greater intensity in fact than at any time in my life. I also laid my hands on his head, which I later discovered is contrary to Zulu custom. I finished praying, and as I turned around in the dim light I felt a shock go right through my body as I looked straight up into the faces of three Zulu men. They were standing behind my back. I had to control myself not to scream out loud. They looked down at me with expressionless eyes, but I had nothing to fear. Nkosi Mgadi introduced his son, and his friends. They were not hostile and we were allowed to leave in peace.

"For ten days I could not get back to the *nkosi* because the telephones were not working. Thieves had stolen all the copper wire. Eventually, however, I did get through and suddenly a man answered. It was a young-sounding voice.

" 'I'm trying to get hold of Nkosi Mgadi, old Nkosi Mgadi,' I said.

" 'This is old Nkosi Mgadi,' he replied.

"The tears poured down my face. 'Have you recovered?' I asked, incredulous.

" 'Yes, I'm well,' he replied.

"A few months later I asked an African teacher I knew, and who lived in Mpolweni, whether Chief Mgadi was still in a good state of health. 'Oh, yes, it's wonderful,' she said. 'He went on the radio and told everybody how he was healed one night by a white woman who came and prayed in his house.'"

3

FOOTBALL, FUNERALS, MIRACLES - OVER THE RAINBOW

Sipho and Thando, two Zulu brothers, not yet teenagers, squat on their haunches beside the potholed track in the midday sun. They screw up their eyes in a competition to get the first glimpse of the lorry approaching in the dust along the mountain road.

There is tranquillity in their valley, KwaXimba, which might persuade the traveller that he has stumbled into paradise. As the sun rises, children fish with hand-lines in a river that tumbles through the boulders into swirling pools, women wash their clothes in chattering groups, cattle and goats graze on the bush grasses. But Sipho and Thando often go hungry, and soon their clothes will be little better than rags. Both boys are orphans of the AIDS pandemic, although no one has told them so. They only know that their mother, and then their father, died of what they were told was tuberculosis, leaving an older sister in charge of four younger siblings. Some uncles buried their mother in the garden, and a few months later their father joined her.

For Sipho and Thando it is a time recalled through horrendous nightmares – visions from the subconscious that feature repulsive skeletal demons arisen from graveyards, stalking them from the shadows of the dark. The boys wake up screaming in the night. Their last memories of those funerals are the coffins, the ritual Zulu burial, the singing at the graveside, and the putting to rest, with customary respect, of the bodies of the dead. Two mounds of red earth, close to the hut where Sipho and Thando live, reveal where their parents were interred side by side beneath a mound of stones.

The boys cannot go to school now, because their sisters do not earn enough money to pay the school fees. Relatives bring mealie-meal to the mud hut, which is rapidly deteriorating, and the men who come to see their sisters sometimes bring cabbages and potatoes. The child-headed family survives — just — but the younger ones can only hope their sisters don't get sick too. The garden is untended, nothing has been planted, and the fowls have been killed. Both boys are unwell and suffer constant pain. The brothers experience debilitation through tapeworm. They are emaciated, yet their bellies are distended. Skin irritations, including ringworm and scabies, itch on their arms and legs, and everywhere they are covered in sores.

Today, however, hunger and pain are not in the thoughts of Sipho and Thando. They are excited. Today is special, like no other Saturday they can remember, and it makes them feel happy. For once, there is a fluttering sensation inside their bellies. They grin at each other. The boys are waiting for a four-ton truck to pick them up and take them, along with 50 other Zulu boys, to a football ground.

Most of the lads that Sipho and Thando will travel with in the lorry cannot read or write. A few have only basic schooling. But ask them questions about football! The demi-gods of the world in which they exist are African football players like Mbulelo Mabizela, Siyabonga Nomvete, Arthur Zwane and John Moshhoeu. Football offers them hope, and it feeds their dreams.

Nkosi Mlaba, councillors like Simon Ngubane, and important people from as far away as Durban, including the mayor, and some soccer stars, are also going to the football ground today. There will be singing, dancing and food — and maybe, just maybe, a chance for the boys to fulfil a dream. They might play in a real game of football, and kick a proper ball. The youngsters know it is all something to do with the white *gogo* they call Mawethu, from Cato Ridge, who owns the truck upon which they are about to climb. She has started a boys' soccer league, which is all they have heard. They are not sure. However, Sipho and Thando are certain they want to be part of it – whatever it is.

There are thousands of children like Sipho and Thando, who have lost their parents. The other orphan boys want to play football too, but there is no money in the valleys where they live. Community life, as the Zulus in the rural areas have known it for hundreds of years, is in decay. There are funerals every Friday, Saturday and Sunday. Children are dying. The impact is devastating.

A generation of young people has gone absent from school in the valley, because no one can afford to pay the fees. The children are turning towards each other to find comfort. A false sense of security comes from being in gangs. It leads to drug taking, violence and crime. Marijuana grows every-where. Then there is the temptation of glue sniffing to alleviate the hunger, the pain and the misery.

The white *gogo* has met Nkosi Mlaba and the local council-lor. She told them: "We must get these children into some sort of organized sport. They love soccer. They are soccer fanatics. The easiest thing to do is just give them an opportunity to become part of a football team. It's the biggest gift you could give any of them. All we need to do is get it started. These are our leaders of tomorrow. They are wonderful chil-dren, let's give them an opportunity, but we will need a mir-acle. I must find someone with influence in the world of professional football, perhaps in England, who can help us."

A few miles from the dilapidated hut where Sipho and Thando live, an old African woman is sitting on a mat in the shadows and staring across the hills through an open door. The room is cleared of its meagre furniture in preparation for a funeral. A Xhosa, this woman came to the valley many years before to marry a Zulu. Like many African mothers, she carried the burden of bringing up her children alone. The nearest work was in Durban, nearly 30 miles away. To keep them alive she had to leave them in the house alone. *Leave them behind, leave them behind. Don't look back.* When it was dark, they sometimes experienced deprivation and terror — but it was the only way to protect them.

The Xhosa woman was torn, her emotions in turmoil. Some of the children did not get a proper schooling and one of these was Sibongile, her eldest daughter. The children grew to become young adults but gradually began to die in the late 1990s. Now four of the eight are gone. In a few hours Sibongile will return in her coffin from the undertaker for the funeral. The African woman feels the presence of spirits.

Soon the white visitors will come to pay their respects and this reminds her of the day when she walked in desperation from her valley to the orphan settlement run by a white *gogo* at Cato Ridge. She had heard about this woman, and the orphaned children who lived with her. She had begged the woman for a job. The white woman told her she was too old. She begged some more. The white woman gave her work helping out in the kitchen. It was the turning point in the long and hard life of Gogo Beauty, who was to become a much-loved caregiver at God's Golden Acre.

Sibongile was discharged from the local hospital because they said they could no longer help her. She was admitted to the hospice at God's Golden Acre for palliative care. Soon Gogo Beauty and her younger daughter Zani were told that infection had spread to Sibongile's brain. She would die within the next few days, they said. Gogo Beauty insisted Sibongile be taken home and within days she passed away, surrounded by her family. She was 29 years old and left two surviving children, aged eight and twelve.

During the days following the death of her daughter, Gogo Beauty remains on a mat on the floor of her living room and is attended to, day and night, by neighbours. In Zulu culture, the bereaved mother or wife should not be left alone until after the funeral. People come to offer comfort and practical support. They sing and pray together. Sibongile's body is there, having been returned from the undertaker that afternoon.

The funeral next day is long and emotional. All the mourners are seated under a tarpaulin erected at the side of the mud-and-stick hut. "KZNFC" is painted in bright yellow on all the benches provided; it is not the provincial football team, but KwaZulu-Natal Funeral Club. Grannies contribute a regular sum so that they can bury their children, or grandchildren, with dignity. The service over, the coffin is carried along the dirt track down the slope to a prepared grave in the garden. The coffin is lowered – more singing – then the grave is filled, the mound covered with large stones, and a crucifix planted. The mourners' memory of Sibongile will live on.

Now the group of orphans whom Gogo Beauty is supporting on her small income is growing, but she does not complain. The phone rings at God's Golden Acre. It is the hospital in Pietermaritzburg. An eight-year-old girl called Thandi, who has been physically abused and abandoned, needs a home. On arrival, her sunken eyes and her swollen yet frail body tell the inevitable story of neglect and starvation. She is so withdrawn and timid that Gogo Heather cannot reach into her mind and get her to respond to the new surroundings, even though she tries hard to counsel, stimulate and care for her. Thandi won't sing or join in any of the games. Her tiny body makes her look strange; she feels the difference between herself and the other strong, more robust children.

At night Gogo Heather and the African caregivers sit beside her bed for hours, comforting Thandi as nightmares rack her mind. She cries out in anguish. Gogo Heather writes in her diary: "I can still hear her strangled cries. I can still feel the hopelessness and pain as I stroke her tiny little body helplessly, trying to reassure her, wishing I could in some way take away some of the fear and terror that rack her little mind. Thandi's nightmares continue for several hours until finally she falls into a deep exhausted sleep."

Time passes and Thandi starts to gain weight. Her sores begin to heal. New clothes improve her outward appearance but her mind is still locked away and communication is difficult. Gogo cannot take her to a male doctor for examination, as her fear will escalate into panic within seconds. She is terrified of men. Natascha, a Dutch missionary girl, and Gogo Heather are the only ones with whom she will relax.

Gogo still cannot find the secret of how to get her to smile and laugh — no matter how hard she tries. Thandi's tiny pointed face remains serious and sombre. During December, Natascha and Gogo Heather take all the toddlers to Durban. Thandi comes along too. She is still fragile and only feels secure when she is close to Gogo.

There are problems on the journey. The old Mercedes that Dorcas South Africa has donated to God's Golden Acre breaks down, and the party are forced to spend an extra two days in Durban. While they wait for the repairs to be done, Gogo takes the children to the beach. She wades into the shallow waves, holding Thandi's hand. All the toddlers are shrieking with laughter and trepidation. Suddenly, very close to her, Gogo Heather hears the strangest cackling sound. She turns around to see what is making this strange noise. It is coming from Thandi and she is laughing. Gogo Heather writes:

Her face is beaming with an expression I'll never forget, as the waves swirl around her. We all just stare at her, totally dumbstruck, and then we all join in laughing and splashing, tears of joy and seawater mingling together. We watch as this miracle is taking place. It is as though the water is washing away all the memories that have frozen her mind. The healing has begun.

Today Thandi is a well-adjusted little girl; she sleeps soundly and plays happily with all the other children. My son Brendan, who is six feet two and very athletic, loves teasing and playing with her and it is such a blessing to hear her squeal with laughter as he pretends to chase and catch her. I thank our Father for this miracle and we continue to see the miracle of his wondrous love as we take care daily of the little ones he has entrusted to our care.

In another valley fourteen-year-old Andile collects what wood he can find in the dry scrubland. He bundles it up before making the three-mile trip back to his grandmother's rondavel. He has already collected water from the well that is 20 minutes walk from the hut. Andile has plenty of time to do these daily tasks, for he no longer goes to school.

The boy has a limp but walks home painfully to find his grandmother pouring water into a pot. She looks at the bundle of sticks carried by Andile and mentally calculates there will be just enough fire to heat the mealie-meal. A small child, a girl of about four, runs out of the rondavel to Andile. She is dressed in rags and her legs are no thicker than most of the sticks that Andile has collected. Her hair is matted and her elfin face is creased in a smile.

"I saw my mummy today," she announces in excitement, whispering the words in his ear as if revealing a secret. Andile shakes his head and says nothing. There is nothing to say. His mother and father are buried in the garden. His older teenage sister is dead too. Now there are just the two of them and their grandmother – who is nearly blind. He walks with the girl into the hut and says quietly to his grandmother: "I must go now."

Some miles away at God's Golden Acre great excitement is afoot. The Golden Acre Singers, a new choir that Gogo has put into place, drawn from the youngsters who live with her as well as others from the nearby rural areas, are all taking part in a talent contest to identify talented performers. A music producer from England has arrived to record vocal and backing tracks. He will then return to Birmingham to edit the music, with other tracks already recorded in England, into a CD album.

There are more than 40 people, including children and young adults up to the age of 23, in the new community theatre at God's Golden Acre, all of whom are overwhelmed with excitement at this opportunity. The music producer and the choir work hard all day, recording tracks and rehearsing for each of the nine titles. Late in the afternoon the producer notices an adolescent boy standing quietly apart from the choir. He is not part of it and does not sing. He looks at the floor to avoid eye contact. The music producer ignores the boy – he has much work to do in the four remaining days he has in South Africa.

The boy is there again the following day in the late afternoon and his appearance this time evokes a response from the producer. He speaks to Gogo Heather, who is helping to direct the choir. "Who is that boy?" he asks.

"He wants to be in the choir," she replies.

"Then why doesn't he show up with everyone else at nine o'clock?" asks the record producer.

"Andile is an orphan from the valley. He has to collect water and wood for his grandmother. It takes several hours, and then he has to walk three miles to get here from his home. So he always misses the choir practice. But he hopes to be a singer one day and he is talented," she explains.

The music producer looks at the Zulu lad and feels a knot in his throat. The boy is still avoiding eye contact.

The producer speaks with his companions, two Rotarians from England who masterminded the CD album. The record producer says to Gogo Heather, "We want to help this boy – ask him if he would like a bicycle." She suggests it might be better to buy the boy a musical instrument so that he could learn to play it and earn money as a street performer. However, she confers in Zulu with the lad, who listens to her question and shakes his head before replying.

She turns to the three Englishmen. "He says he would rather have a school uniform because without one he cannot go to school."

Now Andile has both a bicycle and a school uniform. He is one of the lucky ones.

4
CHRISTMAS WEEK

The woman spoke. "We call it the silent killer. Someone is lying there dying in about every third dwelling, in the darkness and cold. You don't see it... somebody in a bed, just dying quietly. It's not noticeable, not visible – and that's why it's very hard to get the world to react to it. It's not like a disaster where there's a flood and things are visible – where the houses are floating away and there are bodies being washed down the river. Here every night, people are just dying, and every few days there are dozens of people being buried."

A white Land Rover, driven by a small blonde woman of heavy build, turns off the tarmac road at the bottom of Sankontshe valley in KwaZulu-Natal, and begins the tortuous ascent of a slope along a potholed track. Her hands grasp the steering wheel of the vehicle as she continues talking, while looking intently into the mist and driving rain, through the arc created by the windscreen wipers. Streaks of lightning illuminate the misty horizon in the Valley of a Thousand Hills, the rural hinterland that lies between Durban and Pietermaritzburg.

White people keep away from places like Sankontshe, especially after dusk. Indeed danger lurks here for any stranger, whether black or white. Three years before, two nuns were butchered in a neighbouring valley. The journalist from the United Kingdom, who is travelling in the Land Rover, feels uneasy, but Heather Reynolds of God's Golden Acre, as she drives through the gloom towards her remote destination, is preoccupied by other thoughts. Has she brought sufficient food and presents? This is her only concern. She is thinking about the Zulu families, and their children, waiting for her Christmas visit. The vehicle is loaded with food parcels and presents for the unfortunates who live in poverty at the bottom of the social scale in this rural African community.

"Sankontshe is just one area in the Valley of a Thousand Hills, and we refer to them collectively as 'the valleys'. We'll go to a few of the most remote homes and give out food and presents to people we know are desperately poor," she says.

The rondavels, and larger settlements known as *umuzis*, are scattered in profusion around the valley, some as close as a few yards apart, others in solitude on the higher reaches of the hillside. Traditionally the Zulus do not live in village communities, but the members of an extended family might live in close proximity to one another. The smaller, poorer family groups, those without the benefit of support from an extended family such as uncles, aunts or cousins, or those born out of wedlock, were hit hardest when the HIV virus first manifested itself in the mid-1990s. In the years following the millennium, the mortality rate impoverished those further up the social scale, as the productivity of the working generation diminished. There are freshly dug graves all around the track, and many abandoned Zulu rondavels, some in a state of collapse. It is like driving onto the set of a horror movie – only this is real life.

"There is poverty, hunger and deprivation here," Heather explains. She drives the Land Rover through the potholes at a crawl, and points out a succession of huts, most without glass in the windows. Many of the dilapidated shacks have just one thin layer of rusting corrugated iron roofing – and many of those have gaping holes where the rain is pouring through.

"The HIV virus is unique and devastating because it is

selective, transmitted through sexual activity and therefore targeting the sexually active members of society, between the ages of 16 and 50. These are the income generators, leaving behind the most vulnerable members of our society, the old and the very young. There is no one left to repair the rondavels or tend the gardens, or to provide financially for the family."

"Look over there!" she exclaims. She points to a traditional round Zulu hut built of mud and fronted by a small garden, planted with maize, in which there are four small burial mounds. A gravestone marks the oldest grave, and two more have wooden crosses. The newest and smallest is signified by nothing but the red earth and rocks that cover it. "By the time they buried the child, there was probably no money left for a burial stone, or even a wooden cross," Heather explains.

The shadowy impressions of two human faces appear in the front window of a nearby rondavel. Heather sees them and waves. "If you look to the left of that hut you will see two graves by the neighbouring dwelling with a large piece of roof missing on the corner, and the windows broken. I've just seen people in there. The water is pouring into that house. They are kids and they don't know how to cope, how to rebuild their house. They don't have the means, and there are no adults to show them. They are probably starving, and yet they're not even on our programme."

She sighs: "It's a crisis. South African society in the rural areas is imploding, but many people in other parts of the world don't yet grasp how serious it is, and many richer people in this country don't seem to think it's their problem."

Her first stop is to a child-led family that God's Golden Acre has been supporting for two years. The girl, now about 18, looks after four younger siblings, and her own baby – born before she was 16. Their rondavel was falling apart when a project run by God's Golden Acre, called Houses of Hope, received the funding to build the family a new home. "We built it just in time before the house collapsed. Now she's got a little garden, chickens, and receives a food parcel every month. It's barely sufficient to feed them all, but they get some help from neighbours and will soon be eating what they grow – as long as the rain keeps coming. She has to buy her water because she's so far away from the well, and we help her with that. We also pay the fees for two of the children to go to a school in the valley and they also get a uniform and stationery.

"It's a hard life for an 18-year-old child. Imagine if we weren't there. What would have happened to them? Their house would have collapsed. Where would this girl and her four siblings and infant child have gone? Where? What choices would she be forced to make?" Heather gazes ahead in silence into the arcing wipers as the rain lashes into the front of the vehicle.

The girl has hurriedly put on her best clothes. She smiles politely as she stands framed within the doorway of her candlelit home. There is a picture of Christ on the wall of the living room, a table and four chairs, and curtains given by the group of Dutch volunteers who helped to build this square concrete blockhouse with green corrugated iron roof, that has replaced the traditional rondavel.

There are two bedrooms, and all six members of the family share two beds, a double and a single, each covered with an old blanket. The girl keeps her home spotlessly clean. But she whispers to Heather in Zulu that they are hungry. They have no food in the house for Christmas. Heather explains: "She has been waiting and praying that I would bring food. She says, 'Oh Gogo! I didn't know whether you were going to come.'"

So the girl prays in thanks with Heather, whose supplies, as usual, include a sack of rice, mealie-meal, samp beans, soya, teabags, sugar, candles, matches, cooking oil, body soap and washing soap for clothes. She also gives the girl 20 Rand to buy water. Together they sing:

Haleluya Ameni (Hallelujah Amen)
Usithethelele (You paid...)
Usithetheleli izono (You paid for our sins)
Usithethelele baba (You paid, Father)
Usithethelele moya oyingcwele (You paid, Holy Spirit)
Jesu! (Jesus)
Usithethelele (You paid)

About a dozen children appear out of the mist with a hopeful look and there are cries of delight when Heather gives each of them a present wrapped in Christmas gift paper, and a fistful of sweets. Small faces, beaming with happiness, melt away into the mist as quickly as they came.

Heather drives on and provides the big picture: "There's no work here in the valley. Nothing. Absolutely nothing. So it makes no sense when white people say these girls should get a job and help themselves. Where? Where would they work? Who would look after their young siblings? Most of them have no support whatsoever apart from what a generous neighbour might provide. Ironically many of these girls are entitled to some form of basic government benefit but the bureaucratic rigmarole they have to go through to get it means they just don't know how. So it's down to NGOs – like us at God's Golden Acre – to do what we can to help them."

Most girls bringing up a family follow a predictable pattern, Heather explains. They fall pregnant around fifteen or sixteen, either in a relationship seeking emotional and financial support, or through more casual encounters – sex in exchange for favours. For them it is the only way of coping in a world without adults.

"Although things are beginning to change, thanks to government campaigns, many South African men will not tolerate condoms; they don't care about safe sex. This in turn vastly increases the risk of infection, and the prospect of yet another generation dying from the HIV/AIDS virus. It just repeats itself. Women in this rural and traditional Zulu society obey their menfolk. Then there are the children – whose parents have died – who go to live with older relations in the extended families. Here the young girls are often treated very badly; they become real-life cinderellas, and sometimes get sexually abused."

Heather drives across a hill along a rutted track to the home of a young woman, also about 18. Following the gang murder of her father, and the death of her mother, she looks after two younger siblings, and now also a baby of her own. Her hut had virtually disintegrated when rescue came just in time from volunteers and a team of young African men from God's Golden Acre. They had completed building her new house in Christmas week. Heather explains the girl's situation.

"She lost her father seven years ago when he was 'neck-laced'. She watched helplessly with her mother and two younger brothers, one about eight, the other around three, as the gang put a tyre around her father's neck, doused him in petrol and then set him alight. He was burned alive in front of them. The middle boy just started screaming and screaming. He was like that for hours, and by the end of it his mind had gone. Their mother died shortly afterwards, and the girl, the oldest child, was left to look after her brothers and bring them up for six years.

"When we found them they were still alive, but living in a hut which no longer kept out the wind and the rain. The walls of the shack had gaping holes, but she'd had the dignity to cover them with cloth. The support beams had been so eaten by white ants that you could almost blow them away. The girl was the mother figure, but to get food she needed to have a relationship with a man. By the age of fourteen she had her first baby. She had to use her body to get food for her younger siblings, and she did so.

"I prayed for someone to sponsor them, and their house, and their needs. Then unexpectedly someone did come forward from overseas, and we took her to see this little family. She immediately gave us the go-ahead to rebuild the house and she gave the family a substantial cash donation. She also provided fruit trees to plant, chickens for breeding, a coop, food and clothing. With that small gesture, the family has gone from rags to wearing decent clothes, and to look upon life as not so much a terrible ordeal, but with possibilities and promises.

"As for the brother who was emotionally damaged by his terrible experience, all I can say is that he may never again be normal. But he will look after and feed those chickens, and perhaps feel he has some purpose in life. He was never mad; he has just withdrawn into an inner consciousness for protection from a world he can't understand. We are praying for him, and maybe one day he will become well again."

The girl is slim, very attractive and smartly dressed. She is waiting when Heather's Land Rover pulls up. It is not a traditional round Zulu structure, but, like the previous family's new home, a square concrete blockhouse with two bedrooms, a kitchen and living room, with a corrugated iron roof, overlooking a small sloping garden. Many Zulus stopped building with thatch during the transitional years before 1994 when thousands of homes were set alight during rival political infighting between the African National Congress and the Inkatha Freedom Party.

"Oh thank you, Gogo!" the teenage girl cries in English, as a table and chairs are unloaded, with food sacks and presents for the children. Looks reveal joy and gratitude. There is no income earner here, just what the unemployed father of the baby brings when he is in work.

Heather whispers: "They said they prayed we would come in time for Christmas. There is no food in this house either. Nothing."

Soon over 30 Zulu children arrive at the back of the Land Rover and stand in a respectful queue, their hands cupped together, waiting politely for a present from Heather. The girls squeal as they unwrap the parcels to discover a doll. For the boys there is a plastic car kit. Sweets are then piled into out-stretched hands. The children and adults stand in a circle around Heather and pray. A beautiful child of about nine years of age, in a pressed pink party frock, and plaits, steps forward and leads the singing – a Zulu hymn of thanksgiving sung in harmony and with intense passion.

Siyabonga Baba (Thank You, Father)
Haleluya Ameni (Hallelujah Amen)
Siyabongo Jesu (Thank You, Jesus)
Haleluya Ameni (Hallelujah Amen)
Siyabongo Moya Oyingcwele (Thank You, Holy Spirit)

As she drives away Heather says: "It's an absolutely basic diet. Basic. Basic. Samp beans and rice, maize, cooking oil and soya gravy. Yet that song, *Siyabonga Baba*, means "Thank You, Father" for our blessings – and that's what is so humbling about the whole thing. They receive just £15 worth of food for each family for one month, and a few presents that I lugged over from the Netherlands.

"There's a dignity and standard among these young girls. You can drop in here any time and you will find them clean and tidy, and if they have been in the garden, or putting cow dung down on the floor, they'll quickly wash their hands and slip on a clean top. The Zulu people are incredibly polite too, and that's why they get angry with us when we teach their children different ways. They don't appreciate us showing their children how to do things Western style. Their kids are very, very respectful of adults, do not behave badly, or get out of hand."

The next two hours are spent visiting other Zulu families in Sankontshe, whose circumstances are all etched in tragedy; and which constitute a caseload of despair for the handful of community health workers who try to monitor their plight from within the valley. On a higher level in the management chain, a pitifully insufficient number of qualified social workers are either completely overwhelmed, or in some disgraceful cases, seemingly indifferent to the scale of the problem, and inertia has become apparent.

South Africa's government has a heavy burden to bear. In 2003 in some rural schools children were learning nothing about the virus, neither did many valley teenagers receive instruction about safe sex. Vital life-prolonging drugs have not – until recently – been available for AIDS patients in hospitals. Death certificates have never shown HIV as the cause of death. The majority of the rural black population has been in denial about the deadly illness that is gradually destroying their culture like a cancerous growth.

In one hut Heather visits, the children last saw their mother when she was taken to hospital suffering from tuberculosis fours years ago. No word since. They have no idea what happened to her body, where she is buried, or when she died. The oldest daughter has brought up her two young siblings since she was fourteen, and now more recently her own newborn baby. AIDS is not mentioned, out of respect. The word remains taboo, its ownership a terrible social stigma.

In another hut, its roof pitted with rust holes, the mother of the family, and her eldest son, were shot dead by her brother-in-law because she could not repay a debt of 20 Rand (£2). The oldest teenage daughter is now the mother of the family, and has been so since she was fourteen. Heather explains: "The whole family watched the uncle shoot their mother and older brother in front of their eyes. The oldest girl took over the household. Several years later we were called in as an emergency when the hut was collapsing all around them and the youngest baby was dying. One room at a time had fallen in, and they had retreated into the final room where there was a degree of shelter. We found a sponsor, built them a house, and gave them back their dignity. They now have a food parcel a month and the children are back at school."

A group of children smile and wave at Heather's Land Rover as she drives by. Then a pitiful-looking African *gogo* steps forward out of the shadows and flags her down on the track to plead for food. She tells Heather she and her grandchildren are starving. Heather gives the old woman what she can spare from the back of the Land Rover. Within moments, the *gogo* is joined by a group of children, and several teenage girls with babies. All need help. And so it goes on. One human tragedy confronts her after another.

"The old woman was crying about her home collapsing, and saying she needed some wire for the fence of her garden, and I told her I couldn't do all that. I just don't have the budget. I told her the government must help them. I can only do a little bit, what I can. We give our families on the project their food once a month, and we know that by the end of it they will have nothing. They are literally praying on their knees for us to come."

In another house – built by God's Golden Acre volunteers – a blind *gogo* looks after three grandchildren under the age of six. When Heather arrives they stare vacantly ahead. It is a listlessness that signifies despair. The blind *gogo* cannot manage her home. The chickens she has been given are nowhere to be seen, and the young trees she planted in the overgrown garden have died in the dry winter, parched without water. She is too weak to dig the soil, plant seeds, and then fetch water from the nearest well that is nearly half a mile away, and up a hill. By now the rain is lashing down across the hillside, blowing cascades of spray in random directions. Dark grey clouds race across the sky a few feet above the ridge in this magnificent African panorama.

Heather's hands continue to grasp the wheel, and she peers through the arcing wipers. "These roads are incredibly slippery but thankfully it's easy with this Land Rover. But if we were travelling in a small truck it could be very dangerous. A Land

Rover is one of the few vehicles that can cope with this, and much worse conditions."

At length, they come to the home of Gogo Beauty, the much-loved carer at God's Golden Acre. Her home, middle-class by African standards, consists of a small cluster of Zulu rondavels, and a modern square building. It is a meeting point for several families. A plate of chicken is provided for the two white visitors. Dozens of children are waiting and hoping for a present and a fistful of sweets. None are to be disappointed.

At length an African woman whispers in Heather's ear and she follows her to an *umuzi* less than 200 metres from the home of Gogo Beauty. The house is clean, and stands in a cluster of others, signifying an extended family group. The walls are painted lime green, and a rug covers the linoleum floor. There is a suite of red lounge chairs, a sideboard displaying porcelain birds, books on a shelf, and a portrait of Nelson Mandela on the wall.

There is also a framed photograph of a beautiful Zulu girl holding a smiling baby. On the single bed, in the corner of the dim room, lies the pathetic skeletal outline of this same person. Her name is Beth. She is 19 years old.

Heather and a group of African women quietly gather round the bed to sing and pray for the girl's life. They ask the white *gogo* to lead them in prayer. Heather sings. Beth has tuberculosis. A child about five years old lies tucked in beside Beth, lying with her face at the other end of the bed. A young chicken plucks at the fluff on the blanket that covers mother and child. The group, some weeping, pray in Zulu with such intensity and sorrow that the girl wakes from her light sleep, eyes huge on her shrunken face, and gazes around in bewilderment before finding the strength to brush the chicken off her bed. She listens to the prayers for a few moments, and then returns to her delirious world of intermittent slumber.

Before departing, Heather holds Beth's shrunken hand and whispers quietly to her in Zulu. An elderly African woman sobs in deep gasps as the white woman crouches down by the bed. Afterwards Heather says she had not met Beth before. The presence of Mawethu – it means "our mother" and is the name Heather has been given by the Zulus – had been requested to give Beth strength and faith, and to prepare her for Jesus.

Heather explains: "She was a bag of bones. The little hand that I held, and her tiny arm outstretched, was just down to nothing. Apparently they took her to hospital but she was soon discharged. Her family brought her home to die. She was showing all the signs of AIDS. Her bodyweight had diminished, she was vomiting all her food, and it was just a matter of time before she would be gone. Thank God, the little girl who was lying beside her is healthy, but Beth also has a baby and she is sick. Her mother died of AIDS, now Beth will die, and so will her baby. That's three generations of females in the same family. The woman who was leading the prayers was her aunt, and she was overcome with grief because there are other children in her immediate family who have been orphaned. This is just the latest tragedy to hit them."

What form had the prayers taken?

"There were many pleas to God for mercy, asking for help and strength, and for God to come back again and show himself – to alleviate the suffering and the pain being endured by the family. They really need him now to come and help them because they can't do it on their own. They prayed for God's strength and comfort. There were some really desperate pleas from the heart there, deep down.

"I whispered words of comfort to Beth and prayed that in her darkest moments in the time when she is suffering the most pain – when it's almost unbearable – that she will turn her eyes to Jesus. I told her he is the one who can help her to bear the pain. She should know that he is close to her, always close to her, and always will be. I told her to cling on to him right through anything that might seem too terrible to bear. I think this is very important for people when they are dying painfully. They can turn inwards. When you are dying you sometimes go into a coma, into semi-consciousness, and at that time you can hallucinate about God, and Jesus, which can bring a sense of peace about death, rather than struggling to keep going. It's easier to think of Jesus at a time like that and go to him at peace knowing you are in his care.

"I don't believe that I should create false expectations while doing my prayers of comfort in a situation where somebody is dying as a result of diseases caused by the HIV virus. We see such death all the time. So I am not going to give her and the family false hope. We know in the back of our minds that God can do a miracle, but we also know the realities of AIDS. That family has been hit hard and those old grannies are feeling the pain. They have lost a daughter, now a granddaughter, and soon her baby. They are a big family, but you could hear from the agony in their voices that they have gone through a lot of suffering."

Who's preparing the child for her mother's death? How will they do that in the family?

Heather shrugs: "They've got a philosophical way of look-ing at it. Death is something that the Zulu people have always lived with. They are warriors, and they believe the spirits of their ancestors live on among them. They know that God gives, and takes, gives, and takes again. So they will be teach-ing her that, and to be strong."

In fact Beth survives the festive season and over the follow-ing months her health improves. She puts on weight but remains frail and weak. Soon she is well enough to walk short distances in the valley and it is a precious reprieve from her illness. She died in June 2004.

The Land Rover heads back through the remote tracks in the dark valley towards God's Golden Acre at Cato Ridge, passing hundreds more graves and huts where Africans, who will never receive Heather's ministry, are dying in silence surrounded by terrified children. A ghastly paradox – the magnificent panorama of rural Africa, but one that has become a graveyard for the victims of a new plague; the horror film scenario.

How can you stand this, every day?

It is the question every visitor to God's Golden Acre asks Heather Reynolds.

5
CHRISTMAS EVE

Petrus Venter, a big-boned Afrikaaner in khaki shirt and shorts, picks up a small African child with his huge hands and hoists the delighted youngster into his pickup to take him for a joyride, while roaring with laughter at the question.

Five years ago might he have imagined – in his wildest dreams – spending Christmas in the company of dozens of Zulu orphans?

Petrus, in middle age, has the stern military air of a retired policeman, which is exactly what he is. "No – not by any stretch of the imagination!" he continues, chuckling. "I made it quite clear to Myrtle that there was no way we'd ever visit her sister Heather while she was involved with these black kids running all over the house and all over everybody. I made that quite clear. I was trained to fight African terrorists on our borders with Namibia and Zimbabwe, brainwashed to hate them with a passion, and to kill them whenever I saw them. I voted for the apartheid system, and that is where the hatred came from. I was brought up with it – yet I also believed I was a Christian. It was only later I realized that to be a real Christian you have to live it – like Heather does."

A few years before, when Heather brought baby Chummy, one of her orphans, to the home of her brother-in-law in Johannesburg, she was invited by Petrus to leave the child in the garage. It was only in a later incident, when Heather and a larger number of Zulu orphans were stranded in the city, that Petrus had little choice but to give them shelter and sanctuary in his home. It was an experience that started to change him. "I began to listen to what Heather had to say and realized that they were only kids, just like our own children. It's not their doing that they have been orphaned, or that some of them are HIV-positive. The big turning point came when I saw how committed she was to her mission. She was adamant that she was going to succeed. I asked myself why I was rejecting these little black children and turning my back on them."

At Christmas lunch Uncle Petrus will play a big part in the fun and games – and love every moment. On New Year's Eve he'll run the firework display. "It'll be like last year – they'll be jumping on me, and hanging from me, and singing my ears off," he chuckles. "I think in a way God spoke to me through Heather. I watched this woman driving through her incredible mission on her own, believing in what she was doing, determined to reach her goal come hell or high water, not worrying how, but having the faith that the Lord would provide. This convinced me that through Christianity the finest things can be achieved. Black and white men of my generation still have some way to go to reconcile the past, and only some of us are trying hard. One of my best friends now is a former ANC terrorist and we can laugh and joke together about the years when we would have tried to shoot one another had we met. But it's not that way for the majority, and I think South Africa can only be pushed forward by the young generation, those who have no personal memories of the recent past. The biggest hope is in the universities, where the black and white students are integrated, and youngsters from both ethnic groups are totally comfortable with that."

It is shortly before dusk on Christmas Eve and Petrus Venter is part of a group of around 30 people – children and adults – making their way to a quiet corner of God's Golden

Acre. They walk through long grass along a path skirted by gum trees. Heather and Patrick lead the group, each carrying a small child, followed by their dogs. Heather holds hands with a small Zulu girl in a pink frock. Behind them the orphans laugh and chat with the volunteers and caregivers, with whom they walk hand in hand, singing in harmony.

Siyabonga Baba,
Haleluya Ameni,
Siyabongo Jesu,
Haleluya Ameni.

The crickets also sing a familiar chorus, herbal aromas pervade the encroaching night air, and a giant fireball drifts slowly beneath the horizon. It is a hot evening and the children are tired after playing for hours in the pools and waterslide of the resort. At length they come to three graves, two marked with crosses, the third smaller, and freshly dug.

The marked crosses are where they buried Snenhlanhla, who died a week after her seventh birthday on 16th July 2003, and Manalisi, aged two-and-a-half, who went to Jesus on 26th July 2003. The unmarked grave is that of a baby boy who came to the hospice at God's Golden Acre two weeks before he died just a few days before. A small bunch of withering flowers marks his resting place.

Heather gathers the group of adults and children around their graves. "Snenhlanhla was a great fighter like Hope is now. She just fought and showed such courage. She was sick for two years and I tell you she was so full of life – even to the last days when Wendy would hold her when she couldn't sleep. She was so courageous. She would wake up out of a coma, laugh and try and tickle Wendy, and then fall back into her coma again.

"So we come here tonight just to remember all the little children of the world like Sne who through no fault of their own were taken. On the birth of Christ it's good to bring our minds back to our faith in God and to remember Thulani, Happiness, Manalisi, Sne, Megan and many other beautiful children, to pay tribute to them, and also to all the little children whom we don't know.

"We are here to serve little children who find themselves in dire circumstances. The real purpose comes home when we stand around these little graves and we know that we served them well. We were there for them in the worst, most painful, moments of dying. They had no tummies left and food dropped into their mouth and went right through them.

"It's not really a time for crying, or feeling sad, because they have moved on to their home in heaven with our Father. We are the ones that remember the pain and the suffering. We are the ones who cling to the happy memories and because we remember them we feel sad. There's a little song I wrote for the children that explains they are now in heaven and it's not an end for our children when they die, but a beginning."

> There's a new star that shines, oh so bright,
> A new star that lights up the night,
> A new star has reached heaven's door,
> She's home, she's home for evermore.
> There's a new song she will sing
> For her Saviour and her King,
> A new life she's found there, in our Father's care.

The following is an extract from the journals of God's Golden Acre volunteer Susan Balfour, written in August 2003:

Snenhlanhla, who had just celebrated her seventh birthday, passed away during my visit. We all knew it was coming. At Christmas, Snenhlanhla was battling, and the doctors informed us that she only had two months to live. But Snenhlanhla never failed to surprise us. She joined preschool, and blew us away with her intelligence and her amazing sense of humour.

Then, three months ago, her condition deteriorated. She was oxygen-dependent all that time, and was cared for in the hospice. The day after her seventh birthday, she developed an abnormal (terminal) breathing pattern and was transferred to the high care room. Though clearly in pain, coughing up pus and blood continually and usually a very miserable little girl, there were windows of hope during the day, when she would laugh and giggle and joke and tease us.

"You're a fruit," her favourite volunteer, an Irish girl called Ruth, told her.

Both Sne and I were confused by this, until Ruth explained that in Ireland they call crazy people "fruits".

Snenhlanhla looked at Ruth and thought for a moment. "Then you're a banana!" she told Ruth, pointedly!

I can't even begin to tell you how her special little spirit touched us. Her humour, her resilience... she taught us so much. She inspired us to carry on bravely and cheerfully. In the darkest moments, when Snenhlanhla cried hoarsely that she couldn't breathe, Wendy, the hospice nurse, reassured her that she was doing really well, that she didn't have to fight.

I did a night shift with her once. She lay on her chest, as I sat propped against a beanbag. That was the only comfortable position for her. But Sne refused to sleep.

"I'm frightened," she told us, her eyes brimming with terror.

"It's all right baby." "It'll be better soon." "It's so nice in Heaven."

But all through the night, she fought. Her breathing was laboured, gasping, irregular, and every now and then she would sit bolt upright and search the room desperately to make sure that Ruth, Wendy and I were still there.

Every time she did it, my heart broke all over again. "It's OK, darling, no-one is going anywhere," we told her, over and over. We reassured her constantly that we all loved her, and that she was going to be with her mummy and Jesus in Heaven. Sne asked us to pray for her, so we did, and Wendy played some of the little girl's favourite praise and worship music.

Wendy and Ruth stayed with her day and night. They never left her. 24 hours a day, one of them sat with Sne. 24 hours a day, there was someone to hold her, rock her, read to her or stroke her forehead.

Heather and the Zulu *gogos* slipped into the tiny room one afternoon and sang for Sne, in gently layered harmonies. She was on morphine at that point, and in such a lot of pain, but the music soothed her troubled spirit, and Sne's breathing, though still laboured, became steady.

She was surrounded by an awesome measure of love and compassion. I just don't know how to describe to you all that I experienced in that room. It was phenomenal. I feel so privileged to have shared in it.

Over the days that followed, Snenhlanhla became unresponsive. Then, late one morning, in Wendy's arms, she looked up at a mural of Jesus on the wall, and then at Wendy.

"You will fly to Jesus," I had promised her. And in that moment, Sne knew it was true. She was filled with peace. She closed her eyes and breathed her last breath – a gentle death in the arms of someone who loved her. For that, I am thankful.

We all cried as we washed her – tears of sorrow and relief. I closed Sne's eyes and stroked her beautiful face. The tension had melted from it. The air in the room was now lighter: the sense of despair had lifted.

Already, we were preparing to accept another terminally ill child into our home – a two-year-old boy. It's not rare to us anymore, but it's always unthinkable somehow.

Lala ngoxola sisi omncane. Siyakuthanda Kakhulu. Sizokhumbula. (Rest in peace little sister. We love you so much. We will miss you. We will remember you.)

6
CHRISTMAS MORNING

As the sun climbs higher in the sky above
the eucalyptus trees on Christmas morning,
the orphans of God's Golden Acre are beginning to stir for
their breakfast, having dreamed in anticipation of the joyous
day that lies ahead. There will be a roast chicken lunch, a visit
from Father Christmas, a carol service, sweets and of course
presents, opened and enjoyed in the company of the carers,
volunteers and other grown-ups who love them and make
them feel special. It will be another hot day and the boisterous kids will rush around the waterslide, splashing one
another and the volunteers in the resort's swimming pools...
The dark shadows of terror and shame will be banished for
these daylight hours.

Christmas Day at God's Golden Acre is always arranged and
orchestrated by Heather. However, she has other children on
her mind as she sits at the wheel of the familiar white Land
Rover and heads down the rocky track out of the estate. Her
destination this Christmas morning at sunrise, while most still
slumber, is a remote cluster of homesteads high in the mountains, overlooking the valley of Sankontshe. The vehicle is
loaded with food and provisions – and presents and sweets for
children.

"There's one little group of families that I didn't get to
before Christmas, and who to me are very important. They'll

be wondering why I didn't get there, but it doesn't matter because this will be a lovely surprise for them. It's a visit that has a lot of significance for me because, of all the families that I have helped over the years, these have had the most impact. It's about how you can help to change people. I arrived at their small and remote community at the top of the mountain back in January 2000, having been advised by the community health worker that they needed help, and some of the children were sick. When I got to their homes, I discovered they were a group living on the fringe of rural African society. Local people disapproved of them.

"Many were just young teenagers of fourteen or fifteen, and it was clear that the girls were exchanging sex for favours, and the boys were surviving through crime. It shocked and saddened me to find the young girls living that way. You could see by the painted nails and the way their hair was styled and dyed, by the clothes they wore, and the sexual way they moved, that they were in the sex trade. They turned and stared at me with utter disinterest, and even animosity.

"Their faces revealed what they were thinking: 'What are you doing here? We don't need you and your kind.' It was as if they didn't want me there because they feared I was judging them. People like that don't want 'do-gooders'; they don't need to be told what they are, and what they should be. They had for sure already been told many a time – written off in contempt as bad by other Zulus in the valley. Promiscuity, drugs and alcohol abuse – it was all here in this group of outcasts. There is a Zulu song called *Ntombi Hlope*, and these girls would have been called that. It is a term used for people for whom there is no respect or honour in the Zulu culture. Their young faces, hard and mean, revealed a short lifetime of abuse.

"As for the young men, they had the shifty look of thieves about them, which is exactly what many of them were. It turned out later that some of these lads had been responsible for much of the pilfering and stealing around Cato Ridge, including some burglaries at God's Golden Acre, and in one case it was my evidence in court that put two of them in prison.

"However, these young teenagers all had kids, and not only did they have a lot of children, but among them were a large number of orphaned children – left behind by adults who had died of AIDS. Many of the children were riddled with tapeworm, ringworm, scabies, and they were covered in sores. The worst cases were brought back, after hospital treatment, to God's Golden Acre, for a period of recuperation before returning to the community.

"So there was this totally dishevelled bunch of people and children who were dirty, poor and totally disinterested in a society that had rejected them. They were not expecting anything except condemnation from me, the community health workers, and everybody else. So I would get there every month, hand out the food parcels, ignore the hostile looks in the eyes of the teenagers, and just focus on the children.

"The older ones had gone into a way of living that was totally unacceptable to society. This stand-off went on for about six months, and eventually I tried to get closer to the children – I said one day, 'Come on kids, let's have a song. Let's sing a song together.' They looked at me blankly. These kids didn't sing. They didn't know church songs. This was an outcast group of people. To give the children credit, they did try to sing, but it was no good, it didn't come from their heart. I decided not to pursue it. Years went by, and I would still go to their community each month with food parcels and sweets, and talk to the kids. At Christmas I would invite them all up to our parties to join our kids.

"Then one of their houses fell down – it literally collapsed. So I found a sponsor from England and we rebuilt the house for them – and at last they were really happy. It was the first time I saw these teenagers smile and laugh. I felt they were realizing, at last, that in the world there really were people who cared about them.

"Then an amazing thing happened. We were due to plant fruit trees on their land, but when I arrived they hadn't dug the holes for the trees to be planted in. That was part of the agreement. They were supposed to prepare for the planting, and we would bring the fruit trees for them. But they'd fallen down on their side of the deal and I got really mad. I felt the least they could have done was to dig the holes.

"So I told the community health worker, 'That's it! I'm leaving with the trees. They don't get any fruit trees.' I was fuming. These trees were worth 25 Rand each and there were plenty of people in the valley who wanted them and would look after them. But before I drove away, I had second thoughts. I realized that the whole community wasn't at fault. In fact it was the community health workers who should have checked that the digging had been done before we arrived.

Then all hell broke loose. Everybody in the community was offering to dig the holes, and by the time my anger expired, they'd dug all the holes so fast that the trees could be planted after all. I'd never seen holes dug so quickly! I relented.

"The next thing that happened was that a little wooden bench was brought over by the children for me to sit on. This had never happened before. So I sat down on the bench and all the kids started to crowd affectionately around me. They were now four years older than when I first came. So the ones who had been four were now eight, and the ones who had been eight were now twelve. They had got used to the white *gogo* coming around, and it was apparent now that they cared for me. They were all gathered around me. I said in Zulu: 'Shall Gogo teach you a song?'

"They all cried out 'Yes. Yes.' So I started singing, and they followed me, even though they spoke hardly any English.

This little light of mine,
I'm going to let it shine,
This little light of mine,
I'm going to make it shine.

"The next thing, the older girls, the mothers who were now 20 or so, all came out, and they were trying to catch the words too. At the end of it, a whole lot of us were singing, "This little light of mine", and we were all singing together. Suddenly I looked at the mothers properly for the first time in years – I'd always tried to avoid looking directly into their eyes because I hated their cold, hostile looks – but now I looked closely, and it dawned on me in a flash that they were no longer dressing and behaving like prostitutes. I suddenly realized this whole group of people had changed their lifestyle!

"We had built them a house, we were laying a water pipeline up to their settlement, and trying to raise money to get them connected, and we had given them food through the outreach programme. Their kids were now going to school, because we paid the fees, and they'd been given uniforms. As a consequence of all this, the young parents had got back their self-respect.

"Now here we were, singing Christian songs – a whole community of lovely people. In the end they had found God in their own way. I couldn't tell you the joy I felt, the warmth that enveloped me, when they were all singing and I looked at them, and the incredible change that had come over these girls. They were all dressed cleanly and were respectable young women. Now, each one of them could walk down the road, hold her head high, and be any ordinary girl. And the kiddies were singing from their heart.

"Over those years with all the good nutrition the children had received, they were normal, healthy youngsters. In fact they were beautiful – their skins were glowing, their eyes were bright, their hair was shining, and they were growing up in a healthy environment thanks to our rural outreach project. Not only that, when I go up there now I always find that all the plants and fruit trees are well tended. They are so proud, they keep some of the best and most beautiful gardens in the entire valley. If it turned out that this was the only group of people in Africa who had benefited from my help, then my whole life would have been worth it."

Part Two

7
LIFE ON THE TRADING STATION

Heather Reynolds was born among the Zulus and spent the first nine years of her life living in their midst. Her parents ran two trading stations and the one where she lived stood on the summit of a small hill ten miles outside Mtubatuba in KwaZulu-Natal. It overlooked the rolling plains and foothills of the great African kingdom, and bordered the Umfolozi Game Reserve, home of the black and white rhino.

For months of the year the sky was a blue ocean with islands of white clouds on an endless horizon. Beneath this vastness, the bush was an exotic flora patchwork of shades from khaki brown to dark green. Hills and ridges rose and fell into valleys where great rivers tumbled towards the Indian Ocean.

The sights, sounds and smells of rural Africa, as they'd existed for thousands of years, were locked in a time warp. However, the end of an era, with its political upheaval, was approaching like a stalking leopard, unnoticed by ordinary men and women in the rural areas.

The white girl, who in later life would become known among the Zulus as Mawethu, "our mother", was a familiar figure among the Africans with her cropped hair, snub nose and enquiring brown eyes. She might have been mistaken for a boy, because she wore her older brother's hand-me-downs. Heather was born in January 1952, the second youngest in a family of five. John and Brenda McLellan were only unusual in that their oldest son Kenny, born in 1940, was severely handicapped, suffering from cerebral palsy. David came after Kenny in 1946. Myrtle was born in 1949, then Heather, and finally Basil in 1954.

Trading stations in the veldt were reminiscent of provision stores in Hollywood Wild West films. Africans and a few white farmers would purchase food, ironmongery, clothes, domestic items and stationery. Usually the families running the trading station were the only whites in the neighbourhood, so Heather's friends and contemporaries, apart from her brothers and sister, were black. Selina looked after the younger children while their parents worked, and Togo the cook was strict about hygiene and being tidy around the kitchen. Hands had to be clean before they could eat. The housekeeper, Maliya, was big and buxom, in the African mama style.

Heather's earliest memories are of playing with Selina's children around the trading post. She was bilingual, speaking fluent Zulu by the age of four. Myrtle remembers of her younger sister: "Heather used to read a lot in her bedroom, or she used to paint, and she kept to herself. She did not spend much time with me because I spent a lot of time with Mum, cooking and sewing. Then my dad got Heather into the garden and she became good at that. So although we grew up together, we were quite separate, different people. She had her thing and I had my thing. That's how we went through school days too."

In 1961 the family moved out of Zululand to Madada in Pondoland. Here the children helped to run the trading post managed by their parents. The African children used to come in with their parents and that was how Heather got to know them. She would walk barefoot down the track to meet them and bring with her a bag of sweets. They would all squat on their haunches under an acacia tree, out of the heat of the sun, sweating in the humidity, brushing away the flies and insects.

Heather would sit in the middle and tell stories about Africa, or tales and legends that she'd read. Other times she would tell them about her boarding school and adventures there. The African children wanted to hear about her life, and compare it with their own. They would listen wide-eyed as she told them about her school, the pranks and japes, and the sport.

"It wasn't really the done thing to spend time with black children, and so I used to sneak off out of my parents' way. The Africans did not own much furniture, and no one slept on a bed. Most families in the village had meagre belongings that might consist of a few tin plates and cups, three or four grass mats and blankets, wooden stools fashioned from planks, and an ancient metal pot that was usually dented from generations of use."

After work the family would have supper, as it was called, and then Kenny, who had been sitting in his wheelchair all day, would be lifted up and lain down on his bed. Brenda and Heather would wash him, and afterwards, they would all sit on the bed around the oldest son. John McLellan would turn on the radio, get into his own bed, and they would listen to the BBC World Service news. Outside, the crickets, frogs and other nocturnal creatures of Africa provided a symphonious hum in the background to the radio, along with the "pud-pud" of the generator that supplied the power for the lights. Some time around 10pm John McLellan would switch off the radio and go to sleep. The children would sit with their mother, and she'd hand out fruit or sweets. Their father was careful with money, so they were not allowed to keep the light on late, and he insisted the generator be shut down. This created a problem for Heather, who was an avid reader of novels. It meant using a torch under the bed covers until the early hours of the morning. Myrtle remembers: "She was the cleverest of all us children, a great thinker, who would sometimes surprise you with what she would come out with!"

8
CHILDREN IN
THE WILDERNESS

Holidays and camping expeditions are another vivid childhood memory. Settled by the Pondos in the north and Xhosas in the south, the Wild Coast was a black homeland virtually untouched by time. In the 1960s the white government did not regard it as worthy of development. In the vast wilderness, dotted with occasional villages of mud and thatch huts, cattle grazed on the grasslands, and Africans toiled by hand and with oxen to scratch a subsistence living, growing corn maize in small fields, and vegetables in their gardens. Transport was on foot, or horseback, except for occasional whites in their pickup trucks.

Inland, the McLellans explored rivers and estuaries winding through spectacular gorges and forested ravines. In wooded areas, they found prolific bird life, and on the coast, beyond the rocks at sea, fish eagles sometimes perched on the numerous shipwrecks. Heather and her brothers became expert at spotting and identifying the exotic birds that dived into the veldt grassland for insects, sang on the wing in the sky, or called to one another from acacia, white stinkwood, and Natal mahogany trees. In the valleys a dense thicket of evergreen species enveloped the landscape, providing an environment for insect- and seed-eating birds such as weavers, wild canaries and black-eyed bulbuls, whose dawn call resembles that of the European blackbird.

The children became aware of the rich varieties of plants, many of which they learned had been imported during Victorian times as ornamental species for the gardens of the wealthy, before migrating into the wild and becoming common weeds. It was the fishing, however, that most stirred the imagination of Heather's brothers. "I used to go off with David and Basil when I was eleven or twelve and we lived in the Transkei. We clambered from the main tracks down wild paths, watching out for snakes, and it was always a great adventure – kids alone in the wilds of Africa. Eventually we'd get down to the bottom of these valleys behind the Wild Coast in Pondoland, and spend the whole day fishing in the swirling pools of deep rivers like the Mzimhlava and Mthentu.

" I hated to kill anything. My brothers discovered one day that as fast as they were collecting their fish in the holding pond I was trying to set them free again. When I thought they were not looking I'd use my foot to push away the walls of the holding pond they'd built until the trapped fish could squeeze between the stones and dart back into the river. When they caught me they threatened to leave me behind the next time."

David told her: "You idiot, instead of mucking up our fishing have a go with this rod. Here – I'll show you how to cast the line and put the bait on the hook."

"I stood there praying not to have a bite. Somehow the fish always chose my bait and I had to drag several ashore to meet their fate. I was in tears and quietly asking the poor things to forgive me."

On their walking expeditions they would sometimes stop at a hut for water and talk with the local people. They were always welcomed, and Heather never felt threatened by the men. Within two decades the stirring of political activism was to make such informal social interaction in these same rural areas difficult.

As a child Heather looked up to her brother David. He was perhaps an inch under six feet tall and a sportsman like her father, exceptionally well built, a good rugby player and an all-round athlete. He always worked hard at school, although he was not academic like his younger sister. Basil, like David, was also an athlete, but slim and rangy.

"We had our love of nature in common but I do not think my brothers, David and Basil, really understood me. I was academic, bookish, and content to sit in my room, quietly absorbed. I was also an artist, always painting, and then slipping off quietly to spend time with the African children. I felt different from the boys, even though they were my heroes."

At the trading post there was a crisis for Heather when John McLellan had to slaughter a sheep or pigs. The girl could not bear the thought that a creature she knew was going to be killed. She would rush up to her room and put her head under the pillows so that she would not hear the sound of the pig squealing, and the gun going off. When they told her, laughing, that the sheep had not tried to resist but had lain on the ground passively, she could not bring herself to eat the meat.

Heather also soon developed a strong affection for the stray dogs from the African village. These were lean, mangy animals that would hang around the trading station hoping for food. One day a stray snarled at David when he tried to shoo him out of the store, and the McLellan guard dogs went berserk. They were going to kill the unfortunate creature when Heather intervened hysterically, screaming and screaming at them to stop. Another time, David went out to shoot a stray that was disturbing the chickens, trying to steal eggs. Heather pleaded with him not to kill the dog but he went out, and moments later the family heard a shotgun being fired. David had killed it and the next day Heather discovered it was a lactating bitch with puppies. She screamed at David: "I hate you! I'll never love you again!" She meant it.

The next day David walked down the path to where the Africans lived and went to every single kraal until he found the puppies, and then brought them back to Heather and her mother to look after. Animals played an important part in Heather and Brenda's life, and many years later at God's Golden Acre at Wartburg, and then Cato Ridge, stray dogs and cats would always find a home there. She has never been able to turn away any human being or animal, especially a sick one. A consequence of this has been that wherever Heather has lived, her home has resembled a zoo, with wild and domestic animals sometimes following her every step in the hope of food, or petting.

Myrtle recalls: "We all loved animals, but Heather was exceptional. If she saw something die she used to be sick for a whole week. A little pig came to live with us in the house and Dad eventually slaughtered it – since then she hasn't eaten pork. In fact it's only now and then that she'll eat meat, but otherwise not.

"Our love of animals came from our mother who had lots of them. As well as cats and dogs she would look after sick animals like owls and they would all come into the house – like that little pig. There were cows putting their heads through the window hoping for bread. Dad had no say in it – he used to get cross about the dogs coming in and lying on our mother's bed but she didn't take any notice. We all accepted that Mum was a special person."

Wild game was also close at hand in Heather's childhood. Africans would find sick animals in the bush and bring them back to Brenda and Heather to care for. "At the trading post near Mtubatuba when I was very small, animals would knock down the fencing around the Umfolozi Game Reserve. They were getting out all the time."

The Hluhuwe and Umfolozi reserves had been founded before the Boer War in 1895 and were the oldest sanctuaries in Africa. It was there that Operation Rhino was launched during Heather's childhood in the 1960s, successfully capturing and relocating white rhino to other havens within South

Africa. The reserve now holds a fifth of the world's black and white rhino population.

"One night this huge buck nyala appeared in our backyard," Heather remembers. "He seemed to look down his nose at us and appeared unperturbed, before galloping off down to the nearest lake."

However, the most dangerous animals were the rhinos. You'd look up and see one crossing your lawn! Everybody would scream 'Rhino!' and we'd scramble up the nearest tree. You certainly didn't want to be in their way. They would charge anything that moved. You didn't spend time making up your mind where to go – you just ran. A hut, a shed, preferably a tree – anything would do that obscured your scent, or made you invisible.

"Then there were the crocodiles. Dad would organize fishing expeditions and take us children with him. The family truck would arrive at rivers like the Nylazi or the Sombus to find a dozen crocodiles basking in the sun a few yards away. The crocodiles would slide off the near bank and cross the river to the far side. If we were lucky we might see a fish eagle and hear its distinctive cry as it rose from the water with a fish lifeless in the grip of its talons. Other times wading birds would take off in fright at the approaching vehicle. The humans would arrive – exit the crocs and the birds!

"The boys and I would march into the river, splashing about with our black dog Teddy, who used to swim and paddle alongside us. He must have known about the crocodiles but didn't show any fear. To this day I cannot understand how our dad allowed us go wading into a crocodile-infested river, but he did. He'd be totally absorbed with his fishing. We'd be paddling on one side of the river and the crocodiles would be on the opposite bank, basking in the sun, but we felt they were eyeing us up. We weren't scared, but we just made sure we kept away from the other side."

Camping has remained one of the passions of Heather's life.

"I can imagine no more awesome experience than sleeping under an African night sky – transfixed by the infinite number of stars blazing above, spread out in a colossal galaxy. On those early camping trips in the Transkei, we'd listen in wonder as dusk fell to the incredible orchestra of sound from insect to elephant. It was truly the call of the wild."

9
THE FAMILY HISTORY

The McLellans had originally come from Kirkcudbright in Scotland. Heather never met her grandfather, John McLellan, who was an engineer, and her father never talked later in life about him. John junior had been born in 1910 and was only nine years old when he lost his mother in the 1919 world flu epidemic. He was by far the youngest of four children and unable to fend for himself. John McLellan senior decided he could not look after his youngest son and placed him in a convent. He then went off to South America, possibly on an engineering contract. He didn't return to South Africa until he was an old man many years later. The son never saw the father again after he went into the convent, coming out only for holidays when he would go to stay with his cousins on a farm outside Stutterheim.

At the age of 16, John junior ran away from the convent and began to support himself, working in shops. He made his way in life successfully so that by the late 1930s, when he met Brenda May, he was a man with some prospects. John McLellan was a powerful, handsome man, over six feet tall and athletic, with brown hair and brown eyes; he met Brenda May, a piano teacher, at a tennis club. She was 18, six years younger than him, and a small, ordinary-looking girl, but also athletic. Part of their courtship was spent on the tennis court playing tournaments together. From where she stood, perhaps it was love at first sight. Brenda May was a Protestant of German descent and had grown up in a small town called Mt Ayliffe, in East Griqualand, between KwaZulu-Natal and the Cape, where her father was an ironmonger. She was a devout Christian and before the Second World War played the organ on Sundays at the Anglican church in Mt Ayliffe.

The couple married shortly before the war, and as soon as it broke out John rushed off to volunteer, leaving Brenda behind, despite the fact she had already become pregnant. Once he had embarked overseas, he did not see her again for nearly five years. Being a big and athletic man, he enlisted in the infantry, and after basic training was attached to the 8th Army in Egypt where he fought at the Battle of El Alamein and all the successive desert campaigns in Northern Africa. After the African campaign, he took part in the conquest of Sicily and then went on with his regiment to fight on the Italian mainland. Eventually his luck ran out and he was seriously wounded. A German shell exploded when it hit a tree where John McLellan and a section of soldiers were dug in. The shrapnel had a devastating effect and killed most of them. John was taken to the mortuary, his right foot severed. He was presumed to be dead because he had lost so much blood, then someone noticed him twitching and they realized he was still alive. He spent at least a year in Florence in convalescence before being repatriated back home in 1945, having had a series of operations in which the surgeons removed more of his right leg. John McLellan returned a very different man from the one who had departed in 1940.

Heather recounts: "He came home to South Africa expecting to find a childlike wife, barely out of her teens, waiting for him. While in hospital he had written Mum many touching and sensitive letters making it clear that all would be well, and he would soon be returning fit and well. He would come home and be able to look after both her and Kenny. These were letters of reassurance, of telling her not to worry about him. In fact he must have been enduring unimaginable pain.

"Perhaps he was expecting to be the centre of Mum's world, a man who had suffered a disability fighting for his country and who needed tender loving care to help him settle back into civilian life. Certainly Mum had kept herself for him; she was a virtuous and caring woman. However, by now, she was a mature adult in her twenties who had endured the hardship of being a single parent and looking after a disabled child — born while her husband was at war. Perhaps when he did at last return he found himself second on the list for affection."

There had been an accident with Kenny McLellan during a difficult birth. The doctor used instruments to extract the baby and inadvertently damaged his spine. He was paralyzed from his neck down, the accident had left him unable to speak, and his whole body was grotesque.

The child's face was not deformed, but his chest, hips and arms were twisted, his legs shrunken and thin, and his hands screwed up. People looked away from him in embarrassment. Tragically, he was a normal man trapped in a wasted body. There was nothing wrong with his brain. Kenny was Heather's first deep emotional attachment and from the age of six she regarded him as her personal responsibility.

"I helped Mum all I could to nurse and feed Kenny when I was home from school, and I would put him to bed. However, the brunt of the job of caring for him fell on her. I doubt whether Mum ever had a full night's sleep after Kenny was born because she had to turn and change him during the night. His weak lungs, in a distorted ribcage, left him highly susceptible to illnesses like bronchitis and pneumonia, and so he needed constant care. He did not get angry and never became depressed. He was always smiling and ready to listen."

Heather's relationship with her father, John McLellan, was more complex. It was loving, but distant, and also challenging. "Mum had a hard life, running a business, caring for a handicapped son, looking after four other children, and coping with a husband who had a serious drinking problem. She never, ever complained. I can remember only once when these hard circumstances nearly overwhelmed her. After a beating following one of Dad's drinking sessions, I found her crying. She told me she was going to end it all.

"I rushed off in a panic to fetch David and we eventually found her standing by a steep cliff at the back of our house. We talked her round, of course, and I think she realized that Kenny could not survive without her. She loved him dearly and this was her strength in putting up with Dad."

The family never discovered whether John McLellan brought his drinking habit back with him from Italy, as a result of his long period in convalescence, or whether it was because he found it difficult to come to terms with himself in peacetime South Africa. He would drink in binges, and these drinking sessions would last sometimes for several days, and then stop altogether for weeks. Drink could transform him from a quiet and serious man into a loud, boisterous and truculent bully. The violence engendered by the drinking cast a shadow over the family, bringing sadness and dread to them all. The drinking did not end with the school trips. He would start drinking after closing the shop early on a Saturday afternoon, having brought bottles of brandy back with him from town.

It became an ugly ritual. At first Brenda would drink with him, getting tipsy herself, and gradually they would both become louder. The children could see their father's expression turning to one of truculence. The arguments and the fighting would start. The other children would back off, fearful of their father's temper, but Heather would be defiant. "The rows would become violent and then he would beat my mother up. I remember one day something had gone wrong with the generator, or my brother had turned it off for the night. There were no electric lights. We were in my parents' bedroom – Kenny slept next to Mum, and Dad's bed was on the other side of the room. I don't know what provoked him but they began shrieking at one another. He took a burning kerosene lamp and flung it across the room. I dived to catch it. The glass was red hot but I held on to stop it falling to the floor, bursting into flames and spreading onto my paralyzed brother's bed. My hand was totally blistered from the glass. I was so frightened.

"When the rows started, my brothers and sisters would just leave the room, but I wanted to protect Mum and so I would always stay and listen to them fighting. Kenny couldn't leave, of course, and when the beating started he would howl with a mixture of rage and fear for Mum, but was helpless to intervene. So when Dad started beating Mum it was down to me to stop it. I would attack him from behind. Once, when I was very little, she was making cakes and had gone into the pantry to fetch some flour and he rushed in and came from behind to attack her. I dashed over to the fireplace, picked up a large piece of wood and hit him over the back with it several times as hard as I could.

"Other times I used to grab one of my shoes and hit him over and over on his back or neck. He'd get really mad with me and leave Mum, allowing her to escape, and start chasing me. However, with his artificial leg he never had a hope of catching me. Except once. He cornered me and placed his enormous hands around my neck. His face was red and contorted. I thought he was going to strangle me. I was terrified, but instead of pleading for mercy, I screamed: 'Go on then, do it! Do it – kill me! Do it now!'"

It was a turning point in their relationship. The big man just stood there looking down at his tiny but defiant daughter and saying nothing. Slowly his face muscles relaxed, he looked puzzled, then bewildered, took his hands from around Heather's neck and walked away. Despite the drunken periods that demeaned her father, she looks back upon him with fondness. "He was a very positive man. I cannot, for example, remember him expressing self-pity about anything. He never complained about his artificial leg. He suffered from stump sores, but would take a mild painkiller, and get on with his life, walking without a stick and with just a slight limp. Unfortunately, I don't think Dad was able to express loving emotion. It was only when he had taken alcohol that he became affectionate and that was when we would reject him. He would get mad at us, starting the rows. He loved us dearly, but I don't think he knew how to express love, having never had a mother figure to care for him. It wasn't until much later that I understood how his own past had affected him."

10
THE ODD ONE OUT

The sound of the Tom Jones hit, "The Green, Green Grass Of Home", being sung by children accompanied by a slightly out-of-tune piano, wafted from an open window across the trading station. At the piano was a slim, dark-haired girl, Myrtle, and around it stood three other children with tearful faces. A large man with a slight limp marched into the room and his voice seemed louder than the singing and the music: "Come on now, enough! It's time to go. The bus will be here soon." In the South Africa of the 1950s and 1960s, it was not just the children of the rich who were packed off to boarding institutions. Trading station children had to be sent away for an education. The McLellan children regarded the approaching term with dread.

Nongoma School was a single-storey, colonial-style brick building, the classrooms surrounded by several levels of wooded terracing. The teachers' houses, and other buildings, were situated around the perimeter. The boarding houses were on the other side of the road, opposite the school, which was run by the headmaster, Mr Hattingh, and his wife. Heather can recall certain moments, flashbacks, of her childhood. She loved to paint whenever she had spare time, and remembers having a colouring-in book and spending the afternoon working away on a picture. She showed it to somebody older who said dismissively: "Don't tell lies, you couldn't possibly have painted that. It must have been done by someone older than you."

In 1961 when the family moved to Madada, she followed her older siblings to Kokstad High School and remained a pupil there until 1969, when she was 16. She loved sport, particularly hockey, and was in the school team. However, she could be absorbed for hours reading, painting or listening to music. "I remember there was a teacher who sang very well," says Heather. "She had a beautiful soprano voice and I listened enthralled by her."

There were both Afrikaaners and English children at Kokstad High School. However, out of respect for the twin cultures that made up the white minority of South Africa, there were separate hostels and two parallel class streams. For some reason, and Heather suspected it was because her father had discovered it was cheaper, she was placed in the Afrikaaner hostel – even though her language was English and she was studying in that stream of the school. This increased her sense of isolation, and as the years rolled by she retreated further into herself.

What mattered to the teenage Heather were campaigns to save the elephants from dying in Namibia because of the drought, campaigns to save the rainforests of the Amazon, campaigns to save the whales, to stop pollution, and to help the poor. There were few allies to be found at the school. "These were the things I saw as real – these were the things that interested and also worried me. Politics was never discussed at home or in the classroom. Both my parents were racist in the sense that they believed white people were ordained to run society and that the given role of the blacks was to serve them. They would not have been able to perceive Africans on equal terms with the whites socially, but they never displayed any hostility towards them and sincerely believed it was their duty to treat black people fairly.

"Looking back, I believe that God did not intend for me to

develop radical political ideas at that stage of my life, because I might then have embarked on my struggle too early, and this would have diverted its subsequent direction. People were aware of my sense of kinship with the black people, but they did not care to discuss it with me. It used to enrage me to hear them talking about 'kaffirs' and referring to black people as inferior human beings, but I did not realize their views were abnormal. I thought I was the misfit.

"I had never travelled outside the world in which I had been brought up, and so it did not occur to me that the racist laws of South Africa, which discriminated against the black and mixed-race people, were any different from anywhere else. Our society was, after all, the only thing that young people like me had ever known."

As she grew older Heather became aware of religion and showed a precocious knowledge of the Bible that she would sometimes read at night, but the family did not go to church. "Mum would tell us, 'Never forget there is a God', and she would inspire us with how she treated people."

Heather progressed through the school always close to, if not top of the class, in all subjects except science. Her world was reading, reading and reading, painting and poetry, with hockey, netball and tennis thrown in to keep her fit and satisfy her strong competitive spirit. In class, as she went through the school, she was considered by some teachers to be a rebel because she often questioned the established order of things.

The teachers were aware that the classroom rebel was academic and they regarded young Heather McLellan as a star pupil who would matriculate and go on to take her place in higher education. It came as a shock to both them, and her family, when she decided at the age of 16 to leave school with her junior certificate of education, the equivalent of the British GCSE qualification. She took the decision to leave school because she doubted that her father would be prepared to pay for her fees through university.

"I had desperately wanted to go on to university, was a leading pupil in standard nine (lower sixth form), and was expecting to matriculate the following year and go to Durban University. My ambition was to become a geologist, or go into teaching. In retrospect I believe God was guiding me, even at this stage, and by steering me away from Durban University and a career as a geologist, he was keeping me for other ways in which to serve him."

Looking back, Heather recalls her childhood and adolescence as a time of loneliness, haunted by violence and shame. Her father's drinking, his violence towards her mother, and the ritual killing of animals either for food or because they supposedly posed a threat to food supplies, had left her in a state of depression. She longed for a peer group soulmate but never found one.

" I believed I was a misfit, which separated me from others. I felt awkward with people of my own age, and I could not explain to myself why was I so easily moved to tears. Then on top of that, there was this bizarre sense of experiencing the pain and grief of others. When I witnessed any kind of accident, like a fall or a cut, it would come on me as surely as though I had suffered it myself. I would get this numbness. At first I thought everyone experienced this sensation when others were hurt, then I discovered that I was the only one, and I felt a freak. It has remained with me through life. I have learned to deal with it now, but when I was younger it terrified me.

"To this day, I still get deeply affected by the lives and troubles of total strangers. I find myself going to absurd lengths to try to help people I don't even know. I know it's not how normal people react and I don't understand it. I don't choose to be an oddity, and I am not proud about it."

It was the end of Heather's childhood and the end of an era for the McLellan family. David and Myrtle had left home, and her parents were about to move on too. Later in 1969 they were forced to sell Madada to the Xhosa Development Corporation in the process of the black homeland being founded. By this time the McLellans had made enough money to buy a farm and supermarket 20 miles from Cathcart on the Thomas River in the Ciskei. Heather moved out of the home in the Transkei and went to stay with her aunt and uncle in Pietermaritzburg. She knew it was far too young to be leaving school but was excited by the new experiences that awaited her. She got a clerical job in an office, and had to learn how to type.

The head of the house was Brenda's younger brother, Uncle Vic May. He had always been a favourite with Heather. He was a lot younger than her mother, and his young lodger didn't feel there was a huge age gap between them. Vic and Rina, his wife, were ordinary working-class people and Heather felt safe at their house, living with her small cousins, one of whom was her godchild. After a few months, however, Heather felt an urge to move on and set her sights on moving to Durban.

The city is a major international port, with a cross-flow of young people from many parts of the world, and at that time it was in the full swing of the "flower power" era. Heather embraced the whole idea of this with a new excitement she hadn't encountered before. It all seemed to be about loving people and bringing peace – not war – to the world. She draped her now much longer hair with flowers at every opportunity, and embraced hippy make-up and hippy clothes. She started smoking and drinking but avoided the drugs scene. For the first time she felt a sense of total freedom. She was making the rules that governed her life, unconstrained by parental and institutional convention.

"I loved the songs of the Beatles and enjoyed the innocence of it all. I think I could have gone on enjoying the 'flower power' scene in Durban for longer, but after six months news came from home that Kenny was getting very ill, and was about to be admitted to hospital in Kokstad. I rushed home and I could see that he was sick. I remember looking at him and thinking: *He's going to die if he goes into hospital because he can't talk and no one will be able to understand him. Maybe I can go and work as a nurse at Kokstad Hospital. Then I can look after him and pull him through!* I was the only one, for example, who knew how to get the phlegm out of his throat.

"So I applied for a job and was accepted. I started nursing, and though I really enjoyed the caring side of the job, I still could not get rid of my phobia of blood, and other people's painful feelings somehow get transmitted through to me. It was really, really hard. On top of that, I had this whole thing about death. I had a fear about watching life leaving somebody's eyes. The staring eyes, the stiffness of the body, were not things that I could cope with emotionally. I also hated to see anybody cry – like when Mum used to weep when an animal died on the trading post."

Somehow, working in a hospital, she had to overcome those feelings, the fear of blood, and death. In the casualty ward, children would often be ambulanced in after a car crash, covered in blood. Heather hated it and was about to resign when she came up with an answer. She would swap duties with the other nurses. "Most of the other nurses could cope with blood, tragedy and death, but hated the smell and sight of clearing up when incontinent or sick people had made a mess of their clothes or bed linen. Now, here I had my chance! After all the years of looking after Kenny I was oblivious to the smell and sight of bodily fluids. So I used to swap duties with other nurses. I would do the things they hated and vice versa! It worked like a treat for a while. I was also allowed to look after Kenny in the hospital, and gradually we made him stronger."

Then something unfortunate happened. Heather still had not been able to overcome her emotional feelings, especially for sick babies and children. One night she was on duty in the paediatric ward when an 18-month-old baby with a heart defect died suddenly. His mother let out a long agonized and wounded cry. The young father collapsed in grief too. Then the grandparents also lost their self-control. Heather remembers: "I was crying and sobbing with them, and I realized with embarrassment that this was unprofessional. I was supposed to be strong for them, a shoulder for the baby's parents to cry on. I knew then that I could not cope with being a nurse. I was not cut out for it. So I resigned, and decided I would go back to office work or find something new."

It was at this time that Heather met the man who would have a profound effect upon her life for the next six years, bringing at first happiness, but later great sorrow and misery. She would marry him twice, and divorce him twice. Her first husband was a man who, perhaps without realizing it, would play a major role – as John McLellan had also done – in moulding the future Heather Reynolds.

She would become an atheist as a young woman, debunking Christianity, and doing her best to divert others away from religion too. The next six years of Heather's life would be painful and challenging.

11
LOVE AT FIRST SIGHT

He was a tall, dark, handsome stranger and he came into her life with a knock on the door at the small flat in Kokstad that Heather was renting while she worked at the hospital. He stood there with her neighbour, another girl, whom Heather knew quite well.

"Excuse me for disturbing you, but have you got any change? Sorry to bother you," he said, smiling. She was attracted immediately by his dark hair and smiling blue eyes. Barely over five feet three inches tall herself, she had to look up to his lean bronzed face. His name was Sarel Olivier, he was in his early twenties, and he literally swept her off her feet.

"Sarel and a male friend were visiting the girl next door and apparently he told her he liked the look of me. She came over shortly afterwards to ask if I wanted to join them on a night out. I politely declined that invitation, but two or three more followed in the next few days – and eventually I accepted. I soon fell completely in love with him. I was on fire with passion whenever he touched me."

It was, and remained while it lasted, an entirely physical relationship. They were opposites in every physical as well as spiritual sense: he a tall, dark man, and she a petite blonde. What clinched their relationship for Heather was that Sarel soon made it clear he was very happy to come with her to visit

Kenny in hospital. They would spend hours there, and she was extremely pleased to find that Sarel had great patience with Kenny. It was clear the two men were bonding despite her brother's handicap, and Sarel seemed to love her brother.

"For the first time, I was in a physical relationship and I couldn't think about much more than just this guy. I was in a vacuum with him; the other Heather, the thinker, the artist, and the conservationist, was put away. At first, I didn't seem to mind the fact we had nothing in common spiritually or intellectually. If I did try to talk about any of the many things that interested me, he would change the conversation. So I let it go. The major issues of life somehow became less important."

Looking back on those years in the late 1960s and early 1970s, she realizes that if she had stayed in Durban things might have been different. However, in East Griqualand, a rural backwater, the vast majority of young people knew and cared nothing of politics, or of the storm clouds looming on the horizon due to the apartheid system, and the growing international abhorrence of racism.

Sarel was Afrikaans and worked as a telephone technician, installing lines in the Kokstad area. This was a good job, although it meant a lot of travelling, and the couple felt that he could earn enough to keep both of them, allowing Heather time to look after Kenny during some months to give her mother a break. So they decided to get married after just eight months, and make their first home in an apartment in Winterton, Natal. Heather's mother and father didn't approve of the plans. "Perhaps they sensed that because I was a serious-minded person, it would not be a good match. I should have listened. This was indeed only my first affair, and there needed to be several of those before I got married. They didn't dislike Sarel at this stage – but they also thought we needed much more time.

"However, I must have started paying attention to their misgivings, or maybe Sarel's indifference to the things I held so

dear began to sow seeds of doubt. The day before the wedding, I became very upset and felt we should not go through
with it. I went to see Mum and confided in her. 'Mum, I want
to call the wedding off. I want to cancel it. I don't want to be
married,' I told her. She was horrified at the prospect of halt-
ing the whole bandwagon and said she thought everything had
gone too far. She didn't think we should cancel it. I cried — but
she said it was probably only wedding nerves. And so we were
married early in 1972. I think it's significant that if you look
at the photos of that day, you will not find one of me smiling.
I had realized I was making a mistake. I still loved Sarel but felt
we should not be making it so final. Mind you, there were lots
of happy times in the following months."

They both enjoyed outdoor pursuits, and would travel long
distances to stay in interesting places all over Natal and further into other provinces. In the summer they would camp in
the nearby Drakensberg Mountains. The young couple would
lie in their sleeping bags, watching a majestic sunrise, listening to the sounds of the bush, drinking in the intoxicating
mountain air. "We loved our time together when we were
camping in the mountains. Sarel also continued to enjoy his
relationship with Kenny. I just wanted it to work for everyone."

However, an element of disillusionment began to under-
mine their relationship by the end of the second year. On the
physical side, the passionate fires were ebbing away. There
were none of the great heights that Heather had expected. She
felt their bonding should have become closer in some spiritual
way, but the opposite appeared to be the case. She did not
understand what was absent. What she never realized was that
what was missing was the intellectual core of their relationship. They were not kindred spirits; there was no meeting of
minds. There were more and more silly arguments, which
later on became more and more aggressive. Sarel really
enjoyed provoking her and making her lose her temper. This

really gave him a kick and she got to dread it when he got into that mood. She began to recognize the pattern but never learned how not to react. When he made her lose control she got so angry she felt she could almost hit him.

"For example," she recalls, "on one occasion I came into the kitchen and found a bowl covered over by a cloth. When I removed the cloth I was horrified to find a sheep's guts ladled into it with the head stuck on top. That was his idea of a joke because he knew I could not stand anything dead, especially staring eyes."

She once threw a plate at him and he so enjoyed that spectacle he laughed and laughed, and she felt for the first time that she hated him. She hated the way he would do certain things for no other reason except to get her really angry, and would then tell her that he loved her, and loved to see her fighting mad. At times like this she felt totally repulsed, she felt she could hit him, she felt so much anger and humiliation. She also felt utterly alone.

The problems in the marriage also began to manifest themselves as a result of the couple's long absences from one another. When Brenda began to develop a heart problem and needed to go into hospital, Heather would take charge of both Kenny and John, sometimes for a month. Mostly though, she would bring Kenny to stay with them for a while until her mother recovered. Meanwhile Sarel was frequently working outside the area.

At that time, they got involved enthusiastically with a new charismatic church. The pastor and the leading members of the church told them that if they had sufficient faith they could help Kenny to walk, despite the fact that he was severely crippled and deformed. Naively, Heather became convinced that this miracle could really happen. In church they used to undertake strident prayer sessions for Kenny in which they would exhort him to walk. "Get up, Kenny, get up, Kenny. Walk! Come on!" they used to pray aloud, with the pastor leading exhortations. The group aroused such expectations in Kenny that at first he really believed he would get up and walk. In his eyes there was hope.

To this day Heather feels deeply guilty about what they did to her oldest brother. "Now can you imagine this severely crippled young man, 30 years old and in a wheelchair all his life, with the pastor telling him he is going to walk? I look back and realize it was cruel – how could we have done that? Then, when he wasn't able to get out of his wheelchair, it was almost implied that his own faith might be inadequate – nothing was wrong with their prayers, the church leaders assured us. It just required more faith and effort on Kenny's part. We did these prayer sessions with Kenny several times, on each occasion building up his expectations, exhorting him to have another try."

One day Heather noticed a different look on her brother's face when they took him to prayers. She said: "Come on, Kenny, shall we try it again?" From his body language it was clear he did not want to go on. Heather will never forget that look in his eyes, realizing in a moment how insensitive and stupid they had been, and how disillusioned Kenny had become. It left her very distressed, and it widened the gulf between herself and Sarel. The marriage was clearly in trouble, and there was a disturbing distance between them spiritually.

12
BETRAYAL
AND DIVORCE

The couple moved to Escourt, an historic town in the foothills of the Central Drakensberg. One day Heather came back from a long spell at the farm looking after Kenny and found that some of the photographs from her camera film had been developed before she completed the roll. When Sarel got home she asked him why, and asked for the negatives. He said he'd lost them. Instinctively from his response, she knew he was lying. It became an issue with her because there were photos on it that she wanted. "Stop lying!" she demanded. "Where are those negatives?"

Sarel searched, and eventually found them. However, there were only 16 negatives. He tried to claim that the others had not come out. "But where are they? I want to see them. I'm not a fool!" she shouted.

"I was imagining all sorts of things," she now recalls. "It was the first time in our relationship that I'd suspected him of betrayal. I was still a young girl, not into this kind of behaviour, and I was ragingly jealous and upset. By now it had become an obsession, and I started to phone people to try to find out what was behind it all. Their reactions made me feel there was something going on."

Sarel had become friendly with the pastor and his wife, and someone suggested: "Why not ask the pastor's wife? She knows a lot about his business." So Heather phoned her, and the pastor's wife was clearly cagey. Heather thought immediately: *She knows something for sure!*

When Sarel came back home, Heather had had time to think through a strategy and she play-acted the whole thing. "Why didn't you tell me there was another woman?" she asked. "I have just spoken to Maria and she told me all about it." Sarel then confessed. He begged forgiveness, and said he had met a girl from Mooi River and they had gone away for a weekend. Heather demanded the photographs and he told her the girl had got them.

"OK," she replied. "We're going to drive to her place in Mooi River now, and I want those photographs." So they went over to Mooi River and knocked on her door. When she answered the door the girl was obviously shocked and guilty, but instead of anger Heather remembers feeling hurt. She was just a plain girl.

"There was nothing about her that I could fathom to justify his adultery. What did he see in her? If she had been a glamorous or sexy woman, I might have been able to understand more about why he had done this to me. I knew I was not beautiful, but I did not feel inferior to her. I was also in good shape because I was very active, loved mountain climbing, hiking and was a keen badminton player. 'How could he do this to me – prefer her to me?' I kept asking myself."

There were photographs of Sarel and the girl on the film spending a weekend on the South Coast. Later, a bombshell exploded in Heather's mind when she discovered that the adulterous couple had stayed with the pastor and his wife. "This shocked me to the roots of my being. How could a man of the church, a man of God, not only condone, but also encourage adultery in this way? I had gone away to be at my mum's bedside when she was having a heart attack and they had sanctioned Sarel's deception!"

It was an episode that knocked not only her confidence in herself, but also her faith in God, and it triggered a period of her life in which she began to move away from a strong belief in Christianity towards atheism. She began to meet, through her job, educated people who endorsed her views. Perhaps as a form of revenge, Heather actively sought every opportunity to dissuade people from religion.

"I wanted to leave Sarel, of course, but he phoned his mum and dad on the night of his confession and they came over and did some counselling. His mother said that she had had the same experience with her own husband, and that she had forgiven him, and they had made a go of the marriage. Sarel was pleading with me to stay and promised there was no longer any relationship with the girl from Mooi River. From then on, he swore to me, I would be the only woman in his life. So I agreed to give him a second chance."

The marriage continued for another year and the couple tried to compensate for this fracture in their intimate relationship, and in Heather's broken trust in him, by travelling. She also managed to get a good job with a well-known international company and found this both absorbing and challenging. At the weekends they would go to the beach, or camp in the mountains. They would hike into the foothills and mountains around Escourt. It was a beautiful town, and one with which Sir Winston Churchill had been familiar nearly 80 years before. A few miles to the north is the Armoured Train Cemetery, where the future British prime minister was "captured" by the Boers while working as a newspaperman.

The "Burg" mountains stretch for over 150 miles. Heather and Sarel trekked across parts of it, from the massive basalt cliffs in the northern reaches, to the awesome sandstone buttresses in the south. At the Amphitheatre, site of the great Tugela waterfall, they spent hours trying to work things out. Sometimes it felt that they had, and at times like this the couple were contented. However, Sarel was restless. He always needed to be visiting or inviting guests to stay, always needing to go somewhere or do something, or wanting to party. He seemed to suffer from an innate restlessness within himself. The idea of working on the house or relaxing with a book or entertaining himself with some sort of hobby was something he would not consider seriously.

Heather recalls: "He needed company and drinks so that everyone was having a grand time. This was how we spent every weekend. I craved for quiet peaceful weekends, to do some work in the garden, and spend time with our animals. We had four dogs, two cats and a budgie, and they needed to be taken care of.

"I think I still must have been in love with him. However, there was an abusive streak in his nature that possibly acted to prevent the scars from healing. I was never physically abused, but he always tried to make me feel negative about myself. In the end he succeeded in making me think that I wasn't capable of anything. I felt I was useless at everything. He would criticize me endlessly. It was a form of mental cruelty, and no matter how resilient you try to be, it eventually gets to you."

To make things worse, Sarel remained a compulsive adulterer. More affairs followed the first one, and every time Heather found out, he would beg, he would plead, and he would cry. She could not work out why he went to other women. She had never refused him, and she felt that their relationship was normal − although for her the images of the other woman were often in the background making her feel inadequate. As a woman she felt she had failed him. At first, after discovering he had been unfaithful she would leave him for a week or so, but he would always manage to persuade her to come back. Perhaps she could not imagine life without him.

Eventually however, in 1975, Heather divorced him and moved to an apartment of her own in Escourt. It made no difference to Sarel. He would not believe she had stopped loving him and he would visit her and plead with her, hoping to rekindle their relationship. Despite her ex-husband's behaviour, Heather was so softhearted that she continued to see him when he was behaving rationally. She argued to herself that since both of them were in secure jobs, and she was living in a comfortable apartment in a quiet town, it was just possible they might work things out eventually and become reunited. Looking back over the years, it astonishes her that she did not have the courage to force the break in the relationship by moving right out of his life. Perhaps it had something to do with Kenny, with whom Sarel continued to have a bonded relationship, and who was going to become increasingly dependent upon Heather, with her mother in ailing health.

Around this time, Heather discovered that she was pregnant, having conceived with Sarel during one of their periods of reconciliation. Heather was ecstatic. At last, her own baby! She would love and nurture it – build her life around this infant. Perhaps it would be the first real step in creating a family around Sarel so they could settle down. She did not tell him at that time because although she really hoped they might succeed in this latest attempt at forging a relationship, she wanted the option to stay free if he continued to look for sex elsewhere. Heather also did not tell the doctor, who was a friend of hers, feeling ashamed that she had conceived a baby when she was no longer married. She was convinced people would see her as immoral, but was excited and happy to be pregnant.

It was a hard job not to reveal the secret, but she was strong enough mentally to keep it from Sarel, and for the moment the rest of the family. The bombshell came a few weeks later when an angry man, a stranger, came knocking at her door. "Do you realize your husband is having an affair with my wife?" he snapped.

Heather was devastated. Here she was, pregnant. They were supposed to be starting all over again, but they were back to square one. Shortly after the angry husband left, her brother David and his wife Sherril arrived to stay for the weekend. She didn't want to talk about what she had just learned because she knew they all thought she was crazy to have become involved with Sarel again. So she suppressed it, and began to feel extremely unwell over the weekend. They could tell something was wrong and Heather's sister-in-law wanted to stay and look after her, but she sent them away.

No sooner had they gone than she started bleeding profusely. "I thought, *What shall I do?* I tried ringing Mum but my call coincided with visitors arriving at her home, and she could not talk to me. Then the bleeding became much worse and I lay on my bed wondering whether I should summon the doctor. It would mean revealing to him that I was pregnant but not married.

"I did not have the opportunity to call him. Suddenly there was this excruciating pain and in those moments I lost the baby, a living fetus that had died because of me. My stress and unhappiness had ended its life. This experience tipped me over the edge. I just remember thinking, *I don't want to be here!* I couldn't face another tomorrow, or any further part of this troubled life. I had no expectation of an afterlife because I was utterly disillusioned with God after what had happened at the church with Kenny, and then the pastor's encouragement of Sarel's adultery. My contempt for Christianity had, incidentally, increased further when it was discovered the pastor had embezzled money from the church. I just wanted to find peace, to remove myself from what I felt was an evil world.

"I did see everything in a gloomy light at that time. The forests were being destroyed, whole species of animals were becoming extinct largely because of the greed of humankind, there was fighting all over Africa, and many other parts of the world including Ireland. I was exhausted, too, by the mental condition that seemed to make me the world's conscience, and by feeling the physical pain of others.

"I remember being quite cold and calculating as I went about the apartment preparing to end it all. Those who know me well will understand that I am a thorough person, one who likes to do things correctly. I wanted to make absolutely sure that my suicide would not fail because I could not face the shame of having failed.

"Kenny's sleeping tablets were stored in the apartment. I got the pills, a bottle of water and a hosepipe, and drove my grey Beetle Volkswagen deep into the countryside. I knew a place in the foothills of some mountains around Escourt where nobody would find me. Just nobody. It was so remote, right off the dirt road, and in high grass. I went in and parked near a little stream that I had come to know in the dry season when the water was low. The previous summer I had camped by the river when the shallow pools were heaving with fish. Some were stranded on their sides in the few inches of water remaining. On that visit I had clambered into the shallows and worked all weekend, heaving out stones and rocks to make the pools deep enough for the fish to survive the drought. It was probably futile but I had felt I had to do something.

"I fixed the hosepipe over the exhaust, fed this into the car, took 50 sleeping pills, locked myself in, and finally turned on the engine. *If the pills don't kill me, the fumes will. There's no chance of failure!* I thought to myself. *There's no way anyone will find me here. Just no way!* I lay back and could feel this sense of total peace come over me. It was such a feeling of relief now that I had got this far, a wonderful feeling of being able to let go and never having to worry about anything any more, never having to deal with the continual realization that I was a failure.

"I was slipping happily away into unconsciousness, and knew I would never come back again. As I was falling deeper into this peace I suddenly thought of God. *What if he does exist? No,* I thought, *he doesn't. It's all hocus-pocus! But if you do exist, God, then I'm going to meet you now, it's not going to be long! And I will confront you and tell you that you're a liar, because in the Bible you said you wouldn't push anybody beyond what he or she could bear. And I know that you have pushed me beyond my point of endurance. You cannot be a loving God."*

It was Heather's last conscious thought.

13
A FOOLISH DECISION

Heather woke up the following day in a bed in a hospital ward. "This is impossible!" she exclaimed angrily. "What am I doing in Escourt Hospital? The hospital where everybody knows me!"

She just couldn't believe it, and there was her doctor, an old friend, saying softly: "Why, Heather?"

She snapped: "Why am I here? How did this whole thing fail?" She was shocked and angry.

When the doctor saw how angry she was, and heard her strident demand for an immediate discharge, he replied: "No chance! You belong to the state. By law you're a criminal; suicide is a crime. You can be charged."

She replied: "Don't talk a load of nonsense to me. I'm leaving now." Then they forcibly held her down and sedated her.

She woke up the following day in a hospital in Pietermaritzburg, two-and-a-half hours away from Escourt by road. The doctors knew that if she had walked out of Escourt Hospital there and then, she would probably have gone straight back to the apartment and organized a second suicide attempt. She was in a state of total despair and mental collapse. She didn't want to see anybody, and she certainly didn't want to go through the whole thing and explain it. Heather didn't want visitors and was still angry.

The first person to come down was someone called Malcolm

Green, and he told her what had happened. Two teenage boys he knew had been walking early in the morning on a high ridge on his land, and looking down in the valley, they saw a bright light flashing in the sun. They figured out it must be poachers and that the sun was reflecting on the glass windshield of their vehicle. They ran down the hill as fast as they could to catch the poachers before they got away – and found the grey Beetle instead, with Heather unconscious and locked inside it. The older boy shouted: "My God! There's a woman in the car. She's locked herself in! We've got to smash in the side window. Quick, let's grab some rocks from the river and break it before the fumes kill her." Together, the boys smashed the side window, switched off the ignition, and frantically drove Heather up to Malcolm Green's homestead. She was then rushed to hospital just in time for the doctors to save her life.

Over the following days at Pietermaritzburg Hospital, flowers from friends – and other people Heather didn't realize cared about her – started to pour in. The ward was ablaze with colour. She was so ashamed, so embarrassed. All this love, all this attention – and what was she but a failed suicide? Once more she had failed!

Her boss, the managing director of the company she worked for, came to see her. He was full of compassion, saying: "Heather, you can take as much leave as you need, and it will all be fully paid. Just get well and don't worry about the time it takes. We'll be waiting for you when you come back."

She recalls: "It was like that from everybody. Whether I wanted to or not, I was not going to be allowed another suicide attempt, because now I was under close observation, and being overwhelmed with kindness and compassion. So the healing process started, and I went home to Mum, and later the Greens invited me to go and stay with them, instead of going back to the apartment in Escourt."

While she was at home with her mother Heather was strongly denying God. This worried Brenda McClellan. About six weeks later Heather's mother developed a huge boil under her arm; she was feeling incredibly tired, and her kidneys were failing. She was weak and it was clear she did not have long to live.

One evening Heather and her mother had a long conversation about faith. They agreed that when Brenda died she would return, to show Heather there was life after death. Their talk continued for several hours and Heather cried bitterly, telling her mother over and over again that if she was going to die, then there would be very little left in life for her. Three days later, Brenda McLellan died.

"A strange calm came over me, and it was as if my inner consciousness was making me strong because I had already said my farewells. I was able to cope with it. Despite the trauma of Mum's death I continued to grow stronger, and I think the realization that Kenny was going to need me even more gave me that vital inner strength. However, for the moment he continued to live with Dad and me on the farm, and then when I went back to work in Escourt he went on to live with my sister Myrtle and her family in Ladysmith."

Life began to get back to normal and Heather did eventually allow Sarel to re-enter it again. He seemed to be more reasonable now, and pleaded with her to come back to him for a fresh start. Few women who had been on the end of such mental cruelty from a partner, and endured so much misery that it engendered a suicide attempt, would have contemplated renewing the relationship. But Heather explains: " I had no close friend, family or familiar faces nearby and Sarel represented someone I could lean on, a comfortable shoulder. I certainly wasn't in love with him any more but I did have this lingering affection for him, and above all he still loved Kenny. I recall weighing all these things up, looking at the pros and cons, and coming to the conclusion that although ours was a deeply flawed relationship, there might be sufficient intent to make it work on both sides.

"My suicide experience had changed me. I was tougher than

before, more self-reliant, and believed the events of the past few months had had a positive effect upon me. I knew I should control my own life better. Others were beginning to rely upon me, and my new targets were based on practicality rather than emotion."

The priorities were clear. A proper home would have to be found for Kenny, and there was no one better qualified than Heather to provide it. Her mother had gone and John was alone, looking after himself – and running the business. The time was fast approaching when he would need to retire, and again, Heather felt she could look after him and provide him with a home. Her sister Myrtle had a young family and a relatively small home. Sarel appeared to fit well into the overall picture, and although Heather would never love him deeply again, she was moved by his pleading and apparent humility, and felt able to make a further commitment to him.

"What a fool I was!" she now admits.

Sarel and Heather were remarried in 1976. "We heard that a large house in Merrivale was on the market and we went to look for the owner, a man called Charles Kirton, who was chairman of the Natal Weightlifting Association. Charles owned a gym, so we went there and met him and he introduced us to a short, wiry guy with a beard in his early thirties called Patrick Reynolds. He was one of the Natal weightlifters with whom Charles was working out. We appeared to have interrupted an important training session, and it was clear from the way he scowled at me that this guy Patrick wasn't very pleased. He looked irritated, and was obviously wishing we would go away. Charles was happy to talk because he wanted to sell his house, but the scowl on Patrick's face deepened as the minutes went by. We eventually left and went to see the house."

They were introduced to Charles' wife who said half-jokingly: "OK. If you're taking over the house, how about taking over my job?"

"So what do you do?" asked Heather.

"I'm working in a local hospital as a secretary and typist. I also do some of the administration, and help the superintendent. It's a disability hospital actually," the woman explained.

"That could be just the answer to my problem," said Heather. "I have a brother with a disability who is living with me – so at the moment I am unable to work. If I could take over your job, and take Kenny with me when I go there, it would solve everything. Do you think they would let me take him to the hospital with me on a daily basis?"

"Oh, yes, surely. That wouldn't be a problem," the woman smiled.

So Heather contacted the Umgeni Waterfall Care and Rehabilitation Centre in Howick and was asked to go for a job interview with the secretary in charge of administration. And who should that be? Yes – Patrick Reynolds! He was the secretary at the hospital, the man who had clearly been so impatient at the gym. She thought: *Well, I've really blown this. I won't get the job. And to be fair I don't have very good typing skills, or much experience of the sort I think they require.*

However, fate was on Heather's side. She did get the job and she took Kenny with her each day. Patrick Reynolds turned out to be a good boss, considerate and loyal, but a total introvert. The following few months were a good period. Now she had a settled job, Kenny was happy, her father had moved in, and she was able to release her creative energies, especially in the garden. Patrick and his boss Cats Nelemans, the hospital superintendent, and Cats' wife Trisca, became good friends to Heather. She enrolled for painting classes, and who should be there? Yes, Patrick again! He turned out to be a highly talented sculptor in wood, and although he was still an amateur, his work was very highly regarded in the district.

"In a way he became my confidant," says Heather. "I started talking to him about personal things. He was a listener, he didn't talk much, but I found I could discuss any subject with him. I grew to love him as a friend."

Then, later in 1977, things began to unravel. To her great distress Heather discovered some grocery bills in Sarel's car that strongly suggested he had started cheating on her again. She confronted him and insisted that they move to separate rooms. Then she found out she was pregnant once more.

"Because of all the emotional upheaval, I started to have slight bleeding and due to the danger of miscarriage I was given sick leave. I managed to persuade Patrick to let me carry on working at home, and he used to come over with the typing that needed doing. I couldn't afford to lose my job now. I was a married woman, I had a home, I was pregnant, but I didn't want anything more to do with the man who was going to be the father of my child. This time I was much tougher than before." Heather desperately wanted the baby and was scared of losing it through fighting with Sarel, but she was determined now to resist him.

The atmosphere in the house grew tense because John McLellan, still physically powerful, saw himself as her natural protector, and he began to loathe Sarel. He made no effort to conceal his contempt for him. Heather had to confide in someone, and that person was Patrick Reynolds. However, the friendship was entirely platonic. In fact she had already made up her mind that if divorce from Sarel was coming, she would never, ever, ever have any kind of relationship with a man again. She was totally disillusioned.

Finally, one night there was a heated argument over some of Patrick's artwork that she had acquired. Sarel was suspicious that there was something between them and he raised it for the first time.

"What the hell are you wasting your money on this for?" Sarel demanded.

Heather replied angrily: "It's my money, and if I want to buy a couple of pieces of artwork, I can do that. I don't ask you why you waste half your money on booze and stuff like that!"

Sarel had acquired some workable wood while camping in

the forest and shortly afterwards in a telephone conversation Heather suggested he might give it to Patrick to create a sculpture. She recalls: "Sarel then went nuts, absolutely crazy, going on like a madman about Patrick. My father came into the room and told me to slam down the phone – which I did. Sarel rang back moments later, and my father let rip at him: 'Don't you dare accuse my daughter of doing something like that!' he shouted at him. 'She's seven months pregnant – she's hardly likely to be going out looking for a man, you idiot. She's not going to talk to you now, and if I had my way she'd never talk to you again.' Then he slammed the phone down.

" 'Right,' said my father. 'That's it. We're leaving. I'm going to go to town tomorrow and find us a place. We're getting out of here this week.' Frankly, I was nervous. I didn't want to fall back under my father's control, especially since he had started drinking again with his old service chums. Furthermore I was pregnant and in a very vulnerable condition that meant I could easily lose another baby. On the other hand, I was deeply insulted and wounded to have been accused of having an affair with Patrick. So, in many ways I did feel that I had had enough."

The next day Heather went to see Patrick at work, told him about the row, and asked for time off to move. He knew that the three of them – Heather, her father and their maid – would find it hard to lift heavy furniture, and he said: "Who's going to help you move?"

"Nobody. We'll manage on our own," said Heather.

"Well, would you like some help?" he asked. She accepted, thinking that being a weightlifter, he would be able to load up furniture that they could not possibly shift on their own.

The next day Patrick came, but the neighbour, who was a good friend of Sarel's, telephoned him to warn him Heather was moving out. After a couple of hours, Sarel arrived at the house and another serious confrontation developed. John McLellan warned Sarel to leave his daughter alone and not to approach her.

"I suspect he was quite prepared to use his crutch on him," says Heather. "He was still a formidably big man, and I think people around him always suspected that he was capable of inflicting considerable damage with it."

Sarel pointed to Patrick, who was quietly loading furniture onto a vehicle, and said accusingly to Heather: "And so what's with you and this guy?" Patrick just ignored Sarel's presence and went on moving the furniture onto the truck. When they'd finished they all drove off, leaving Sarel brooding in the house. Heather had taken just her personal belongings, a few inherited things from her mother, and they moved into the house that her father had found. She left nearly everything behind. "Frankly I didn't really care. I just wanted out – the time had come. Indeed, I never went back to that house," she recalls. It was a major turning point in her life. She was leaving behind years of heartbreak and frustration.

Sarel, however, still believed he could win her back. "Our departure didn't deter Sarel, of course, once he had found out where we were staying. He would come round and beg me to go back to him. He would plead and cry for hours. In a way I felt sorry for him, because he was a man who had desperately wanted a child, and was now going to be a father – but would not be in a position to enjoy a normal fatherhood. I think it was fate's cruel hand on this man's life and it chose to manifest itself at that critical moment. He desperately wanted a child, and now I had gone. The pleading, the cajoling, the threats, went on for several weeks but now I was determined not to succumb. One day I realized the only way to get Sarel out of my life was to move far away, possibly to Cape Town."

It was a fateful decision that would change her life for ever. Heather went into work the next morning and said to Patrick that she had had enough; she didn't think she could cope with Sarel any more. The only way to deal with it would be to leave the job, leave the town and move away. She said she thought she would go to Cape Town and make a clean break from Natal.

Once, a long time before, Heather had made a joke with Patrick, enquiring who cut his hair because there was a slight step in the cutting on one side of his scalp.

"Oh, it's the woman next door," he replied.

"Is she your girlfriend?" she asked.

"What's it to you?"

"Have you ever thought of getting married?" she asked.

"No, not really," he said.

"But have you ever wanted to get married?" she persisted.

"There's only one woman I've ever thought about getting married to," he said after a pause. And so she left it there, and never asked him again about his private life.

Now, some months later in his office, she was about to tender her immediate resignation. Patrick looked at her and said: "Do you remember asking me about ever wanting to get married?"

"Yes," said Heather.

"Do you remember me saying there was only one woman I ever wanted to marry?"

"Yes," she said.

"Well, now she's telling me she's going to Cape Town."

Heather laughed, thinking he wasn't being serious. "What? You're crazy!" she said, still laughing a little bewilderedly.

Heather recalls it was such a shock that she didn't have time to measure her response, or say something to avoid hurting his feelings – and later she realized her laughter had certainly done that. She hadn't handled it well, and went off to tea, leaving him in the office. They didn't really talk for the rest of the afternoon, and then it was time to go home in the evening. Just as it was time to leave, he stood in the doorway and asked: "Have you thought about what I said?"

She told him that she didn't consider there was anything further to be said. She didn't think it could possibly work, and she would certainly never, ever consider getting married again. She said that although she knew him as a friend, she didn't really know him on a personal level and so she couldn't consider it. She reminded him how she was (at that time) a heavy smoker, and he wasn't a smoker and would hate living with someone who was. She also reminded him that she was eight months pregnant and that her brother and father were living with her and that there would never be a chance of a relationship surviving under these circumstances.

Heather recalls she wasn't attracted to Patrick at that time. That's not to say he wasn't attractive, but she had been through something so horrific that she was not interested in any man. Patrick was just a good friend. They could talk for hours across a range of cerebral subjects, totally immersed in ideas and thoughts, and they shared many interests. But it never once occurred to her that this was exactly the kind of partner who could bring her fulfilment in every way. She had just never looked upon him as a man, a member of the opposite sex. Patrick Reynolds was a soulmate.

"So there it was. I had turned him down pretty bluntly, but I really didn't think there was much feeling on his part either. He had never indicated or demonstrated any affection or attraction for me, so I think I was reacting as though he had suggested this idea of marrying me off the top of his head — without thinking it through. There was no emotion involved." As far as Heather was concerned she had filed for divorce, was free, and intended to stay that way. She didn't even appease Patrick by saying she'd think about it. So she walked out and went home for the weekend.

On the Monday morning Patrick walked in to work and Heather was shocked by what she saw. She had never seen him looking so terrible. He was ashen, and appeared sick. "What's wrong?" she gasped.

"Don't ask me what happened," he snapped back, with a cold look in his eyes.

Then the realization hit her. This man cared about her, and she had broken him. She just could not believe it. There was

this guy, usually so remote and aloof, and here he was, looking stricken, haggard and awful. She was appalled at what she
had said and done, and realized too late the depth and extent
of his feelings.

"I am so sorry," she blurted out.

"I really don't want to discuss it," he replied quietly.

Heather felt the full force of his hurt, and wanted to make
it better. Her eyes welled with tears.

"Surely we can talk," she pleaded.

"I don't think there's much to be said," he replied.

"Look, you've put me in a predicament," said Heather. "I
don't even know you. We've been friends for two years but on
an entirely different level. Patrick, I can't bear you being hurt
like this – why don't we go out to dinner, why don't we start
getting to know one another? At least we can try?" She was
somehow searching for a way to ease his misery, and now
hers. "Let's go and have a coffee after work and talk about
this," she suggested.

He agreed. So they met after work and it gave her an
opportunity to explain why she had reacted in a negative and
off-handed manner, and how she now regretted that and was
sorry. She had not been able to accept that he loved her that
deeply, but now realized his feelings were genuine.

"Why would I ask you to marry me if I didn't feel deeply
for you?" he asked.

"Look," she said, "before yesterday you never gave me the
slightest idea about how you felt. There was nothing to suggest it in what you said and did. How would I know you loved
me so deeply?"

Patrick Reynolds, she was about to find out, is an incredibly honourable and moral man. He told her then that he
would never have considered speaking to her about his feelings while she was married, and would not have done so
before she was properly divorced – had she not announced
her intention of moving out of his life. The two of them went

into new and deep discussions. He argued that going to Cape Town would not help her because Sarel only needed to apply for a transfer and could follow her down there. She would be away from her friends and there would be less of a support system in the big city than in Merrivale. She listened to him and agreed. Patrick then suggested that he should move in to Heather and John's house as a paying guest with his own room because he could give her support in the pregnancy, taking her to hospital when she needed to go there nearer the birth, and also helping to look after Kenny when she had to go into hospital.

"But what will that look like?" she asked, worried what people might think, and about her reputation.

"Let's do what's best for us and not worry about that," he replied.

So Patrick moved in, and Heather met his family. Sarel, of course, was now convinced there was something going on between them. Heather was nine months pregnant with Brendan, but because that was the way Sarel's mind worked, he was convinced the new set-up was all about sex. He must have been shocked by the strength of her reaction. "I'm not having an affair with Patrick," Heather told Sarel, "but I've filed for divorce from you, and if I want to I *will* have an affair – either with him or a hundred others. I'm entitled now to live my own life without you and that's the way it's going to be!" Sarel had discovered to his cost that Heather now felt much more confident in dealing with him. Then it finally dawned on him that Patrick was going to be a feature in her life for ever. He had lost her.

Sarel arrived outside Heather's house, carrying a metal bar. She walked out towards him and he strode up with a threatening expression on his face. "I'm going to kill him. He's not taking you away from me!" he shouted.

She screamed back: "I don't belong to you any more! It's finished."

Heather was frightened now because Sarel was a big man. Her father was not around and she thought Patrick might be killed, or seriously injured, if Sarel lost control of himself. What made it so much worse was that Patrick was completely innocent. She ran into Patrick's room at the back of the house. He looked up calmly as she shouted: "Sarel's here, he's got a metal bar, and he says he's going to kill you!"

Heather was trying to find in her mind some way to appease Sarel and prevent the confrontation. She walked hurriedly around to the front of the house ahead of Patrick, but he gently took her by the shoulders, put her firmly aside and said quietly: "I'll deal with this."

He confronted Sarel, asking: "What exactly is this all about?"

"I'm not going to allow you to steal her from me. She's mine!" Sarel snarled.

Patrick's voice was quiet and assured. "She's certainly not yours. Face the truth, Sarel, you've never wanted her. You've always wanted someone else. You ruined her life, and you're still ruining her life. You treat her without any respect and dignity, any true affection and love, and you certainly don't deserve her. Now you are even putting her baby under threat."

He continued: "Heather is everything that I've ever wanted, and now I am going to look after her, care for her and the baby. I'll treat her properly, give her respect, and love, and everything that she deserves."

The quiet words had the power of ten sledgehammers upon Sarel as he realized the truth of what Patrick said, and that this time there would be no turning back of the clock. He seemed to crumple, to wilt before their eyes, with tears welling up. Heather recalls: "I'll never forget it. Patrick and I were on the veranda of the house by now, and we walked down the steps together. I felt so sorry for Sarel. He turned away, walked in a dejected manner down the drive, and drove off in his car. I was astonished. Here was this new man in my life that I still felt I hardly knew, who in a few quiet words – but words expressive of such strength and conviction – had charted a new way forward for me. He had shown total courage in the face of aggression from a man much larger than himself, and armed with a weapon that could have been lethal."

A few weeks later, Brendan was born and it caused some confusion in the hospital because Heather had two men visiting her, both playing the paternal role. She was determined to get Patrick involved with Brendan from the first moment. On the other hand, she couldn't say no to Sarel because Brendan was his son. "He would sit at my bedside and cry and cry. I think, somehow, Brendan must have felt the incredible tension. Then Patrick would come in and find me with a face swollen from tears. I could feel the incredible pain that Sarel was suffering, but I knew I just could not go there again. It was over. He loved his little son so much, and was so remorseful that, maybe, he would never have had an affair with a woman again, but this was now only part of the equation for me. I was through, for ever, with power struggles and provocation."

Heather had seen the harmony in Patrick's life. There was another path waiting for her.

14
A NEW LIFE
WITH PATRICK

The divorce began to go through, and in due course Patrick asked Heather to marry him. She resisted it and suggested they might just live together. She told Patrick she could never have an intimate relationship with a man again. Why didn't they just live together as friends, with no physical relationship?

"I've never asked you to have a physical relationship with me," he replied.

Heather looked at him and realized he was quite serious. "Then why don't we just live together?" she asked again.

"No, I want to marry you," he insisted. "I will be your husband. I will protect you, and love you for the rest of your life. But if you never want to sleep with me, then so be it."

A few months passed, and he would say to her with increasing frequency, "Well, have you thought about it?"

Eventually Heather thought to herself: *Look, this thing could possibly work. We get on very well together, share so much in common, and if he is prepared not to want anything from me, then perhaps we could get married. He puts up with my father's drinking, and my brother's illness. If I could still sleep in Kenny's room, then everything could be fine.*

So she said to Patrick: "OK. Let's take it a step closer. You know a lot about me. I don't really know anything about you – or your personal habits. Let's take a trip together overseas to Europe, maybe about seven weeks on maximum leave." This was a test. Heather reckoned that when companions were travelling at that pace continually, and in close proximity physically, it would be hard to hide things away – not to see one another in their worst light. Patrick might get on her nerves, and if she also happened to be tired and hungry, it was a recipe for conflict.

So they travelled from South Africa to England, to Germany, Denmark, Switzerland, to Sweden, Norway, Austria... and just kept moving – backwards and forwards, always tailing back – to see the effects of this stressful trip upon their relationship. It turned out to be the most memorable and romantic journey of their lives! The schedule was irrelevant. Heather fell deeply in love with Patrick and then was sorry that she had planned it so badly – because they were having so much fun. "It was amazing," she recalls. "I had found my soulmate! The trip was the most fantastic, wonderful time. He was so considerate, so gentle, and so marvellous in everything. I told him one night I would give him my answer to his marriage proposal when we arrived back home."

As soon as they got out of the airport and into his car, he said: "Well, what's your answer?"

She looked at him, and smiled: "Yes. OK. Let's go for it!"

They had arrived back in South Africa just before the New Year in 1979, and the divorce papers had already come through. Now, Patrick's feet hardly touched the ground. That very day he was on the telephone to the Methodist minister in Howick and arranged the wedding in the minimum time permitted, which was three weeks.

Patrick and Heather were married at a quiet service for just family and a few friends in January 1979. She was married for the third time, and at the age of 27 had at last found happiness and a solid family life with Patrick, her father, Kenny and Brendan. Bronwen, their daughter, was born in 1980. They moved from the house John McLellan had rented, to Umgeni

Waterfall Care and Rehabilitation Centre. The secretary's residence was a smart and spacious, double-storey house with a large garden.

Who was this man Patrick who had come into Heather's life and why was he important to her development as a person?

"He is a total introvert," she explains, "with really strong principles and values. He never compromises. You tend not to notice Patrick, because he is always in the background. He is a listener and seems to engender respect among all who know him. If he says anything, people normally listen. However, even though he may be an intellectual, he doesn't enjoy working on cars or doing maintenance; his skills lie elsewhere. Tell him to make a scale model of your house, make a model of a ship etc., or even a toy chainsaw, but don't ask him to cook and don't ask him to fix your car."

Patrick Reynolds has been a great reader of books all his life. He consumes them. Friends say that if there is nothing to hand published for him to look at, he'll read bits of paper on the desk. He loves literature, history, mythology, astronomy and the sciences. Heather had never explored this world and meeting him was the beginning of a long and intensive process of self-education. At school she had been in the top stream but life had been regimented, with sporting commitments. She recounts: "I got totally caught up in astronomy, and I literally devoured every book I could lay my hands upon. Soon, I came upon quantum physics and was fascinated by it. Patrick introduced me to Darwin and evolution. At school, we had not really discussed evolution. Now I was devouring everything I could find about it. At first, it reinforced my conviction that Christianity had been a blind alley. I read about scientific explanations for how the universe had started through the "Big Bang" and how human beings had evolved. Patrick and I together explored all these things but I became disillusioned when I had read every book about it.

"The Darwinian principle of survival of the fittest and its

concept of natural adaptation is unquestionable and very few people will argue with that conclusion. But I still needed to be convinced that everything came from one living cell and that random mutations were responsible for every major adaptation, and provided perfect DNA. For example, the perfect wing of a bird and its changed bone structure, the eye, the lungs, etc. – these are not adaptations but incredibly complex and sophisticated body organs, plus functions. That is where I found it easier to believe that a creator designed and masterminded everything – rather than that billions of random mutations just happened at various times."

Heather was also still deeply disillusioned with the church. She then started reading the ideas of many other scientists on evolution, such as Fred Hoyle. She discovered that there were others whose work remained ignored and unpublished in the mainstream. They were often denied a proper platform upon which to put forward their views and ideas. She realized then that there could be no sense of fulfilment in the quest for knowledge about the creation. So she moved on. "I then got involved with subatomic particles and found that here was a world in which I could blow my mind!"

However, the most inspiring quality of Patrick Reynolds was his talent as an artist. Heather was deeply impressed by the wooden sculptures – many depicting the human form – which he created in his spare time. She was convinced his work was the result of a natural gift, and it became an essential part of her programme to provide him with the maximum creative time and space to carry on his work. She began to feel they should move away from the hospital to give him more space and opportunity to develop his artistic work.

Before any decision could be made, there was news within the family concerning her father and it was sad news: "At this time my dad had gone back to live with Myrtle and some time later he went into hospital for heart treatment, and died after a short illness. I always regretted not having that final, definitive conversation with him because in later life I came to realize what had made him behave in the way he did, and why he took to drinking. He had never known love as a young, orphaned and abandoned child, and so he had found it difficult to give hugs and show affection when sober, although his heart was full of love for us. I now can see that when he was under the influence of alcohol his inhibitions dropped and he wanted to hug and cuddle us – but that was when we all rejected him. No child wants a drunken parent hugging and kissing her.

"Of course when we rejected him he would be hurt and angry and that was possibly the beginning of many of the misunderstandings that led to awful quarrels, with him chasing us all out of the house. These are some of the possible conclusions that I have reached when analyzing his behaviour now. There were things in his personality that were due to his awful childhood – perhaps he had not even understood that himself. Counselling would probably have sorted out all that unhappiness. I wanted to tell him that I understood, and that Mum and I forgave him. He had sometimes brought shame and sadness to our family through his drinking, but my overriding memories of him are fond ones.

"I admired his loyalty towards those he cared about, his honest and straightforward nature, and the way he tackled life without allowing his disabilities to sap his energy and resolve. Dad never complained about anything – except other members of the family spending money – and he set us a fine example. I loved him deeply."

It was now clear that Heather and Patrick needed less space than before, because her father would not be returning, and Kenny was staying with Myrtle, while Bronwen was still in her infancy. Soon the opportunity presented itself for them to buy their first home together, and they bought a family house in the nearby town of Merrivale. It was a beautiful home with a large garden and double garage, which they converted into a studio. Most weekends would be spent blissfully, with the children playing around them, as Patrick worked in his studio and Heather painted her landscapes or worked in the garden. She continued to enjoy her art, reading, gardening and badminton, and she also found time to respond to stiffer challenges that included mountain climbing and flying.

Heather was in her late twenties and at last, thanks entirely to Patrick's support and encouragement, able to enjoy the kind of self-fulfilment that had been missing during her first marriage. Her self-confidence increased in leaps and bounds. She remained an atheist, although she always wondered about her failed suicide attempt and questioned whether there was a remote possibility that it had failed through divine intervention. Then she had an important experience that would change her life profoundly and bring her back to God.

15
HEATHER RETURNS TO GOD

Dusk was approaching, and Heather was late for a badminton club committee meeting that was being held in Pietermaritzburg. She was driving fast along the motorway with Brendan, who was still a toddler. He was strapped into a baby-seat in the back. Ahead, she saw two trucks, one behind the other in the left-hand lane. She was expecting the second truck to pass the one ahead of it, so she slowed and waited for the driver to pull out. But he didn't.

"Come on, come on, get on with it," she muttered impatiently as she slowed down.

Still the second lorry driver held his position. Heather started to accelerate and was in the process of overtaking when the second lorry pulled out in front of her without any signal. She literally "stood" on the brakes, swerving to the right, leaving a cloud of blue smoke and missing the truck by inches. She was shaken but very relieved.

The road into Pietermaritzburg is long, steep and winding. Heather had to brake at each curve to control her speed and soon realized something was wrong with her brakes. They were spongy. She had to pump repeatedly to produce any effect. As she approached a stop sign at a major intersection, they failed completely. She wrote later:

Then I saw headlights approaching at speed. I knew that a collision was unavoidable! Brendan, my precious son, was directly in
its path. In an instinctive attempt to avoid the collision I acceler-
ated. The oncoming car struck the rear passenger door – close
to where Brendan was sleeping – I remember vividly the terrible sound of the impact. The car spun several times and finally
came to rest on the pavement. There was a deathly silence. I realized I was unhurt, just dazed and shocked. But what of my baby
– was he alive? In frantic anxiety I jumped out and opened the
rear door. With my heart filled with dread I fumbled in the dark
interior for an interminable moment. I could not find him. I
said: "God, if you are there, please let my son be safe. I ask for a
miracle. If he is unhurt I'll search for you."

And then my hands found him, untouched, his eyes wide
open. I shook him to make sure he was alive; his little mouth
quivered as he began to cry. My heart filled with joy.

I turned towards the car that had hit me. I didn't know if anybody had been killed or injured. Perhaps someone had gone
through the windscreen – my heart filled with dread once more!
Two men were walking towards me, one of them a very big
man. They were both dressed in tennis outfits.

I have always hated any kind of public humiliation, and now all
these cars were stopping, and a crowd was gathering. I was
responsible for this accident. I expected them to be furious and
even abusive, but they didn't speak, they just kept walking
towards me. I wondered again, had anyone been killed? The big
man loomed over me; by now I was quite terrified. Was he going
to assault me? But instead of shouting or cursing, he laid a hand
on my shoulder, and asked in the gentlest voice, "Are you OK?
Are you hurt?"

I had just wrecked his brand new silver Jaguar sports car,
written if off – and yet this man's only concern was whether
anyone had been injured. It was the last thing I expected him to
say. I replied: "I'm fine."

"Anyone else in the car?" he asked.

"Just my son in the back and he's OK."

"Then let us thank God that no one was hurt."

He placed his other hand on the shoulder of his friend, and together we bowed our heads in prayer. Suddenly all the pain, and the hurt, and the anger of those former years dissolved. Here standing in front of me was what I had searched for in Christianity. This was the sort of person I had always hoped Christianity would produce. In some way, this big man had expunged all the earlier pain I had experienced as a young woman. I started to cry.

He probably thought I was crying because of the shock, and this may have been partly true. However, I was thinking, *This is how I would like to be. This is the sort of Christian I would like to become.*

I whispered to God: "From this day on I will seek you, in truth, and with an open heart and with an open mind."

When the police arrived, the big man said to them: "Her brakes failed. It was an act of God." They checked the car and confirmed this.

The next day he telephoned to see if I was OK.

The accident seemed to mark a turning point in the Reynolds' lives because within weeks things were to change for ever — and for the better.

Heather had taken a job that seemed to offer her a career path. She loved the challenges it presented, and although some might not necessarily see her in a corporate role, she had come across a project that excited her for two reasons. It would test her abilities as a good manager and organizer, and it would benefit the poorer members of society. This was a new innovative group insurance policy that was affordable and targeted the African market. Heather was fluent in both the Zulu and Xhosa languages. She worked with a team of enthusiastic young men, and as they travelled around KwaZulu-Natal they were extremely successful in developing the programmes from scratch. Unfortunately, the boss was one of those people who liked to socialize and was often in the canteen chatting with the guys. He also took the credit for the endeavour of others, and was disinclined to do much work himself. Looking back, Heather agrees that she had become rather ruthless with men who treated women without proper respect. She was not – and never had been – a feminist but having survived terrible ordeals with Sarel Olivier, men ceased to intimidate her.

"At that time South Africa was a chauvinistic world," recalls Heather, "and women accepted that. However, I had made up my mind that I was never going to be subjected to male dominance again. Men were no longer something to fear. I had won my freedom from that. I put up with my boss, provided he did not interfere with the way I ran things, but unfortunately he began to see me as a threat. People were coming to me for answers, and also for solutions to problems. Often he found himself out of the loop through his own loose management style." She realized it was only a matter of time before he would forfeit his job over this mismanagement, and she would be asked to take over the reins to manage the business properly. However, a shock was around the corner, and it came in 1983.

"When first recruited for the job, I had told the management that I would never be available to work on Saturdays because it was family time. I had promised to give 100 percent, five days a week, Monday to Friday, but also made it clear I could do no more than that. This had been accepted, and I had been hired."

Now, the boss called her into his office and announced that he wanted everyone on the team to work on Saturdays – because of the huge increase in business, which Heather's team had generated. Cunningly, he had worked out that she would not want to lose her weekends with Patrick and the children, and realized it was the only way he could get rid of her. This came at a time during which Heather had been working a lot of overtime and seeing a lot less of her children than she would have liked, coming home late and leaving early in the mornings.

One previous Sunday afternoon, as Heather and her mother-in-law Agnes were sitting chatting, Agnes had asked her: "Do you know Bronwen took her first steps?" Heather was stunned. Trying to hide her devastation, all she could remember was a story she'd heard some years earlier, about a friend who'd missed her child's first steps, and Heather could recall feeling terribly sorry for her. Now she sat in the same position, and nothing she could do could turn back the clock to undo it. With this in mind, her priorities had been highlighted, and now, as the unfair call to work weekends came, her resolve strengthened.

"I was so angry. I phoned head office and spoke to the man who had jointly recruited me for the job. I said to him: 'Do you remember that the day I went for my final interview, I made it clear that I would not be prepared to work on Saturdays?'

" 'No,' the man said, 'I don't.' "

Heather felt that was the end. She had no leg to stand on. If the head office man could not remember their verbal agreement, she had no option but to resign – because it would be the word of two managers against hers, and they were senior.

"OK. Then I'll resign," she told them – furious that she had not asked for a clause to be written into her contract. That night she went home really angry. She had put her heart and soul into the job. She told Patrick what had happened and they talked about it. Then she remembered that a friend, Rob Wareing, a portrait artist who had recently painted Heather, had told them a few months before how he had become a full-time artist.

"I'd just wanted to get out of it," he'd said, referring to his full-time job. An electrician, he had put down his tools and announced: "That's it – I'm finished with this." Next day, he started life as an artist.

Although Heather treasured their weekends together, she used to loathe Sunday evenings when Patrick had to put down his tools in the studio, no matter how important the work, or how critical the stage he had reached, and close it down for another five days. She had come to realize he desperately needed the opportunity to operate as a full-time artist. He had a folder full of ideas that he wanted to sculpt, yet if he carried on working only at weekends he would face nothing but continuing frustration in the future. Very few of his wonderful ideas would ever be created. Patrick Reynolds' speciality is for the human figure, usually female and often in adolescent or child form.

Shortly after they met, Heather had bought one of Patrick's best, well-known pieces, *The Bicycle Girl*, which he originally sculpted in wood. It is now available to everyone in bronze, and is a great favourite. She says of her husband: "He has also done some outstanding work of animals. All of Patrick's work is intricate and finely detailed. There is a 'feel' in everything he touches with his chisel that I find unique."

Locally, around Pietermaritzburg, Patrick already had a substantial following – but his problem was in finding enough time to do the pieces people wanted. Heather relates: "I was by now deeply in love with Patrick, and regarded him as a truly great sculptor. It hurt me to see him so frustrated, even though he would never admit it to anyone. Patrick was rarely demonstrative with his emotions, but I could read his true mood. And so, when the altercation with my boss came out of the blue, instead of treating it as a disaster I decided to regard it as an opportunity for us to break free and move on together. Patrick would have his freedom to become a full-time professional artist, whatever the cost, and whatever the risk."

The couple had some savings, some income from pensions, and there would be money from the sale of the house.

Heather and Patrick calculated this would be sufficient to last them for two years until Patrick had completed sufficient pieces to attend a big exhibition in Pietermaritzburg. "Why don't we go off and do it?" she said to Patrick. Her recollection is that he didn't need much persuading! She was up at dawn to read the paper and find out if there were any properties in the "For rent" columns that might suit their plans. Once again fate intervened. There was an old farmhouse advertised, not far away, but in a direction that they had never travelled, in a place called Dalton.

It was set in the foothills about 30 miles from Pietermaritzburg. By six o'clock the next morning they were there. It turned out to be a remote, stand-alone property called Deep Valley that had fallen into a state of considerable dereliction. The homestead was midway up a hill, about four miles along a narrow road from the nearest shop, and nearly a mile from the nearest neighbour.

They fell in love with Deep Valley immediately. It was a German colonial farmhouse, built in cut stone. The white paintwork was peeling off both the wooden shuttered windows and the ornate trellis on the wide verandas. No matter! Here was the perfect setting for a couple of artists to go and hide – and do their thing! "So we signed up to rent the farmhouse, with the idea that one day we might have sufficient money to buy it," Heather recalls.

They agreed Patrick would take the leave owing to him at the hospital as soon as possible and tender his resignation. Heather, of course, had already resigned from her company and did not expect to hear from them again. That day they paid a few months' rent to the owner of Deep Valley, and went back home to Merrivale. As soon as they got back, the phone rang. It was the head office of Heather's former company. The managing director came on the line.

"Hello, Heather," he said. "We'd like you to reconsider your resignation. We want you to take over the office immediately."

She couldn't believe her ears. Patrick said immediately, "You have to take the position." She shook her head. Not for one moment was she tempted to say: "Yes! I'll come back!" The promotion was no longer important. They were artists. They were going to live as artists. They had just glimpsed paradise.

16
THE DEEP VALLEY YEARS

In the coming weeks Heather and Patrick could hardly wait for their move to Deep Valley. Patrick brought with him his chisels, a collection built up during his travels in Europe. They invested in a band saw, a circular saw and a planer. Later, when the local community discovered that a sculptor had come to live in the district, the local boys' school invited Patrick to go along once a week and teach woodwork.

They converted one of the front rooms off the veranda into Patrick's studio, while the other, which had been the lounge, became the bedroom. It meant that while Patrick was working, and Heather was with the children in the bedroom, they could still communicate, especially if he wanted to work late. She remembers: "Those were balmy days before the climate began to change. Now, in KwaZulu-Natal, the weather is not predictable. I would bring my easel out onto the veranda, painting in the shade of the hot sun, while Patrick worked in the studio. The hours would glide by in tranquil bliss. Even in the months of winter, from May until August, the weather was generally sunny, although some days it was freezing cold."

Heather has always been an organizer, and her skills extended to running a kitchen that most other women would envy. She learned to bake her own bread at Deep Valley, made jam from the garden fruit, chutney from the vegetables, and even found time to bake biscuits and cakes. The children remember elaborate icing on their birthday cakes. They would enjoy English-style birthday parties in the garden, when all their friends from school and the local farms around would be invited. Here in her piece of paradise, Heather was finally content with life.

One night, as she was lying in bed next to Patrick, the figure of her mother appeared. Heather still does not know whether it was a dream, or reality. Brenda McLellan stood at the foot of the bed. Heather relates: "I experienced this powerful rushing sound within my head, and it felt as if my mind was being sucked by a powerful vacuum cleaner. It was such a strong feeling – not scary – and it felt as though I would be swept across the universe in a moment. Part of me wanted to let go, and go with her, but the logical side of me was afraid of not being able to return. I remember saying in my mind, *No, no, Mum, I can't go with you. I don't want to leave Patrick, Kenny and the children. I am all right now. I am too scared to go with you, I am scared I will not come back. I cannot go with you.*"

Heather has never since been able to explain the visitation of her mother, but recalls the promise Brenda made to her before she died. She will never know whether it was a powerful dream or not!

In the first year at Deep Valley Kenny returned to live with them and together they made the garden a priority target, creating it in the English style with a lawn, roses, hydrangeas, and paths intertwining with herbaceous flowerbeds of exotic African flora. It was large, about an acre, and had become quite wild. There was plenty to do. The Africans who had worked for them at Merrivale soon found the travelling out to Deep Valley too much, and so they didn't stay long after helping to train replacements. New faces appeared. "Lena had come to Deep Valley to nurse my brother Kenny, and I was teaching her to understand him because he couldn't speak. One day she told me that her daughter Betty, who was still of school age, had become pregnant and would like an opportunity to work for us. I said OK, so Betty came with her baby, lived on the farm, and we got to love her dearly."

Sadly, as the months passed, Kenny's health began to deteriorate. The last few weeks of Kenny's life are a painful memory for Heather and it brings tears when she revisits them, but she takes comfort from the fact that at Deep Valley he was able to experience once again, in some form, the outdoor life he had enjoyed on John McLellan's farm. There he'd looked after the dairy, and maintained the fencing on the land.

"At Deep Valley," says Heather, "we built a chicken run and Kenny kept an eye on the chickens and the garden, making sure it was weeded and watered daily. However, he had major circulation problems by this time and his kidneys were not functioning well. He no longer had the energy to do the amount of work he'd once been capable of doing, but at least he found a form of fulfilment.

"One day in 1984, we took him for a treat to the Royal Show and on the way back he seemed to be in considerable pain. I gave him a painkiller but while I was talking to him he stopped responding. It was clear he was dying. I jumped into the back seat and tried to revive him. We drove as fast as we could to the nearby hospital, the same one where Brendan and Bronwen were born, but he was certified dead on arrival. A blood clot had lodged in his lung. I loved Kenny dearly and I find it hard even now, 20 or so years after he has left us, not to cry when I recall his life and his death. He was a normal man trapped inside a feeble body, imprisoned for his entire life within something from which he had no hope or chance of escape. And yet Kenny tackled his life with courage, usually with humour and without complaint. My oldest brother inspired me as a true hero."

Fortunately, Kenny's death came at a time when Heather's faith was growing stronger. She was starting to pray regularly, and this often seemed to help in bringing solutions to the family's problems. They were now towards the end of the second year at Deep Valley, and Patrick was completing more of his pieces. Heather was able to assist him in several ways. Soon after she had met Patrick she wanted to help him, and when she bought *The Cup Girl* when they were living at Howick, she asked if he would mind if she did a little more finishing work on it. "It was slightly rough in surface and its hardboard base was unsightly. Patrick is a creator rather than a finisher. So I took the sandpaper and spent hours and hours doing the finishing. It was almost as if I had been doing it all my life; my fingers knew just what to do. Soon I was picking up the knife and cleaning off bits and refining. I could not sculpt, but could help him by finishing his work. By the time we were living at Deep Valley I had learned how to wet and raise the burr, sand it once more, stain and polish."

Most of the figures for that first exhibition in Pietermaritzburg were about one-and-a-half feet tall and included *The Cup Girl*, *The Bicycle Girl*, *The Nude With A Towel*, and *The Girl On A Rock*. Heather and Patrick had attended the Pietermaritzburg exhibition when he was still working at the hospital but he had never been able to produce enough work to meet the potential demand. This time, they knew that if they could create a sufficient number of pieces, it would begin to establish his name beyond the locality. The exhibition attracted artists and dealers from all over the country and the sizeable stand exhibiting the work of Patrick Reynolds would now be noticed. So at least, Heather and Patrick felt, they were on the first rung of the ladder. Patrick's work was deemed to be of sufficient quality to stand alongside sculptors who were better known.

As the time approached, they managed to complete about twelve pieces and carefully wrapped them in blankets before packing them into the hand-made trailer they had recently bought. Ominously, on the day before the exhibition when they would have to travel to Pietermaritzburg, there were dark grey skies overhead that threatened heavy rain. Worse was to come. Shortly before they departed it began to drizzle. Heather explains: "Patrick's pieces have a polish on them, and if they get wet the polish goes white, and you have to start again to get the finish. Furthermore, this was an open-air exhibition and so we approached the coming day with a certain degree of trepidation."

Things went from bad to worse. They were halfway to Pietermaritzburg when the trailer cover blew off, exposing the very pieces it was supposed to be protecting. Patrick pulled up the vehicle and examined the frame. Worryingly, it had buckled beyond repair. They couldn't believe their terrible fortune. "Here we were with all this work standing in the drizzle, knowing it could start raining really hard at any moment. We had travelled beyond the point of no return, having already covered 20 kilometres – so we had no choice – we had to go on. We climbed back into the car, not saying much, but we were totally devastated. This could be the end. This could totally ruin everything. We would have to go back to office work after two years of using up our savings. I could hardly comprehend it. After so much creative effort, one downpour could ruin everything. Patrick was grim-faced as he drove, and I looked at him anxiously. I loved this man so dearly I just couldn't bear the thought of putting him back in an office again."

Then it started to rain heavily, and now they were in a critical position. As on so many occasions in Heather's life her simple faith motivated her to turn to God. "I started praying in my heart, saying, 'Dear Father God... I beg you – if you are out there – stop the rain. Please just stop the rain.' It didn't work. Then I did something that really embarrassed me in front of Patrick. I decided to sing my prayers aloud. I sang the Lord's Prayer: 'Our Father, who art in Heaven... for ever and ever, Amen.' As I finished the prayer we came round a corner, and there were blue skies ahead." The rain had stopped – just like that!

They arrived at the exhibition and to their huge relief discovered that the rain hadn't penetrated the blankets after all. They sold every piece to private buyers, on average for around 2,000 Rand each, which was not a fortune in 1984 but sufficient to justify two years' work, and to provide the Reynolds with the capital to carry on with their cherished lifestyle for a further twelve months.

Eventually the couple realized that Patrick would have to work in bronze and they discussed this with a friend, Dave Falconer, who wanted to start a foundry nearby. They realized that if Dave Falconer could cast and finish Patrick's work to the required standard, then the entire process of creating the figures in bronze would be possible. Gradually the two men began to collaborate. It turned out to be much more difficult than they envisaged, and it took longer than planned. As time went by, the Reynolds began to get into financial difficulties. Things went from bad to worse and eventually they faced financial ruin. But providence intervened.

For some years, Heather had been involved in growing bonsai miniature trees. She was by now chairperson of the Natal Midlands Bonsai Society, and the garden at Deep Valley was full of miniature trees. It had been difficult to find pots for bonsai trees and so a few months earlier they decided there might be a niche in the market, specializing in producing pots to grow them in. Showing great foresight, they decided to invest in a pottery and now it began to be successful, with a growing number of local customers. By the time of the financial crisis caused by the expense of Patrick's conversion to working in bronze, Heather was selling the trees and had opened the pottery.

"With guidance from Patrick, I had trained myself to make the pots, without having any classes. We were just learning as we went, and we found our way through. It was fascinating. I remember the first time we fired the kiln, which we put in our kitchen. We could hardly wait to open it to see what would come out. I prayed hard for good results. They were certainly good enough to encourage us to go on, and I started to make different shapes as I became more skilled. Within a year we were producing really fine pots in various sizes, some terracotta and others glazed in a variety of beautiful colours: shades of beige, blue, greens and earthy colours. Slowly our reputation began to spread throughout the entire country."

From the humble beginnings of the first pots coming out of Deep Valley, the Reynolds began to build a profitable business with customers all over South Africa; some pots were even exported to neighbouring Zimbabwe, during its transitional period from Rhodesia. However, net profit margins were low because higher productivity depended upon intensive recruitment of labour. Here were to be found the roots of the altruism which ultimately would take over Heather's life. All around them the Africans were living in miserable poverty, and now there was something she could do to alleviate that by employing Zulu women, who were more productive than the men. As she recalls: "We became even more labour intensive than perhaps we needed to, but we wanted to take in as many women as we could to give them work. It had become important to me to help the Zulu people and I began to feel within me that it was what God wanted me to do."

From here the idea of a community of needy people working at Deep Valley gradually evolved. Perhaps, during the latter part of the 1980s, this altruism became focussed as a mission for Heather. It was to move a step further forward when a pregnant Zulu child called Zodwa arrived out of the blue from the valley, looking for both a home and a job. She was only about fourteen years old and desperate. She had nowhere to go, and the baby was about to come. Zodwa knew that Heather gave people work tending the garden, and also in the pottery.

"You can't work; you're just a child," Heather told her at first. Zodwa burst into tears and said she was hungry and had to have food.

"Then you must go to your parents. I certainly can't employ you," said Heather.

"My mum and dad are dead; the whole family were killed in a car crash. I'm the only survivor. I've nowhere to go. Please help me," the girl implored Heather.

Heather and Patrick were horrified, and didn't know what to do. They realized that if Heather agreed to raise an African baby in her home, meaning that blacks would be using the family bathroom and kitchen, then the Reynolds could soon expect to become the focus of unwanted attention from other white people living in the community. Heather was trapped between her humanitarian instincts, all the things she and Patrick believed in, like equality between black and white, and her own family's social predicament.

The Reynolds knew they could not turn Zodwa away. "Come in," Heather said, and gave her food. Zodwa stayed and became the first resident helper in the new pottery. The young girl had her baby the following Christmas morning at Deep Valley, and they called her Gracie. Baby Gracie's birth signified a growing split between the lifestyle that Heather and Patrick had chosen, and that expected of them by the overwhelming majority of their white neighbours in the German community. The first to reject them were members of Heather's own family, one of whom told her he would not come to stay for Christmas with a black baby in the house.

The Reynolds had already made friends with several leading African artists. It was one area where, to a certain extent, people could be equal. At the annual art exhibition in Pietermaritzburg, their friend Mizriam Mazibuko, a popular African artist from Johannesburg, had a stand near the Reynolds. However, he parked his caravan outside the local camping ground in the car park and Heather asked him why. He looked at her with bewilderment and whispered: "Heather, where else would I park it?"

"At first I thought, *What on earth is he talking about, where would he park it?*" recalls Heather. "Suddenly, click, click, click, I realized he couldn't go to the caravan park because it was for whites only. Things fell into place." Earlier that day, the Reynolds had insisted he join them for a barbecue, and some of the other exhibitors around them had moved away. Now they knew why.

Despite incidents like the one involving Mizriam, Heather and Patrick continued to keep a low profile in the community and to steer well away from apartheid South Africa's notorious white-run police force. It was racist towards Africans, and highly intolerant of anyone, regardless of race, who set out to disturb the status quo. However, trouble with the local police was beckoning. It all started when Heather's maid Betty began to get seriously harassed by her drunken partner, the father of her child.

"The father of the baby had an alcohol problem and so Betty decided she wanted to break off her relationship, which is not easy in Zulu culture, because a man won't accept this from a woman after she has produced his child. I was part of the process of helping Betty to start off a new life with a new family outside the district. But because the man had made threats that he would kill her if she left him, I told her to report to the police that the threat had been made on her life.

"So I took Betty to the police station one morning to go and make a statement and have it filed, and told her I would pick her up later. By the evening they had still not attended to her. She had sat in the police station all day. So I phoned them and demanded to know why this young woman had not been attended to. I got some sarcastic response, and demanded to speak to the station commander.

"I would just like to know," I said, "why Betty was made to sit at your police station all day and no one attended to her..."

"He butted in: 'Look! I'm not here to nursemaid your black...'

"'I beg your pardon! I'm talking about simply taking a statement from somebody whose life has been threatened.' I was furious.

"As it happened I played badminton for some years with a

colonel in the police force, so I got hold of him. He was up in Pretoria doing senior security work for PW Botha. I rang him: 'Bob, I will not be spoken to like that by this commander on a matter as serious as this. I'm not going to stand for it. I want an apology from that man for the way he spoke to me. And I want an apology to Betty for not attending to her for the entire day. She has rights. She was not attended to because she's black.'

"I asked him who I should get hold of and he gave me the name of the colonel for the district, and agreed to phone him to tell him I would be contacting him. This second colonel then listened to what I had to say, and the net result of my complaint and demand was that the local acting commander was made to drive out to Deep Valley with another officer. They knocked at our door, and he introduced himself and said he had come to apologize to Betty and me. I must have needed my head examining to have done something like that, because I saw murder in his eyes. I knew it would be only a matter of time before he tried to get his revenge, and I was right. Two months later I was caught speeding in a radar speed trap on a freeway near Heidelberg and the magistrates sent notification of a fine by post. But I didn't send it back; in the rural areas like ours, usually an officer would come round with the summons, and then you'd pay the fine.

"It was the Friday afternoon before Christmas when they came and told me I was under arrest.

" 'What for?' I asked.

" 'You didn't go to court. You didn't pay your fine.'

" 'This is crazy,' I said. 'Why didn't you give me my summons?'

"They said: 'Oh. We didn't know where you lived.'

" I said: 'Of course you knew where I lived.'

" 'No,' they said, 'none of us knew where you lived. You are under arrest and you must come with us. You are to go to jail.'

"I was in a panic. I could see no way out. Because it was just before Christmas, and we were going into the weekend, there would have been no court to hear my case for at least a week. I faced the prospect of being in a prison cell for the entire Christmas holiday and possibly into the New Year for a stupid little offence.

" 'Can I go into the house?' I asked, trying to think of a way to delay them.

" 'No, get into the car now. You are wasting our time,' they insisted.

" 'Look, I'm a woman, and it's my time of the month, and I am going to get what I need,' I said angrily.

"I went into the house, locked the door, and got straight onto the phone. I said to the operator, 'Quickly, get me Heidelberg Magistrates Office as soon as you can.' Then I phoned Bob on a club call and told him they were arresting me: 'Please, Bob, you've got to get hold of the Magistrates Office and tell them I am coming in to pay before three o'clock.' I got a call back, and Bob said: 'Here's your number, quote the number, pay it at your local police station and quote my name and rank to those policemen.'

"By now they were banging on the door. I walked out of the house to the policemen and said, 'Gentlemen, I have just been given this reference number by the Heidelberg Magistrates Office, and I am now operating under the instructions of a very senior officer in the police. Here's his name, rank and number. It has been agreed between us, and the magistrate, that I should pay the fine at the police station before three o'clock. As instructed by this senior officer I will accompany you in my car, rather than travel in yours. I am sorry for all the trouble I have caused you – as you could have been preparing for Christmas this afternoon. I am so sorry.' I had foiled them, and they were very angry, but their set-up had failed. I kept my nose clean after that."

Heather and Patrick focused on trying to help people who needed it, and despite the deteriorating political situation the Deep Valley pottery continued to prosper. Heather employed more girls, most of them very young, unmarried, pregnant and homeless. The Reynolds converted the farm outbuildings where the young Zulu mothers could live with their babies. Within a year there were about seven girls staying at Deep Valley. Sometimes, they would just arrive and plead for help, and it was not in Heather's nature to turn anyone away. It was the same with animals. The farm became a menagerie of domesticated and wild animals, some sick, others just continually hungry and noisy.

There was very little employment for girls in the district, but at Deep Valley there were many jobs to do. Another important task was the mixing of the clay, the pouring, and the cutting, on the production line. Then there was the mould-making – and the African women, who had been totally unskilled, became expert potters under Heather's supervision.

More girls arrived and Heather offered them work in the garden with the bonsai trees. The Reynolds were also trying to be self-sufficient in vegetables, keeping chickens and looking after sick animals that they found or that were brought to Deep Valley. By now Heather was travelling all over the country – getting pots to Durban, and further to Cape Town, Johannesburg etc. She would pack the truck with the pots, usually pack in the kids, and just take off!

Deep Valley may have been a sanctuary for African girls, and Heather's animals, but it was also home to Heather's children, Brendan and Bronwen, whose upbringing turned out to be just as unconventional as their mother's had been. Bronwen recalls: "I think every child should grow up on a farm. It was amazing because my brother and I had the run of the place, riding our bikes and climbing trees, going to play in the cane fields, or whatever we wanted to do. It was idyllic. There was the barn where Mum did pottery and we would climb onto the roof, and draw on it with bits of hard clay. I loved the little babies of the women workers who lived in the outhouses. I used to be in their huts constantly, on the floor playing with the babies and children. As a child I wasn't conscious that they were anything different from us, that some of them may have been refugees or orphans, because they were always at Deep Valley growing up alongside us."

The active support of her children, Brendan and Bronwen, as they grew from childhood to adolescence, became a source of great reassurance to Heather. In 1988 she became the chair of the Bonsai Society, and this helped her to develop skills as a public speaker, overcoming a lack of confidence. Now, Heather was quietly drawing ever closer to God. She had grown up in the Anglican faith but as there was no Anglican church in Dalton, her young family joined the local Methodist church, and the children also joined the youth group who met every Friday evening.

Heather began to feel a developing sense of mission – a mission that God had planned, and one that she anticipated would require total dedication. For the moment, however, she was not sure where this lay. She felt she was being drawn along an unfamiliar path. Now was the time to express total dedication to God, to subjugate everything else in her life beneath his calling. "There were so many times when I really needed God and I needed miracles and I needed help." The night of her mother's visitation at the foot of her bed, Heather had vowed that she would serve God for the rest of her life. Now, as she lay in bed one night she remembers feeling very close to God. She reminded him that he needed to show her what it was that he wanted her to do. She told God that if she had to leave her family for him on her life's mission, then she would do that.

"I truly gave my entire life, every atom of my being to him that night. 'I just want to serve you, Father. Take my life and let it become a meaningful one,' I told him. I remember this warmth that filled my body, and tears of happiness were streaming down my cheeks. I felt so close to him, it was almost like he was touching me and enveloping me in his love. Next to me Patrick was sleeping while all this was happening.

He was totally unaware of it. That moment was so profound for me. I had always wanted to serve God since I was young but the intervening years and the strife I endured as a young married woman had created the doubts. Now, all those were resolved. I had proof in my own mind that God existed and I knew that for the rest of my life I was going to be a servant of the Lord."

Heather registered for a Bible diploma at the local Methodist church at Rosebank, where she could join the classes and study theology seriously. She found it hard doing assignments with the demands made by the factory, and the bonsai sales had also started to take off.

As the Reynolds invested greater time in their pottery, and more pregnant African girls arrived to live at Deep Valley, they became less involved socially with their neighbours. Most white people around Dalton regarded them as eccentric. By now, the white community was anticipating a bloodbath in the rural areas as the country moved through the transitional period to majority rule and a black government.

"I was very conscious of trying to avoid getting identified with one faction or another," says Heather. "We didn't know who was right or wrong between the black political groups, and we also took great care not to get involved in the crossfire between them. It was extremely dangerous for white people to become involved, and there were many violent attacks on whites, and even murders. We knew many of the victims."

Heather Reynolds, however, is not one to watch the world destroy itself for long. By 1989 she felt she had a role to play in helping the victims of violence. The white regime was gradually losing its grip as the world expressed its revulsion of apartheid. Militant political activism increased dramatically. South Africa was entering into the strife of the transitional years, the final phase of the apartheid era, and it was clear that majority rule was going to come at some time in the future.

In KwaZulu-Natal the Zulus split into several factions, but

mainly into two political groups: the Inkatha Freedom Party
and the African National Congress. Tribal Africa, old Africa,
lies just off the beaten track in every direction to the horizon
in much of KwaZulu-Natal. It was in these vast tracts of land
that the black-upon-black violence occurred. The Valley of a
Thousand Hills at that time was inaccessible by anything more
than dusty tracks and many of these became quagmires during
the wet summer months. Danger lurked in many of those
remote rural areas, as factions within it resisted the political
creed of the African National Congress.

New socialist principles sought to remove the absolute
power of the king, and break down traditional Zulu tribal
structures to impose a more democratic system of local government through the election of councillors. Inkatha, or the
IFP as it is known, at that time stood fiercely against the ANC.
Serious conflict resulted, in which thousands died. Nowhere
was the violence worse than in the valley of Swayimane. The
Zulus had their own laws, their own king and their own *nko-
sis*. Many were violently opposed to change.

Fortunately, neither the ANC nor the IFP regarded Patrick
and Heather's intervention in the valley as political. Fighting
units did not stop the couple as they helped to support children, some of whom had been orphaned. On some occasions
they brought bodies back from hospital to the valley for a
Zulu burial. Heather recalls: "A house would be burned
down, and we would be asked to go and help. Patrick would
go to the Edendale Hospital mortuary to fetch the body, and
try to get it back to the valley for burial. In the Zulu custom
you must bury a dead person within a certain period, because
it is important for the wellbeing of the soul, or spirit. There is
still profound ancestral worship among the Zulus, and it has
been integrated into their Christian faith.

"There were police roadblocks stopping people because it
was very dangerous for strangers to drive in that area.
However, we had got to know the valley so well that we knew

which side roads to go down and where there wouldn't be a blockade. The police couldn't man every single entrance into the valley. You'd go from one zone – perhaps a river or a road or a hedge would delineate it as the ANC area – then the next moment you might cross into the IFP zone. You'd go through several of these pockets until you reached the house where you would drop off the body. You'd pray that nobody was going to shoot at you, because trigger-happy people might not have any idea whether you were friend or foe.

"We cultivated a network of informants who would let us know how and where to find the victims of the civil strife. We became known and also trusted by many of the people living there, who were terrified by what was going on. We were aware it was dangerous but we put our trust in God. You never really knew as you rounded a corner, or came to the crest of a hill, whether there might be huts on fire, an ambush prepared – if armed men would shoot first and ask questions afterwards. Some gangs and fighting groups did not know who we were. We were just white people in their land, which to them was justification to kill. There was terrible hatred – *umuzis* (homes) were coming under attack from armed groups who had identified a neighbour, often wrongly, as being on the other side. Thousands of homes were burned down and people killed summarily.

"The unrest didn't stop until Nelson Mandela's government took control and then the politicians and Zulu leaders worked out a peace formula that permitted a dual system of local government in which the Zulu *nkosi* and *induna* were able to work alongside the elected councillors."

One day in 1993, in the cold weather, a group of 38 destitute women and children arrived at Deep Valley, pleading for shelter and food. They had walked 20 kilometres from the Swayimane, in driving wind and rain, to find sanctuary with the Reynolds. After an attack upon their *umuzi*, they had been left with nothing but the clothes they were wearing. Heather opened up a big shed, and made a base on the floor from the newspapers used for wrapping the pots. Then she piled on underfelt and old carpeting obtained from the few friends who were still prepared to help her. They managed to find some old sheets, and then laid more newspaper over those. In fact she created a duvet of newspapers. The entire band of 38 people crawled in underneath it. They had nowhere else to go and stayed at Deep Valley for nearly two weeks.

Every morning the Zulus would sit under the same eucalyptus tree in the garden as Heather walked past to go to the pottery. They looked upon her in silence, but in hope and expectation that she would help them. Heather had given her life to God, to serve his will, and she turned to him now. She said: "Father God, just show me how I can help these people."

Heather wept at their plight. "They had lost everything, absolutely everything. Their clothing and their few possessions were gone and only Deep Valley stood between them and starvation. I telephoned the Red Cross, but they said they had been inundated, there was fighting going on in several localities, and a state of emergency had been declared."

Heather said to Patrick: "I've got to see if I can start a self-help scheme and get these people to earn some money." She reckoned that with Patrick's studio work, her pottery and bonsai garden, and by encouraging the Zulus to learn craftwork and a variety of skills, they could jointly develop a complete business project. Heather prayed to God to help her get work again to earn sufficient funds to finance the project because it would take time to train the refugees, and this large new group of nearly 40 people would need food and clothes. She had been successful in the insurance business, and thought there might be something in sales, with good commission, that would earn the kind of big money they needed.

Heather didn't know what she was looking for but felt she would recognize it when she saw it. Help soon came, but from an unexpected source.

17
A LIFE-CHANGING JOURNEY

Myrtle rang from Johannesburg and said she had been working as a "temp" for a company called Roadfix. She explained they were selling a plant that manufactured asphalt for road repair projects. The company offered a total manufacturing kit or package, from crusher and mixer to conveyor belt, which was simple to operate, and the finished mix of gravel, asphalt and tar could be transported on the back of a truck in bags. It was extremely suitable for filling in potholes, and ideal for the pan-African market, where nearly all roads have gaping holes.

The cost of the entire package was just over 1 million Rand and, Myrtle said, the company was looking for salesmen to go to Northern and Central Africa and the Gulf.

"What's in it?" Heather asked.

"Ten percent commission on the million," Myrtle replied.

So I just have to sell one to some government, and get the European Union or something to fund it, and I'm home and dry, Heather thought to herself. It seemed just what she needed. God had answered her prayers! It was a one-off thing, she was looking for something big, and this was certainly the sort of solution they had envisaged.

So Heather went to Johannesburg to have an interview with the Roadfix management. She walked in and they thought it was a joke. In fact they all laughed. She was a woman, white, and the countries they wanted her to go to, like Uganda, were all very anti-South African. In fact many of these countries were providing training camps for guerrillas to fight the South African regime.

The problem for the Roadfix bosses was that no one else had asked for the job – they were stuck with Heather. So they came to an agreement that she would travel initially to both Kenya and Uganda, then on to Egypt and Dubai. They agreed to pay all of her travelling costs, but she would have to find and fund her own accommodation, and then she would receive her commission upon successful completion of the contract. Heather thought that was fair, and so she booked a ticket. Her brothers, and their families, then woke up to the fact that their sister was going off to Kenya and Uganda in Central Africa and they might not see her again. So they started trying to dissuade her from making the journey. They warned her that if she disappeared nobody would ever know what had happened to her. She looked at them and said: "Listen. I believe that this project is for God. If you think I am going alone, then you are wrong. He will be at my side."

On the face of it she now agrees that her family had good cause to be angry and scared for her, but she was convinced this was a journey God was calling upon her to make. She told them: "I trust that God will keep me safe, I'll be successful and I'll come back safely." Kenya was not dangerous, and it is not a difficult place for white South Africans. Uganda was a different proposition and presented all kinds of problems, involving both risk and logistics, for a sales expedition that was totally disorganized. Heather had no idea whom she was going to meet, who might be suitable contacts to approach, how to get in touch with the Transport Ministry, and how she was going to get about once she got there. On top of all this, she was a white woman – and a South African one at that.

She told her brothers: "The only person here who can stop me is Patrick, my husband, and if he is willing to let me go into this unknown country and raise the money we need, then there is no further argument. He could object, but he hasn't, so I'm going!" It was only then that her brothers realized just how radical she was. Her view had become both fatalistic and faithful. Even now, in the valleys where Heather goes to do her pastoral work, to help orphans for God's Golden Acre, or to set up foster homes for abandoned children, she is prepared to accept death. "I don't believe God allows his servants, his followers, or his children to be killed unless there is a reason for it. So off I went on my sales mission for Roadfix."

First, Heather flew to Nairobi, Kenya where she met government officials and gave them the plan. She then headed for Entebbe. She was late for the plane and rushed across the tarmac in the sweltering heat to the waiting aircraft. People on board were both hot and cross. They believed she'd kept them waiting on the ground needlessly. Heather got onto the plane and there was one seat left. She found herself next to another white woman; everyone else on board was black. She sat down, highly flustered, but after a while the two women started chatting.

The woman asked Heather what she was going to be doing in Uganda, and Heather told her she needed to speak to somebody in Parliament. "My first aim is to try to get somebody from the Department of Transport to have a look at this asphalt plant because they could produce the stuff, use it for their own roads, and sell the excess to Rwanda and Kenya and other neighbouring countries and make money. It could be a profitable concern," said Heather, her sales spiel rolling off her tongue.

Her travelling companion said: "Oh, that's very interesting, and it could be quite easy to arrange, because my husband is working in Parliament at the moment."

She added: "As a matter of fact, he's coming from Parliament to Entebbe to pick me up. I'm then going to drop him off back there and drive home. You must come and stay with us."

This was marvellous. Heather had only just arrived on the plane, and within a few minutes, she had a place to stay, and a route to members of the government. And so her new friend's husband picked them up from the airport. Heather met him, and he drove the two women to Parliament. They waited until there was a tea-break and then he introduced Heather to the deputy minister of transport, with whom she had a brief meeting and made arrangements to have a further meeting at the tennis club on the following Sunday.

That evening the host said to Heather: "Why don't you use one of my vehicles and a driver and have a look around Kampala?" This was just what Heather needed. They scouted around the provincial part of Uganda within striking distance of the capital, and went to see the source of the Nile, among many other features of the country. She did not get to see the famous gorillas, which was a great source of disappointment but the trip there was fully booked. However, everything she had read about Uganda, and its verdant beauty, was confirmed.

In the meantime Heather had the arranged meeting with the deputy transport minister at the all-African but nevertheless colonial-style tennis club, and discovered that it was exclusively male. She walked in, expecting to be laughed at again, or worse, but they were courteous and gave her lunch, and listened to her. "We talked through the whole procedure and they were very interested and suggested we might make the project possible by linking up with Chinese funding and investment. The minister and his team could see that the process was extremely relevant to Uganda where the road network is riddled with potholes. I came away with the distinct impression that the men had seen an opportunity and would come back to me in South Africa if they could secure the Chinese investors. If they were successful, they said they would send the Chinese team to South Africa to negotiate a deal on their behalf. They then provided me with a car to take me back to my friends' house."

The following day was the last of her visit. Heather and her driver bodyguard had by now visited all the interesting places to go locally. What would he like to do, she asked? He said he'd like to go and see his family. He was a resourceful man and soon produced a car and so they went off shortly after dawn. His village was incredibly far away. They went right up past Mbali, far into the bush along dusty track roads, and it was near there that they passed a small village. Heather relates: "There were children from the village all around. But I noticed that there was something about these youngsters that worried me – they weren't laughing. They were absolutely quiet. Normally, if children see a strange woman, they will at least talk among themselves. But there was this eerie silence. The children stared – but without expression. Eventually I couldn't stand it, so I asked the Ugandan driver: 'What's wrong with these kids?' "

The man said to her: "These are the AIDS orphans."

Heather asked: "What do you mean – orphaned by AIDS?"

He replied: "Well, the parents have died."

In an instant it became clear. Heather will remember it for the rest of her life. "Now you see, at that point, in South Africa in 1992/93, we were faced with political upheavals in the country and the change from apartheid. We'd heard about the HIV virus and AIDS-related diseases, but it was in San Francisco, in the gay community, or in Central Africa. I hadn't made the connection until that moment. With a start, I realized I was in Central Africa! I was just horrified. 'And so, who's going to look after them?' I asked.

" 'Nobody,' he said.

" 'But surely,' I insisted, 'there must be churches or some-body.'

"He said: 'Yes, there are. There are some Roman Catholic missions but not here.' "

Heather was stunned. She realized that Uganda was a vast country and that a few missionaries, here and there, were but a drop in the ocean. She decided to look inside one of the village huts. She was about to come face to face with the effects of possibly the world's greatest catastrophe since the bubonic plague.

"There were two children lying on the floor on a mat. One lay on her side, was completely motionless, and I think she was already dead. The other was so sick he had probably less than another day to live. His body was covered in a dirty cloth and his eyes were glazed. I came close to him and stared long and hard into his mournful eyes. I have seen many like him since, and know I will see many more in my lifetime. However, this was a first time for me. I thought to myself: *These children are starving to death.*"

As Heather looked at the dying boy, who might have been three years old, she realized her journey to the hut had been no coincidence. God had guided her there to show her the way forward. It was the mission for which she had been waiting. The words of Jesus came into her mind: "Anything you did for one of my brothers here, however humble, you did for me." (Matthew 25:40, New English Bible)

"I made my pledge with God. I knew now that this was the work I was supposed to do. He had brought me here." She broke the silence in the hut as she said aloud: "God, from this day on, I will help every child in need, every child that needs a home, every child that needs food that crosses my path. I will see to it. I promise you."

Later she told Patrick: "I made that pledge easily and willingly as I looked at the poor child dying on the mat without the comfort of an adult. We were silent and didn't speak. There was no common language for us to communicate in."

What struck Heather hardest was that this was an unnecessary death. A child's life was being taken away because he was unable to get food. He was starving to death because he had no parents. Here was just a little person wasting away in front of her from malnutrition. Just alone in a room! In that moment her thoughts were like snapshot images. She was out-raged at what she saw as the total failure of Western society and the Christian church. She wrote later:

> We have reached the moon, we have a spaceship out in the solar system, past Neptune and Pluto, we have communications sys-tems so fantastic that we can put encyclopedias on silicon chips, we can cut the cornea of an eye with a laser. We are incredibly advanced technologically – but we can't see to the feeding of starving children in the world. All over the Western world, peo-ple are getting on with their ordered and well-fed lives and they are oblivious, or worse, indifferent, to what is happening here.

It shocked Heather so much she felt sick. She felt ashamed for humankind. Then she looked at herself and thought: *I'm part of that society.* Her mind was racing: *There are a billion Christians in the world, and millions of those in the West are earning good salaries, enough surely to give substantially – and yet we can't come together to help the starving!*

She walked out of the hut, weeping in both grief and rage. Slowly, she composed herself and told the frightened body-guard driver that they could now go on and see his family. She didn't say anything to him about her experience, or her feel-ings. In fact, she doesn't recall much about meeting his fam-ily.

She vaguely remembers getting back to her hosts late that evening. They were cross and worried. She apologized that she would have to leave almost immediately to get to the airport. Heather was no longer at the dinner table in her mind. She was already on a mission. Something had happened inside her. She was struggling to cope with emotions and what she had discovered. "I left my hosts and I checked into a hotel. I had to be completely alone."

She telephoned Patrick and was crying down the phone as she said: "I've got to come back to Uganda. We've got work here. There are children starving and dying. And they've been left alone. It's the HIV virus."

He said: "Look, let's talk about it when you get home."

Next day, she took a flight back to Nairobi and checked into the Stanley Hotel. Once in her room she collapsed and cried for hours for the little children of Uganda. Over and over in her mind she thought to herself: *These young children are little more than babies and they are trying to cope, to stay alive, but their parents are dead. They have no support through their grief, and thousands of them are becoming sick, some with HIV. They have no food to eat.*

It was the awful fact that they were dying alone. The little boy she found would die alone. There was nobody to hold him, nobody to comfort him. There might have been an older brother or sister around, but there was nobody attending to him. Heather couldn't speak his language, so there had been no communication between them whatsoever. She felt helpless, hopeless and guilty that she had not been able to do anything to save him. She sat on the edge of the bed and thought. What, logically, could she do quickly? She recalls: "I thought to myself, *I can't wait until I get back to South Africa. I'm going crazy!*"

Then she thought – maybe she could write a letter to the *Natal Witness*, and tell them what she had seen, and hope and pray that there would be somebody out there who was not interested just in politics, and who would pick up the cost, maybe sponsor a trip for her to get back there. She didn't know whether it would work, but she understood she was doing God's work now. She knew nothing about fundraising, but she must, and would, succeed.

Then she thought: *I need a name for this project. It must be something African.* She thought of many African words and expressions, but then realized she was thinking in Zulu. Hopeless! Then, all of a sudden and from nowhere, "God's Golden Acre" came into her head – it just wafted in.

Heather immediately rejected it. "Can you imagine?" she says. "From a marketing point of view at that time it would be a crazy name to choose because people would think it was some kind of fundamentalist sect, perhaps like those crazy people who had all committed suicide in America." The name didn't reveal that it was about children, or suggest anything about her mission. Mentioning God's name would make it unacceptable for a donor who might not be "into" Christianity. So she tossed "God's Golden Acre" right out. It kept coming back – a bit like a tune someone can't get out of her head. Heather prayed: "God, are you trying to make this thing impossible for me, having been an atheist? Is this your way of making things hard for me?"

She told God: "Believe me, I know about marketing. This is the wrong way to market. This name is not right. Red Cross, Salvation Army... they tell us a little bit about what they are doing in your name. 'God's Golden Acre' doesn't tell us any-thing about children, about helping little children..." The name kept coming back. Eventually Heather said: "OK, Lord. If it's going to be 'God's Golden Acre', I will follow you."

Heather had never written a song in her life or created a tune. Now, with incredible speed, her head was filled with both. "I thought then, *God's Golden Acre, give a child a home proj-ect, don't let them die all alone.* This exact moment in my life became another great turning point. I will remember it vividly for ever. As I sat on the bed in that room in the Stanley Hotel, my world began to change course, and I believe God came to me. I can't even read music. But a song, music, a tune, came into my head, almost word perfect. I don't know how long it took, how long I sat there, but a song just came out from within."

Give a child a home, give a child a home,
don't let them die all alone,
on God's Golden Acre they'll get to know their maker,
give a child a home,
give to God on high,
give to God on high,
we'll meet him by and by,
on God's Golden Acre
we'll work for our creator,
give a child a home,
give a child a home,
give a child a home,
let them into your heart,
to God's Golden Acre,
that's where we are going to take her,
give a child a home,
to God's Golden Acre,
that's where we are going to take her,
give a child a home...

This song has since become the vehicle of Heather's simple faith in God. It is not a tune copied from any other in the world. It came to her in that moment in the Nairobi hotel, and to her was a miracle. When times were hard – and they would get agonizingly tough in the coming years – the song inspired her. She would sing it, or the orphans would sing it, and then she would feel reassurance. It underpinned her faith.

Since then Heather has written over 20 songs and this has provided her with the strength to believe that he would also give her every quality that she would need in her struggle. "So it was more than a song. It was also a promise to me, showing me God's way of how he can change you, and give you some gift like that. At that moment in the hotel room the song also took away the grief and depression that I was feeling."

Part Three

18
THE ESTABLISHMENT OF GOD'S GOLDEN ACRE

The next day, Heather flew back to South Africa and the first thing that she discovered when she got home was that the refugees had moved back to Swayimane. To everyone's relief, they had found support in their own community in the valley. The second thing she discovered was that the Reynolds' time at Deep Valley had come to an end. The landlord had notified them that he needed the homestead for his son, who was getting married. It was the end of a highly significant twelve years for the Reynolds family, of ups and downs, great happiness and joy, and sometimes despair. They were sorry to go, but realized that as one cycle was ending, another was just beginning. The Reynolds viewed the future with both determination and optimism.

The new home, and what was to become the first proper location for God's Golden Acre, was a farmhouse called Kort-Kraanzkloof, by a little gorge and in a beautiful setting, in the village of Wartburg. It was also within the German community, about 20 kilometres from Deep Valley. The Wartburg farm was a big settlement, and easily large enough to accommodate all the Africans in the community. It had a spacious farmhouse, lots of subsidiary buildings, and an outbuilding for cattle that the Reynolds converted into a pottery.

Meanwhile, anxious for the finance to get started on her project in Uganda, Heather followed up the lead she had made for Roadfix there to find out if the Chinese had come over and signed a contract with the company for 1 million Rand. It soon transpired that the Chinese had indeed come over to Johannesburg at the invitation of the Roadfix directors. Myrtle was in the office and knew about the meeting. Heather waited for her 10 percent but nothing happened. A month later she phoned up and was told: "Oh, the company has gone bankrupt." She made a few more enquiries about the people involved, but nobody seemed to know anything about anybody or anything and she reluctantly came to accept that she had lost her money.

A few weeks after their move to Wartburg, Heather and Patrick were sitting and talking, and watching TV. It was a Sunday night and a programme came on about AIDS. It explained that Acquired Immunity Deficiency Syndrome developed from a viral infection caused by the HIV-1 virus. This virus slowly killed off the autoimmune system with the result that immunity, and thus resistance to any normal infection, was drastically reduced. A paediatrician called Dr Neil McKerrow was being interviewed. He was talking about statistics and they were horrifying. He said that an estimated 2 million children were going to be orphaned in Southern Africa in the next decade, and people had already started dying.

Heather thought: *What!* The doctor was so sure of his facts; he was even talking about so many deaths a day, and about the figures peaking. These were horrendous statistics. Of course, Heather and Patrick had heard of AIDS, and had talked with the girls in the pottery in order to support AIDS awareness. They had stressed to them the importance of being careful. But the Reynolds didn't realize that the virus had moved into South Africa.

The programme credits revealed that Dr McKerrow was a well-known paediatrician at Edendale Hospital in Pietermaritzburg. The next morning Heather phoned him and told him she'd seen terrible things in Uganda, with a whole village full of children left without adults. Dr McKerrow said: "Yes, that's so, because people have been up there to study and see what is happening."

Heather said: "Well, I want to go and start an orphanage there and help the children."

There was a pause, then he said: "Heather, you would be better off to stay here, and help Zulu children. You tell me you live in a rural area. Go and find out what is happening. You'll find there are children who have been orphaned by AIDS within a few miles of where you are."

She said: "What?"

"Oh, sure," said the doctor. "Within a few years your valley – the one you are taking care of because of the civil war – is going to be affected. My advice to you is to stay exactly where you are, because you already know the people in those rural areas, and that will be a great help. You could help your own people."

He continued: "Listen, as hard as it may seem, forget about Uganda. Just stay where you are; we need people like you here. You speak Zulu. You know and understand the Zulu culture."

"But," Heather stammered, "where do I start? I haven't got a clue where to start."

He said: "Look, it's your vision. You and God."

"Yeah, but I need some practical advice."

He paused and then said: "OK. The first thing I would say is, make sure you tell everybody what you are going to do. Always, if you are going to do anything, let everybody know, because already many people in several organizations are doing good work."

He added: "They are looking after people who already have AIDS here in South Africa. Get hold of the AIDS Training Centre. Speak to Toni, and ask her to help you. Ask her to send invitations to key people. Then get them together and tell

them where you are coming from so that they will know you
– and know about God's Golden Acre. Then, people might
trust you. But don't just start something and end up feeling
isolated. If people aren't sure who you are, you probably
won't get the support you need."

Heather thought that was good advice. "But nobody's going
to come if they think I'm some eccentric or radical Christian
woman who has just come from Uganda and…"

He interrupted: "Well, that's your problem…"

She said: "Neil, I need somebody like you to come and talk.
If you were coming to that meeting, people would come."

"Well, you haven't asked me yet."

She asked: "Are you a Christian?"

"No," he replied.

Heather felt foolish suddenly. She'd being going on and on
about how God had sent her to Uganda, how God had given
her this and that, how God had guided her every step – and he
was an atheist!

She persisted however: "Well, would you come?"

"Sure," he said.

"Would you chair the meeting?"

"Yes."

Neil ended the conversation with the following advice: "By
the way, don't put all your energy into opening an orphanage.
Consider the cluster foster care concept. That means creating
small family units around a foster parent and giving that small
nucleus, of perhaps six or seven people, all the help and support it needs to sustain itself."

The next day Heather contacted Toni, the secretary of the
AIDS Training Centre, and they set up a meeting at the training centre in Pietermaritzburg. Toni helped Heather to build
up her address book, and offered to send out all the invitations
announcing that Neil was going to chair the meeting. Heather
eventually met him on the day of the meeting. He was one of
a very interesting group of people who attended. She didn't

expect such a response, but to her astonishment the small hall was full. She recalls: "Neil chaired the meeting and introduced me and my concept of God's Golden Acre. I nervously got up to speak. However, being nervous is a stimulant. I suddenly felt fired up and off I went, straight into it. Afterwards I invited a smaller group – who I thought might be in a position to help me – to sit on the God's Golden Acre committee."

As far as the meeting went, Heather later realized that she had made a mistake. When she stood up to give her talk, her passion took over and indeed overwhelmed her. "I didn't just say that I wanted to start a cluster foster care centre. I jumped too far ahead, possibly because I had had time to think through my longer-term plans, about making the centre and its satellite community sustainable. So I told them how I planned to help the children, but then bring in life skills, resource centres – how we could earn money, as we do now, for instance, with the Young Zulu Warriors, and with art exhibitions – and how we would train these children to become skilled to do jobs, such as being motor mechanics and builders etc."

Heather sounded to them like a woman who had got nothing, but wanted to do a huge project, rather than start with something limited and nurture it into something bigger. They were asking themselves whether or not she was big on dreams but short on reality. Next day, Karen Stone, the lawyer, phoned her up. She said to Heather: "It was just overwhelming. You came across with so much passion about God's Golden Acre, and with so much stuff, that you overwhelmed me!"

Heather had learned a valuable lesson. If a person has got huge vision, others often can't get their heads around it. They won't just jump to it. Most people can accept one goal at a time. So give them small goals. Nowadays, she always reminds herself that while she might have the big picture, it is better to be cautious, and add on piece by piece, slowly, until the whole picture is finished.

Now, she had created doubts in the minds of some people.

Thanks to her extreme and wild enthusiasm, there were those who thought she was going to be a loose cannon, and not perhaps wholly reliable. A few days later, however, Professor Ron Nicholson agreed he would be chairman of God's Golden Acre, and a Dutch missionary doctor, Dr Gerrit Ter Haar, volunteered to be deputy chairman. Both subsequently turned out to be brilliant – wise, kind and gentle – and Heather numbers them both among her most special friends and mentors. Dr Ter Haar's background had been in medical missionary work in the Transkei where he had developed a hospital and community health service amongst the Xhosa people. He had come out fresh from the Netherlands as a young man in the 1960s and was a capable administrator in his field.

He recalls: "After retirement I moved to Pietermaritzburg and started a health programme for a local radio station and in the process interviewed all kinds of humanitarian people – amongst them Heather. I think we had an immediate rapport, a lot in common." Then he discovered to his astonishment that all the Reynolds' personal financial resources were being drawn into helping the children who were brought to Heather, and also those whom she helped in the valley. From that moment he became one of her closest supporters and admirers. "I planned to raise funds for her so that her personal income could be separated from the project funds," he wrote.

Heather recalls: "I started to put my management board into place, to create a proper constitution for God's Golden Acre, and to initiate policies that would give us goals and a procedural way to operate. None of it was an easy process – I even encountered problems with formulating a constitution, until a lawyer came to my rescue. I knew I would have to have an acceptable constitution in place if we wanted to raise money. The problem was, I'd never written a constitution in my life, and although my management board had said they were prepared to support me, they couldn't help me with a constitution."

At three o'clock one morning she was still struggling with it. She said: "God, I have done everything I can. I don't know what more to do about this constitution. I don't have the expertise to write one." She fell asleep with it still incomplete.

The next evening, Heather went to the local Wesleyan chapel to give a talk. Afterwards a man came up to her and said: "I don't know if I can be of any use, but if there is anything I can do for you let me know."

She said: "Well, what is your background?"

He said: "I'm a lawyer, an advocate."

So Heather confided: "Well, I've been up till three o'clock this morning trying to write a constitution and I have got the basic things done, but I have no idea how to finish it."

"Oh, no problem at all," he replied. "Come to my office tomorrow and if you don't mind waiting for a few minutes I'll stick it in my 'in' tray and work on it."

However, Heather's vision for God's Golden Acre, its aspirations, and her trust that God would help her in achieving her goals often received a sceptical reception from non-Christians involved in the fight against the AIDS pandemic. Heather acquired a reputation for being too reliant upon her faith. "It was extremely humiliating," she says. "I clearly remember one awful, awful moment. I was sitting in a CINDI (Children in Distress) meeting in Pietermaritzburg. I knew people were impatient with me and my thoughts. I had sat patiently, waiting for my turn to say something, and I started speaking, and then this woman with a sneer on her face – I'll never forget it – said, 'Oh Heather, Heather and her God... they're going to solve the entire AIDS problem.'

"I was no great speaker. I was crushed, and felt humiliated. She just put me down with her actions and her words, and sometimes with that particular woman, when I was speaking, you could almost feel her sneer, it was so obvious. And all I was trying to do was to make useful suggestions. My work would be at the coalface in the deep rural areas and they were working in the urban areas; sometimes our problems were not quite the same. I became extremely disillusioned with an organization I had supported from its inception.

"Even Gerrit himself had to defend me at times when I was speaking to somebody about my vision. Eventually, however, we were ready to take in orphans from the valley. We were in business. The first visible signs of the AIDS pandemic were already appearing in the valley. By 1995 you could see the familiar pattern of people losing a lot of weight, becoming weaker, and frightened people asking themselves: Is it AIDS?"

Heather had realized earlier that she should become more knowledgeable about AIDS-related diseases and the HIV virus, and learn about how it was going to impact on the local communities. So she joined every organization she could find in Pietermaritzburg that was concerned with it. "I went to every conference. I went to every seminar and every work-shop. There were all sorts of ideas being thrown around about the value of nutrition, high vitamin C intake, high antioxidants, and various medications. Patrick and I were really focussed on studying to find ways of helping the children to survive. For example, we spent quite a lot of money on getting things with high antioxidants in them to treat children that were very ill, to see if we could boost their immune systems. We used powdered baby milk with a high fat content believing it might help to strengthen the babies. We didn't have a lot of success at that time, but then most of our little children were very ill.

"As I began to visit the valley I found there was a social stigma about the HIV/AIDS virus. This in turn was leading to isolation and rejection. Those who were afflicted experienced shame from contracting the virus – and usually rejection by family and friends." In those early days in the valley Heather was almost always entirely alone, the only white person for miles in a world where normal life had broken down for an increasing number of family groups – as the adults began to die.

Heather was in Swayimane one day at the homestead of the Jila family when a group of fourteen or so youngsters, who knew some of the girls at the pottery, approached her. They had heard about Heather's work helping the victims of the violence and then of AIDS, and so they asked her to take them on as their choirmaster. These youngsters, several of whom were related, it turned out, had been selected and trained initially by an old man who had been killed during the violence, and they wanted to carry on as a choir with a new master.

"At that time," says Heather, "I was quite shocked because I did not have a clue about music. I did not know what to say. I had no experience and wondered what I would do with them. I looked at this bunch of little people and thought, *What have I got here?* What could I do with a Zulu choir? These children had nothing. Some were orphans. The others came from families impoverished by the civil war. You could see the expectancy on their faces. I would have devastated them if I had made an excuse. They reasoned I would know exactly what to do with a choir, because in their minds I knew everything. To them, it just required me to say yes!

"Thoughts were racing through my mind: *What will be expected of me? What am I supposed to do?* I couldn't say no! I wouldn't have been able to get the word out of my mouth. Their passion and commitment made it impossible for me to refuse."

Heather's response was automatic, and later she would realize it was a defining moment. "Yes! Of course, I'd be delighted," she told them without much conviction. "Stand over there and let me hear how you sound." They formed into a group, and she sat on the one chair in the room. Then they started singing.

"The moment I heard them, I experienced an almost indescribable feeling. My spirits were soaring, yet I was choking

Heather as a baby in the garden of the trading station run by her parents near Mtubatuba in KwaZulu-Natal.

An early picture of the McLellan children taken at the trading station near Mtubatuba in KwaZulu-Natal in the 1950s. At the back is Heather's oldest brother Kenny, second row left to right, Myrtle and David, front row Basil and Heather. When they were older, the children roamed far and wide during their holidays – fishing expeditions to rivers like the Mtentu were especially popular.

Heather, born in 1952, with her older sister Myrtle, born 1949.

The family group pictured at Heather's first marriage to Sarel Olivier in 1972.

Heather's parents Brenda and John McLellan.

Sarel and Heather after their wedding. No photograph shot that day showed her smiling. A few days before, she had asked her mother to 'postpone' the marriage.

Heather and Patrick's wedding in 1979 was altogether a happier occasion for the bride – who knew she had met both her soul-mate for life, as well as a faithful husband.

Heather and Patrick found Deep Valley in a newspaper advertisement in 1983 when they decided as a young couple to give up office work and become artists. It was a rather ramshackle German-style farmhouse but they lovingly restored it into a comfortable home and created a pottery for bonsai pots.

The Deep Valley years in the 1980s are remembered for the 'English-style' tea parties for the children in the garden with homemade bread and cakes. This occasion was a birthday party for one of the children.

Moving in! Proud mother Heather shows her two toddlers Brendan and Bronwen round the gardens at Deep Valley in 1983. The family recalls the long hot summers and blue skies.

Brendan and Bronwen had the run of the glorious garden at Deep Valley which was redesigned by Heather.

Bronwen, born 1980, recalls her mother's strong Christian faith from a very young age.

Bronwen as a woman says of her mother....*there isn't a daughter alive as blessed as I am, and none loves her mum more than me.*

Building a business. The pottery at Deep Valley became a thriving business – Heather's pots for bonsai trees were being sold all over South Africa by 1988.

Heather became an expert self-taught potter, creating a wide range of pots for bonsai trees in a variety of shapes and glazed colours.

From a very young age Heather regarded her disabled oldest brother Kenny as her special responsibility. Even in childhood she took over the duties of looking after him from Brenda McLellan whenever possible. Towards the end of his life Kenny came to live at Deep Valley where he looked after the garden and the chickens. He died in 1984.

Wherever you find Heather you will find animals. She is a Good Samaritan to her fellow humans, but when it comes to four and two-legged creatures she will never turn one away.

Patrick and Brendan developed a strong bond over the years as father and son.

After the move to Wartburg and the establishment of God's Golden Acre in the mid-1990's, Mary Van der Leeuw became one of Heather's earliest supporters and a member of the board. When Heather decided Khayelihle should be the new home for GGA in 1998 it was Mary who said…*Heather, if it's your vision, we'll stand by you.*

Marianne Jenum and Vibeke Blaker from Norway were among the first volunteers to work at God's Golden Acre at Wartburg and over the years have become successful ambassadors and fund-raisers for GGA in their country.

The lively lads! Sbo, Siphamandla and Siyabonga, three young teenage boys who Heather brought from the valley to live at Wartburg in 1997. They slept in the back of an old 'combi' and became close to Marianne and Vibeke - after being caught spying on them in their bedroom.

A classic picture of Heather at Wartburg. She grew accustomed to sharing her bed with one of the baby orphans – and usually one of the dogs managed to sneak in as well.

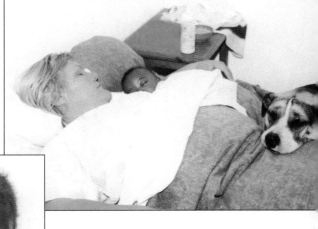

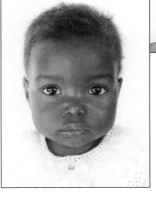

Megan's was a story of tragedy. She was found in the sugarcane with a twin sister who died shortly afterward – but Megan survived into infancy. Heather loved Megan dearly and remembers her as the most beautiful baby she ever nursed.

Cheeky chappie! Marcus is one of the great characters at God's Golden Acre who delights visitors with his outward going and friendly manner. He came to GGA as a premature baby and was one of those who spent much of his infancy in Heather's bedroom at night.

Chummy is one of the most popular children at God's Golden Acre with his handsome face and wise eyes. He has accompanied Heather on several trips abroad and his spellbinding treble voice, once heard, is an experience never forgotten.

The little angel sleeps. Susiwe has had a difficult infancy because of sickness, but the loving and caring manner of GGA nurses, and plenty of good nourishment since she was a small baby, has brought hope for Susiwe's future.

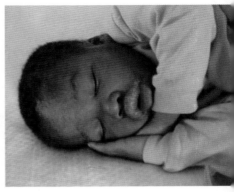

Lucy Foster, seen here holding Thabiso, was one of the first volunteers to arrive at God's Golden Acre, Khayelihle, near Cato Ridge, after it became the new HQ of GGA. She wrote...*you will find 97 happy children – Heather is responsible for most of them being alive!*

Practical help arrives. Volunteer Orin Wilson, who had been a longstanding friend of Bronwen, made a significant contribution in improving the standard of living for everyone at Khayelihle, Cato Ridge, in 1999 thanks to his building and electrical work.

The GGA building team and volunteer built the Hospice and this allowed the sick children to receive a higher level of professional nursing - and also acted as a sanctuary within a sanctuary for the new babies arriving.

Spick and span. When the refurbishment of Mons House at Khayelihle was completed in 1999 it became once more an imposing farmhouse. In the early years Mons House accommodated the children and later became an activity centre.

Gerrit and Anneke Mons from Holland mortgaged their home so that God's Golden Acre could buy Khayelihle, Cato Ridge in 1998. They visit regularly and are always received with joy by the children. Gerrit wrote... *the children call us Oupa and Ouma (grandfather and grandmother) and we love them so much that sometimes we can hardly speak.*

Muslim students were among those who built the pre-primary school at God's Golden Acre. It is now a well-equipped little centre staffed by volunteers where the toddlers and small children are prepared for local primary schools.

The housing and communal dining room projects at God's Golden Acre marked the beginning of a new era after the millennium. It became a cluster foster care community – with each house becoming home for a specific number of children living with African foster mothers and aunties.

Heather is determined that all the children at God's Golden Acre will grow up as Zulus, thoroughly familiar with their culture, customs, and food. Pictured are some of the gogos, foster mothers, and aunties who look after the 97 children living in the community.

Nearly finished
After several ye[...]
sleeping in a
bedroom behin[...]
the office,
Heather and
Patrick were ab[...]
to move into
their own
magnificent
home at God's
Golden Acre
Khayelihle in
2004 where the[...]
can enjoy – at
least some – we[...]
deserved privac[...]

The view of the valley from Heather's new home in the grounds of GGA.

Making a splash! The resort at Khayelihle has been refurbished and is now the major play area for the children when they are home from school. It means that most have learned to swim from a young age and the toddlers soon become accustomed to the water.

Wholesome food. Gradually GGA is trying to become self-sustaining in its food production both in poultry and cultivation of fruit and vegetables.

The new dining room at GGA means that when cultural and sports events are organised visitors can be catered for. When all the community needs to come together – such as at Yuletide and Easter and other special occasions like birthday parties – the true Christian spirit of God's Golden Acre can be fostered in one room.

It's great fun in here! Party-time at GGA!

A joyful place to be. Despite the traumas and abuse that some of the children have suffered, God's Golden Acre is above all a joyful and happy place to be where the children smile and have lots of fun in a big family atmosphere.

Gogo Beauty is one of the legends of God's Golden Acre where she is loved by the children and regarded by the Reynolds as one of the family. She is pictured here with her daughter Zani who also works as carer at GGA.

Gogo Beauty with Marcus who she has helped to bring up in the Zulu culture.

Heather is now a granny figure to the children of GGA. Mothering is the responsibility of the African foster mothers and aunties. At first this broke Heather's heart. Now she carries the responsibility for a more strategic role in the fight against the AIDS pandemic and so inevitably had to give up the day-to-day care of her babies. *Sometimes with all the sadness and tragedy I encounter in the valley, and when I am missing my babies at night, I feel like crying till I die.*

Death has stalked tens of thousands of families in the valley. The graves, created from stones, and usually marked by a wooden cross, are found in the gardens of the umuzi where the Zulu families live.

SNE.11·7·96-16·7·03

In a quiet corner of God's Golden Acre at Cato Ridge the young children who have died there are buried. They are not forgotten, and at Christmas and other religious festivals the children gather around and sing hymns led by Gogo Heather.

The famous white Landrover that for thousands of people in the Valley of a Thousand Hills has become a symbol of hope. Mawethu (our mother) is a familiar and much loved figure to the Africans who live in the rural areas and she is almost always welcome wherever she goes.

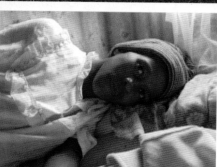

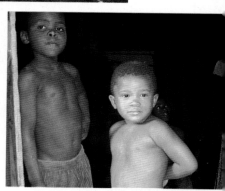

This mother, only in her mid-20's, is HIV-positive and knows she is dying. She is among tens of thousands of young women in the rural areas of KwaZulu-Natal who are infected with the deadly virus. One small comfort for this mother is that her children will be safe with mawethu, who came to her in her moment of greatest need.

These orphans are among the luckier ones in the valley. Heather, working with government community welfare officers will ensure that either they are integrated into a granny-led family group - supported by an outreach programme – or brought into sanctuary at GGA Khayelihle, Cato Ridge.

tens of thousands of cases, he mantle of motherhood falls pon the oldest daughter, sually a girl in her early teens. is a hard and precarious xistence just made possible by upport from outreach rogrammes like those run by God's Golden Acre. The girls usually accept their role with ourage and humour. Heather: *There is a dignity and standard among these young girls. You an drop in here any time and you will find them clean and tidy, and if they have been in the garden, or putting cow dung down on the floor, they'll quickly wash their hands and slip on a clean top.*

The child-led orphan families exist on a simple diet supplied largely by outreach programmes. Heather: *Imagine if we weren't there. What would have happened to them? Their house would have collapsed. Where would this girl and her four siblings have gone?*

Heather remains on
excellent terms with
King Zwelithini Good[
kaBHEKUZULU, King
the Zulu Nation (belc
A party of Japanese
volunteers is pictured
with Queen Buhle (le

The Zulu Theatre, set in the
grounds of God's Golden
Acre, Khayelihle, was
completed towards the end
of 2004 and has become a
cultural focus for the valley.

God's Golden Acre has become a leading cultural centre in the Valley of a Thousand Hills for traditional African song and dance. There are several choirs and dance groups. The child and adult members – drawn both from GGA Khayelihle and the valley – are now performing locally, regionally, nationally, and overseas. Varied sounds of continual rehearsal echo from the thatched Zulu Theatre and Mons House and are among the poignant memories that visitors carry away with them.

They are in rural Africa, their sense and intuitions sharpened by the air, the light, the sounds of the greatest continent on earth, and perhaps 50 metres away the throbbing drumbeat of the boys and girls in rehearsal or a concert. Are they dreaming? Why, no! It's real! It's part of the magic, mystique, and perhaps, the sheer witchcraft of Africa. They feel more alive, more aware, more excited, and perhaps closer to God than anywhere else.

Heather at the opening ceremony of the Zulu Theatre.

Trips to the seaside are an integral part of life at
God's Golden Acre for the children and they are
often led by Gogo Heather who takes charge for a
weekend - or day trip - in one of the GGA vehicles.

THE LIFELINE. Orphaned families led by a granny
figure – or a teenage girl – receive food supplies
once a month that helps to sustain them but is
rarely sufficient to meet all needs. The God's
Golden Acre rural outreach programmes are now
bringing food and clothing to hundreds of families -
but much more remains to be done. There are tens of
thousands in the Valley of the Thousand Hills who have not
yet been reached.

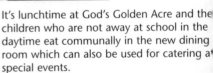

It's lunchtime at God's Golden Acre and the
children who are not away at school in the
daytime eat communally in the new dining
room which can also be used for catering at
special events.

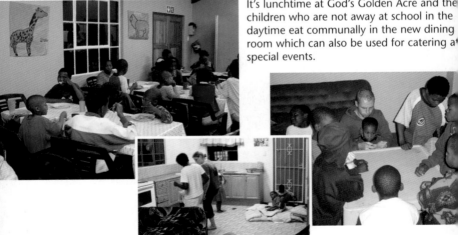

The new houses at God's Golden Acre were designed to make them feel like family
homes to the children. The older boys and girls are segregated and each has a support
team of adults and volunteers.

One day in 2003 Heather was in the huge Kwa Ximba valley and saw a group of boys loitering around and sniffing glue to alleviate their hunger. She took this as a message from God that she should take the lead role in creating a structure to enable the children to play organised league football to give them a better life. Through the author's friendship with Martin Edwards, President of Manchester United, Heather went on to meet several men and women at the top of British professional football, and also from the worldwide sports equipment company NIKE. Collectively they came to her assistance in what she regards as another miracle.

The God's Golden Acre Junior League Association was brought into being thanks to the help and co-operation of the local Thandanani League and Nkosi Mlaba. Soon thousands of youngsters – boys and girls - will be getting the chance to play for teams in organised leagues. Heather hopes the GGA Junior League will become a benchmark for other associations wishing to develop football for youth in the rural areas of South Africa.

Heather at the Football Association in London in 2004 with (left to right) Ann Smith, Chief Fund-raiser for GGA UK, Alastair Bennett, Director of External Relations Football Foundation, Dave Richards, Chairman of the F.A. Premier League, Heather Reynolds, David Davies, Executive Director, Football Association, Jane Bateman, Head of International Relations, Football Association.

In the same year Heather was invited to Old Trafford, the home of Manchester United, by club President Martin Edwards. She seen with him holding the world famous FA Cup.

Oprah Winfrey has played an increasingly important role at God's Golden Acre since her first visit there in 2002. She is now a close friend and supporter of Heather and 'mother' figure to some of the orphans.

Not often caught on camera! Patrick Reynolds is retiring man of few words who prefers to work quietly in his studio at God's Golden Acre. He is regarded as one of South Africa's leading sculptors of the living form and in the early years of GGA his work largely subsidised it.

While many Western children cannot get out of their school uniform quickly enough when they get home, African children in the Valley of a Thousand Hills regard their school uniform with the highest level of pride. For many it is their most treasured possession because it gives them a sense of belonging and is a ticket for an education.

back tears. I thought to myself: *They are not just good, they are wonderfully good!* Somehow, at that moment, Heather knew that these young men and women were going to become an important part of her life. "I taught them phonetically because they couldn't read, or understand the English. They'd learn the songs by ear, picking up the words from me as I sang slowly, and going over the lines again and again. They were all very quick to learn. They would sing at funerals, they would sing at weddings, and other Zulu festivals and events."

One night the sky was darkening across the valley as Heather neared the last drop-off point for the members of the younger choir who had practised together that day. As she stopped the "bakkie", a woman made her way hurriedly towards the car. The desperation on her face was all too familiar. She knew of a family that was in dire need of help, and had a sick baby who would not last much longer without medical attention. Heather later wrote:

In response to my enquiry as to where or how far away the family lived, she pointed vaguely over the hill and assured me it wasn't far. Some older children climbed in the back of the bakkie to give directions and we set off to find them. Two hours later, along a treacherous path that seemed to be fading away altogether as the rocky hillside became more uneven, we came at last upon the broken hut.

As I climbed out of the vehicle, with the engine still running, as we'd had much trouble with the battery and I dared not turn it off, a little girl only about ten years old came out of the hut. She didn't falter, but walked straight into my arms and held onto me. I'll never forget it. Her simple trust – it was as if in some way she had been expecting me.

I said "hello" and asked her how she was. She led me to her younger siblings, a girl of six, a boy of four, and the youngest, a two-year-old girl. The baby girl was very ill, Sandisile explained, but she didn't know what to do to make her better. She handed me the child, and as my hands held her wet and sticky thighs and buttocks, my first thought was that she'd messed herself and wasn't wearing a nappy.

The bakkie's headlights pierced the growing darkness, and as I held the child closer to the light, I realised in horror that the stickiness was in fact a mass of wet, gaping sores. The other children huddled closer, and I saw that their clothing, old and caked with mud, barely covered their little bodies.

We took all four children home with us that night, and after treating the ringworm, scabies, sores and dehydration, they soon blossomed under the care and attention they received. The baby girl, Jabu, became very close to me. After some time, Sandisile told me that Jabu used to be left at home with their father when she took the other siblings to school. Their father had been sick for a long time, and was too weak to do very much except sit at home, largely unresponsive. One day, as she and the others got home from school, they found Jabu sitting next to her dead father's body, singing in her little baby voice the melody to the traditional song, *Bawelile ba Peshe ya* ("They've Gone Across the River").

Sandisile became a lead singer in the God's Golden Acre Singers Choir and received sponsored funding to attend a private Christian school in Pietermaritzburg, where she excelled. Heather's work with the choir, and her pastoral missions in the valley, took her into some of the most dangerous places in rural South Africa. More than once she was stopped by gangs of youths, and the menace of hijacking was always present. However, she relied upon her exuberant personality that often stretched to feigning anger, or even outrage. She seemed to possess an inner strength, and conviction, in potentially dangerous situations. She also discovered that Zulu men didn't quite know how to deal with her when she addressed them abruptly in their own language.

Then came a very narrow escape. One fog-ridden night

Heather dropped off the choir at the Jila homestead after a church service. Before she drove away she was told about a young girl, Wendy Zulu, who was struggling to bring up her siblings Ruth, Sikhumbuzo and Thandeka, alone. Heather had brought a missionary with her – he had been at the church service – but he was frightened about the dangers of driving into the night with no clear idea of how to find Wendy Zulu. Heather was adamant that all the children had to be rescued, and eventually they found the hut where Wendy and her siblings were living.

Wendy told her she had been trying to look after her three young siblings since her father had died. The children were loaded into the back of the truck, and the party was driving to Wartburg in the fog when Heather realized they were being followed. A group of young men in another combi came up alongside and tried to push her vehicle off the road. "They had seen me in the lights of their car and came straight after me. I thought that night was going to be it. They chased me along this narrow road, came up alongside, and tried to force me onto the side. My knees were shaking and the missionary sitting next to me was screaming."

"I told you not to come. I told you not to come," the man wailed. He was getting on Heather's nerves. His hysterical attitude was stopping her from thinking.

"Please shut up!" she shouted at him. She said quietly to God: "Please help me."

Heather slammed on the brakes and in an instant her fear was replaced by anger. She opened the car door, pulled herself up to her full five feet three inches, and glared at the group of youths in fury and indignation. Then she let them have it in Zulu: "How dare you worry an old woman who is rescuing a family? One you probably know! People told me of their plight and I am trying to help them. Go on, look in the truck – what do you see? Your people – the young Zulu family! Don't you realize I am trying to help you and your people? These children are orphans! I have permission from the *nkosi* to take them home. What do you think will happen to them if you take my truck? How dare you interfere! I'm trying to get them back for food and safety, and all you can do on a stormy night is jeopardize my life and yours!"

Suddenly the young men were all becoming apologetic: "We never wanted to harm you, Gogo. We just wanted to find out what you were doing in the middle of the night and see if we could help you." The ringleader added: "If you're ever in trouble, or anyone tries to harm you, just let me know!"

19
THE HORRORS OF
THE VALLEY

The community at Wartburg continued to grow, and Heather began to take in more sick babies and abused youngsters from the valley. Many were healthy, and just needed plenty of love, care and protection. The terminal cases needed somewhere to die with dignity and receive one-to-one nursing.

They converted the family TV room into a nursery. More than 24 babies and toddlers lived in a room that was perhaps 18 feet square. Every morning the Zulu girls from the pottery piled up the mattresses against the wall. They would put them down again on the floor at night. It created an astonishing picture that visitors found hard to believe. There, on the floor without cots, were two dozen babies and toddlers dependent for their survival upon Heather, and a group of African caregivers. The babies needed 24-hour nursing and included many heartbreaking cases.

As they worked tirelessly through the night, bottle-feeding and changing nappies, they knew some of their beloved infants would eventually succumb to the virus, whatever anyone did. Heather would sometimes weep, choking back her sobs so as not to disturb the infant, as the sick baby lay snuffling in her arms, losing its fight for life. Large tears would well up in her sad brown eyes, and stream down her face. Sometimes it seemed she was fighting alone against the world's worst catastrophe since the plague – without support from the rest of the world.

Efforts to raise finance to underpin God's Golden Acre had failed. She recalls all this was happening at the worst period of her life. By 1997 they had approximately 30 children and were feeding them, educating them, supplying nappies, medication, and bearing all living costs. Yet they had no money. The importance of her work was going largely unrecognized in the outside world. One day without warning, a workman from Eskom, the power company, was sent to cut off the electricity supply because the bill had not been paid quickly enough. She asked them to wait so she could boil a kettle for sterilized water for the babies' bottles. They refused.

The electricity was disconnected on several more occasions during the Wartburg years, putting the lives of the sick babies at great risk. "We had our electricity disconnected three times and the phone cut off frequently because we couldn't pay our bill. We even had our water cut off once. I didn't dare let our board of management know how bad things were."

Babies like Chummy, Susiwe, Tommy, Michael, Siyanda, Fikile, Nosipho, Thulani, Gadiga, Siswe, Nkosi, Scelo and Happiness found their way to God's Golden Acre at this time. Some were HIV-positive, and among these were Megan and her twin sister, who were found abandoned in the sugar cane. Basetsane, her twin, had died there, but Megan survived for nearly a year, before she too passed on to heaven.

Heather recalls the time with sadness: "The little girl, Megan, was three months old and the most beautiful child I had ever seen. Like a tiny doll, her perfect features were so delicate you felt you had to hold her very carefully, like glass. Even now, her face fills my mind, and I remember her funny disposition that endeared her to everyone who saw her. Being so young, there are few specific stories about her life, except to say that she was my baby, and in the year that I had her, she managed to touch my life so deeply that I carry her memory close to my heart, and cannot allow myself to think on her too deeply, as the tears come too quickly.

"She was brought to me with an enlarged spleen and swollen glands, and the rollercoaster ride of watching her fight the disease, having her good days and her bad days, close to death on many occasions, was heart-rending. Her vulnerability and innocence in the situation into which she was born broke me, and I hated the powerlessness I felt against this silent killer. A Canadian volunteer named Laura Harlos was with us at the time, teaching our preschool children, and she too fell in love with our precious little baby. Her parents baptized Megan and really bonded with her in the time that she was with us.

"Fifteen months after she had arrived at God's Golden Acre, Megan finally lost the battle and faded away. The worst of it was that after she went to Jesus we wanted to have the funeral. She was taken to the Pietermaritzburg mortuary but the staff there lost Megan's body, and we were never able to grieve properly. We spent weeks trying to find her body, but it was never recovered. This baby that we so loved was lost. We will never know why or how it happened. They have these pauper burials where two or three people are interred together. Maybe a mistake was made there. I don't think we'll ever know.

"Those are the most crushing experiences in this work. To have a child sleep in your bed with you, to watch her fight death almost daily, and to know that there are thousands more just like her is almost enough to make you lose hope altogether. But the miracles we witness almost daily at God's Golden Acre, and the success stories that are found in the lives of healthy, happy children who have overcome, is priceless, and keeps us all going. In ten years at God's Golden Acre, we have lost only twelve children in our residential care to HIV/AIDS. God has been good to us, and we pray daily for his hand upon all of the children he has entrusted to our care."

In the early days, God's Golden Acre linked in with Thuli Mzizi, a social worker from nearby Grey's Hospital, who started to send their most acute cases. Some were HIV-positive, others victims of cerebral palsy, and in all cases, it was impossible to find them foster parents.

"Sicelo Madikwa was among those first infant arrivals and is still with us today. He had an older sister, Ntombi, and a brother, Majola, and we took in all three of them. There were no medical records, but we know Sicelo's mother was run over by a taxi. He had developed cerebral palsy at eleven months of age, and this was something that I recognized from my brother Kenny's condition many years before. So my heart went out to this boy. 'You are not going to stay stiff like that, Sicelo Madikwa! As long as I live I'm going to get those arms of yours straight. I'm going to work on them,' I promised him, although, of course, at twelve months old he could not understand what I was saying to him.

"I used to cry when I pulled Sicelo's arms, they were so stiff. I'd pull them a little bit and he would scream and his poor sister must have thought I was being cruel to him. Can you imagine, me holding him, and this child screaming in agony? Ntombi would look at me with horror in her eyes, not understanding what I was trying to do. It must have been really hard for her. She didn't know that I had had a brother like hers."

Sicelo's arms loosened gradually and now his arms are straight again. He can even open his hands. A wonderful singer and dancer, Ntombi is now teaching the younger children, and is one of the leading members of the Young Zulu Warriors who made the UK tour in 2002.

Then there was Siyanda Vundla who was abandoned in a hut as a tiny baby. Heather remembers he bit her when she first tried to feed him. Siyanda was severely malnourished and his little body, from his feet upwards, was swollen with fluid. Heather nursed him back to health and now he is a healthy boy. Another of the children was Nondeka, who had been shot through the spine by her stepfather. She was about nine years old and in a dreadful state and in great pain when she arrived with an appalling sore on her foot.

Heather would weep for hours at every death, but exhorted her team of Zulu helpers to go on with their work. And grim, dedicated work it was. The number of sick babies being brought to them kept on increasing steadily as the scourge of the pandemic ravaged the valley. "Caring and nursing these sick children and babies took hours of our day. Those who turned the corner from apparent terminal sickness, and did survive, created enormous relief and joy within the community."

There are no more joyful stories than that of Thabani, who was born ten weeks prematurely near Ingwavuma, which lies on the border between South Africa and Swaziland. At birth, Thabani weighed maybe just over one kilogram. His mother, a thirteen-year-old girl with learning disabilities who had been raped by an older man, abandoned him at the local hospital less than a week later. Heather recalls: "Thabani arrived at God's Golden Acre in a banana box. Born premature, he was about a month old when we got him from the social workers at Ingwavuma. They were desperate for a place that could take him, as he was very ill. The first thing we noticed about Thabani were his enormous eyes. Slightly squint and seeming almost too big for his head, these dark pools seemed to hold an infinite wisdom beyond his infant age. There was just something about him that drew everyone to him, and we all knew without a doubt that this child would be destined for great things. Some of the volunteers there at the time formed an informal campaign for his presidency... this all at the tender age of four months!"

His health was no laughing matter. Rattling coughs shook his tiny body until he gagged and lost his breath, making every moment of the day a struggle for survival. His coughing made it impossible to keep any medication down, as he'd just vomit as soon as it went in. Tuberculosis ravaged him to the brink of death, and every night was a battle. Becoming so accustomed to his rattling breathing, Heather would jerk awake in shock every time he'd slip into deep sleep and she didn't hear the familiar sound of his heavy breathing. She would yell to Patrick: "He's dead, Patrick, he's not breathing!" Shining the torch on his sleeping face, her heart would settle in relief as she realised he was still alive. Those were long nights, and it eventually took Thabani twelve-and-a-half months to overcome the TB – twice as long as it should usually take.

Now four years old, he has become a firm favourite amongst staff and volunteers, and his deep eyes still command the same reverence. He walks around with a strange gait, capturing the hearts of all who meet him, and the caregivers all still speculate about his mysterious destiny, which might never have come to fruition had he not arrived in that little banana box. Heather wrote:

Many children came riddled with serious illness like tuberculosis, malnutrition, or problems with their lymph nodes, or spleens. It took 24-hour supervision and intervention to save them. We cared, prayed for, comforted and nurtured them all. God called many of the infants to heaven. That was how we saw it in our faith.

Happiness was the first child to pass away, and so it was the hardest, and also because she was not a baby. She was a little girl of six years old. She just wasted away. Being the first one, you question God's motives. This is a child. Why? Why give her this suffering? This beautiful little girl, who we had to watch just waste away.

Happiness had been brought to us by a social worker and she came from Swayimane. She had been born with full-blown AIDS, terrible sores in her mouth, thrush down below, and I felt the pain for this child. Unimaginable. I will remember, for ever, the long hours I spent with her. Happiness, my little girl, sitting on the toilet for hours, with me beside her for comfort – a skeleton of a child. I would sit on the edge of the bath too, and ask her what songs she wanted me to sing. Sometimes I'd sit there for an hour at a time, singing, and then carry her back to the room. She'd no sooner settle down than she was up again, sitting on the toilet. You had to be sitting with her because she would fall over, she was that weak. You couldn't leave her. She couldn't walk back to the room. You had to pick her up and carry her.

At the end it was really the songs that helped her, and the music, and the telling her about Jesus – the whisper in her ear that when she was ready, to just let Jesus come and take her, because she was going to go to this beautiful home and live with him there. "No more pain, darling, no more pain. Close your eyes now, and go…"

There's a beautiful song in Zulu and it goes like this:

When I meet him who I love,
I will then be with him who is my protector,
There's a new name for me,
I will sing my praises to him.

It's got the most beautiful Zulu words and has about six verses. It's the whole thing about when we reach heaven we get a new name, a new dress, and everything will be fine, there's no more pain, and all the bad things will be gone. And everything will be perfect.

Little Happiness went away from God's Golden Acre like the others. Closed her eyes and went to Jesus. That's the way it is, that's the way it happens. The deaths I was involved with were very peaceful.

It was hard to have so many funerals, even though the Zulu way of dealing with it is beautiful. The infant is laid out on the floor and we put a little candle beside the body, cover him or her up, and close the eyes. Everyone who loved that child comes in, sits around, talks and sings hymns. We spend at least three hours in the room. It's a farewell, and it helps to take away the hurt because we know we will all miss the child because we loved him or her. I tell the children we all have to die, and to die is not final, just passing from one world into the next world. For some reason God wants us to live in this world which is not perfect, where there is pain, and many imperfect things, but we love to live here because it is the only thing we know.

I explain to them there is a much better life on the other side, so we don't die, our spirit never dies. Everybody that we know and love is on the other side. That's the perfect place, and where we really want to be, but thank goodness, we all want to hang on to life here because it is all we know. Then I sing them a song I wrote to help ease the pain of parting.

There's a new star
That shines, oh surprise,
A new star that lights up the night,
Because a new soul has reached heaven's door,
She's home, she's home, for evermore,
There's a new song she will sing,
For her Saviour and her King,
A new life she's found there,
In her Father's care.

20
LOCAL HOSTILITY TO GOD'S GOLDEN ACRE

In 1996 a **letter came through** the post informing Heather she was to receive an award from Archbishop Desmond Tutu for the work she had carried out during the transitional years. The reward was in recognition of the manner in which she had helped many people, including refugees, who were made homeless and had suffered during the fighting between various political factions in the valley. It was called the SANLAM Bridge-builder's Award and it exemplified Heather's humane and compassionate role during the unstable years when she set an example by remaining neutral and offering succour to all who needed it.

Locally, however, most white people were cynical about Heather's vision. Worse still as far as local whites were concerned, she was bringing sick and orphaned children out of the valley – creating a community they did not want to be there. The farm's unkempt appearance created further disapproval, with washing hanging on every available fence, and small children, dogs, cats and chickens running around unsupervised. To make matters worse, abandoned vehicles were strewn here and there among the farm buildings, and kids' toys and play equipment was piled high on the veranda.

"Looking back now at the kind of person I was at that time," says Heather, "I do have to admit that many 'normal' whites might have been justified in thinking I was eccentric. What were they to make of a white woman who goes to the valley several times a week to pray among the dead and the dying? Many people were privately saying that Heather and Patrick Reynolds were not quite normal. Stalwart members of the German community were asking why this woman was going to places she had no sane reason to go to, and interfering in the affairs of the Zulus. Had she got some kind of death wish? What was she doing bringing out these sick children who would probably die anyway? And if there really were healthy orphans starving in the valley, why weren't their extended family group caring for them? The Zulus were a proud and independent people, they'd always resented interference – why not leave them alone?"

Among the few Christians in Wartburg who sympathized with Heather was Pastor Hugo Fulter of Wartburg Lutheran Church, whose Bible studies group Patrick and Heather attended. The pastor recalls the day he first met Heather: "When I came into the area in 1995 I heard about Heather and that she was living on a farm, and wanted to start an orphanage. Then one day our Mission Committee went there and visited her. Immediately I thought that we as a church could help her to reach out to the community because the effects of the AIDS pandemic were beginning to escalate in our area."

Apart from the pastor himself, and a few friends from the Bible studies group, however, all the local churches in Wartburg left Heather to fend for herself at God's Golden Acre. Pastor Fulter recalls: "The key for me as a pastor was her strength in faith in standing alone. In the church we have support structures. We've got the organization, houses to live in, a salary, a congregation – but she just stood in faith and said, 'God will provide.' During those difficult times he opened doors, and closed doors, just to see if she would keep her faith. In the beginning, I must say I was a bit sceptical – will God really fulfil her vision? She was, for instance, in debt, and we could not see how she would get out of that, she didn't have transport, and many people were hostile to her. Through all this she trusted the Lord in everything.

"Eventually it was clear to us he was leading and guarding her. Many people were hostile to her because they still had not been reconciled with black people. They found it hard, and they were afraid that the orphanage would draw other Africans, and these in turn would be responsible for more crime, and possibly sickness, and things like that."

Heather understood some of their fears: "We were living in a conservative area and there was uncertainty and resentment among the white community for the political future of the country. They were wondering what kind of society the former terrorist Nelson Mandela, now president after 27 years of imprisonment, intended to create."

Perhaps Heather Reynolds appeared to them as yet another manifestation of the new Africa, a strange woman who seemed to have this intense faith in God and a troubling preference for spending her life among Africans. Displaced blacks, most of them babies and children, were all living in her home, which other white people thought was unthinkable.

Here and there people appeared who believed that what Heather was doing was right, and among them were Ilse Ceronio and her sister Lenthuen Smit, who were both devout Lutherans. Ilse recalls: "She told us about her vision of the black cloud that would fall over us if we didn't care for the AIDS orphans now. She used to say, 'A child that is uncared for, unloved and uneducated becomes a criminal.' She endured real hardship – sometimes on a Sunday she would phone and say, 'There's no food – can you gather some and bring it to me?' My sister Lenthuen usually had something in the garden that we could give. Then the Harburg congregation – a small town 22 kilometres from Wartburg – got to hear about Heather and they really were marvellous. They started by praying, then helped with gifts, and after that by supplying cars and trucks. She needed friends at that time."

However, if local people thought Heather eccentric, the family unit, the board, staff and caregivers at God's Golden Acre remained loyal to her vision. Mary Van der Leeuw and her husband Carl had come on the scene right at the beginning of the Wartburg years. Mary recalls: "Our maid's sister had died of AIDS-related diseases and her baby son was HIV-positive and we were looking after the child at our home. He was really very sick and I'd been phoning round several organizations looking for help – and then someone put me on to Heather. When I phoned her she was totally shocked that they had given us her name because although she had moved to Wartburg, she didn't have any sick children there at that time – only a vision. Anyway, I was so desperate I didn't know what to do with the little boy.

"She gave me some other numbers with the instruction that if they did not turn out to be OK, then I should contact her again. Eventually he went to a hospital in Greytown and Heather asked us to come to a meeting to find out more about her vision – soon afterwards I started working as her secretary."

During the mid-1990s, Heather's two children, Brendan and Bronwen, had been successful students at a small German school nearby and were fluent in both English and German. Brendan was accepted as a scholar at Pietermaritzburg College and became a promising tennis player on the junior Natal championship circuit before injury forced him to give it up. Bronwen recalls that the many trials and tribulations brought about during the momentous Wartburg years strengthened their family unit, but any thought of being a normal family was jettisoned: "As you've heard, the TV room was converted into a nursery. The floor at night would be one big bed. Babies were everywhere, you couldn't easily reach the TV – you'd have to pick your way across the room to turn it on – and then watch your programme quietly with this crowd of sleeping babies on the floor! How could you get angry about the loss of privacy when you realized what they had been through?

"I only went to the valley when I was working at God's Golden Acre quite recently and I just cried. So I think through our childhood Mum protected us from the awful things she saw and the heroic things she had to do. She would come back from the valley and she would be very tired and she wouldn't really talk about it. I think maybe this was because she knew I am also very sensitive and hated to see, or hear about, people being hurt. So I don't think she really off-loaded that much of what was happening. But we knew she had saved those babies in our living room.

"Did I ever rebel against it all? Well, like any teenager in high school you grow up and become more self-absorbed, and it's all 'about me'. And so in that respect Mum and I some-times had a difficult time just because I was your typical teenage girl – having to share a bathroom with hordes of chil-dren when there was only one bathroom. So, yes, I had my moments!

"I think we were brought up from a young age to be aware of God. I personally remember feeling his presence when I was very small and we were still living in Dalton, where we were involved in the Methodist church, and I used to go to the youth group. So I knew him from small, and later I never lost sight of the fact that it was God's calling on our life."

Among her activities with the choir at this time Heather became well known in the evangelical movement of the church; she worked with Bishop Sibiya who ran a training col-lege for priests and was also responsible for a group of affili-ated churches in various parts of KwaZulu-Natal. She travelled great distances in Zululand with the choir, often to very remote areas, to attend all-night services, but always felt safe with her Zulu boys beside her as protection. She recalls: "It was useful because black people got to know me through my evangelical work. Usually I was the only white woman in the congregation in these churches and I would get up on the stage with the choir and sing with them. It was of course unheard of in the rural areas for a white woman to be involved in that kind of church business. It was also a time of reconciliation and healing between millions of black and white people.

"On another occasion, after a big demonstration in a rugby stadium in Durban against violence being perpetrated upon white farmers, we had nowhere to sleep and so people of both races gathered around us impromptu, and we sang right through the night. It developed into a wonderful occasion with white and black people coming together. At about three o'clock in the morning I remember an Afrikaans man who broke down after he'd been singing with the choir. He confessed to having done horrible things and it was a cleansing process."

21

THE NORWEGIAN VOLUNTEERS ARRIVE

owards the end of the time that God's Golden Acre was at Wartburg, some of the pressure was taken off Heather, in her role as a day-to-day nurse, when her first overseas volunteers, Vibeke Blaker and Marianne Jenum, arrived from Norway. Both girls experienced severe culture shock.

Marianne Jenum: "Dr Ter Haar picked us up and he told us that the children slept in the garage and in mud huts. I had trouble picturing myself sleeping in a mud hut. When we arrived, I forgot my worries. Beautiful, smiling children gave us the warmest welcome. There were also dogs, cats, chickens, roosters, and a frog in the bathroom. I was relieved when I found out that we were sleeping in Bronwen's room, indoors. 'Chaotic' is the word that best describes the first evening. There were so many people and animals around and so many things happening at the same time, while I tried to fit as many children as possible on my lap and learn their names."

Vibeke Blaker: "One evening, it was dark outside, and I sat alone on the bed in our room. We had closed the curtains in front of the window, and I thought nobody could see me. Then I heard a loud, deep voice saying: 'Sugar!' It came from outside the window. I almost got a little scared. And then I again heard the voice saying, 'Sugar!' I did not understand who this was and I looked out of the window. The only thing I could see was an old combi-van that was parked on the grass. But after a while I heard laughter, and then three heads became visible from inside the combi. Then I understood that the curtains in our room were transparent. There were three boys living in the van, and it became clear that they had the perfect place to spy on us in our room, and they did! Marianne and I realized that they had probably seen some funny things during the first days we were at God's Golden Acre, for instance us putting lotion on our sunburned bodies before we went to bed at night.

"The three boys living in the combi were Sbo, Siphamandla and Siyabonga. They were all in the class we taught and we became really close to them during our stay. We could not help noticing that they often looked really tired in the mornings. They never fell asleep before we did, and often they made funny noises after we turned off the light, and we had a lot of laughs. Seeing that these children were actually cheerful children made me very happy. It didn't look like they were damaged from experiences in their past; it seemed like they were able to live full lives. Watching how much they enjoyed singing and dancing made me glow, as did the feeling that me coming to South Africa meant a lot to them.

"On the other hand, there were lots of things that made me sad too. All of the children had experienced horrible things before they came to God's Golden Acre, and I wept hearing their stories. I felt that it was 'unfair' that small, innocent children should have to be that sick, and that they all grew up with no parents. I kept thinking about their future; I worried about what chances they would have in life. The poverty was so extreme, and I analyzed my own life in Norway. I felt sort of guilty for living under such pampered conditions and for my love of material things."

Marianne: "At a closer sight, I saw that several of them were very thin and tiny, and one of them had ugly sores on his feet. I was prepared to meet sick babies, and deal with the low risk of being infected, so I tried not to let the sores scare me.

Heather didn't test all the children systematically, so we did not know who had HIV, but we could see that several children were obviously sick. Tiny Nonto was constantly crying and had chronic ear-infections. Gadiga and Thandeka had terrible sores that wouldn't heal, so we worried about them. Mavu and Goodman were skinny and wouldn't put on weight. It turned out they had TB, and after they got rid of that, they've turned into healthy young boys."

Vibeke: "Siyanda and Gadiga were a little bit older; they wanted to be held a lot. I was actually a bit scared of Gadiga. Since he had these open sores, I was afraid of being in physical contact with his blood. I was very afraid of that at the beginning of my stay at God's Golden Acre, but we all grew used to it. There was a girl called Happiness who had died of AIDS-related disease just before Marianne and I came to God's Golden Acre. Heather talked a lot about her, how they treated her at the end, how she died, how they let the other children see her after she died. It made a huge impression. To be honest, I was actually a bit relieved that I didn't stay at God's Golden Acre when Happiness died. I'm not sure how I would have handled it."

Marianne: "One little girl – Pume – was so tiny I was afraid she would break if I touched her. She was only eight or nine years old, but had been a prostitute together with her mum. Heather had made an exception and taken her in – although her mum was alive. The girl was just lying in a hut while men kept going in to abuse her. She was so scared of men that she got hysterical and broke into tears once when Brendan accidentally touched her, and she was so weak that she fell asleep everywhere. It broke my heart when Heather later told me that her mum took her back, and there was nothing she could do about it. I remember actually hoping she had AIDS and would die quickly. Life on earth must have been hell for her, poor thing. She didn't know English, but she usually calmed down when I had her on my lap and sang to her.

"Learning about Pume's life and other similar life stories were our saddest moments. We asked, and Heather told us, their life stories. Then later, we usually talked about these things in our bedroom at night, after the children had gone to sleep. Vibeke and I often cried. We took turns being 'the strong one' – we couldn't both cry and ask difficult existential questions – one of us had to 'pull' the other one up and help the other to see the bright side. This arrangement was our way to deal with the overwhelmingly tragic information."

Heather avoided exposing Vibeke and Marianne to the everyday horrors she herself experienced in the valley, on their first tour of duty. However, the arrival of the two European girls at Wartburg allowed her even greater opportunities to spend more time in the valley, where her presence was desperately needed. Eventually, there were 41 children at Wartburg. The babies still all lived in Heather's home, and the older ones lodged in outbuildings and garages, and of course that old motor-caravan, known as a "combi", outside the Norwegian girls' room, where three of the bigger boys slept. The strong Christian ethic within the community was expressed at mealtimes where there would be prayers before food. In the evening the orphans would wear their pyjamas and come into the lounge to sing, play games, and get their toothpaste and vitamins.

Marianne recalls: "They would fetch their toothbrushes and stand in line. I'd give them toothpaste, and they'd have to say 'thank you'. I don't really know why I loved this so much. Perhaps it was the normality about it: clean children in pyjamas, brushing their teeth at night. Maybe it was how they tried hard to pronounce the 'thank you' correctly, like they really wanted to be good. Maybe what made an impression was that they were in fact thankful for such a trivial thing like toothpaste. I guess I loved to be able to look each and every one in the eye, and give each attention."

One of the happiest moments for the Norwegian volunteers was finding out that the older girls they were teaching in their class in the little school at God's Golden Acre were not HIV-positive. "After having heard Heather talk about all the cases of sexual abuse, and seeing the girls' faces when Heather did her 'Sex can give you AIDS' speech, Vibeke and I had the impression that the girls thought they might be infected. We talked with Heather about testing them. We thought that if they were negative, the girls would be extremely grateful and protect themselves from then on. This was only an idea from our side, but Heather knew some of the girls had been abused and asked them if they wanted to get tested. And they did. Afterwards, a few more of the girls came, and it turned out they had been abused too. So suddenly, Vibeke and I found ourselves escorting five girls, aged eleven to fourteen, to the doctor to find out if they were going to die within a few years or not. It was horrible; we knew that our naïve idea might have a terrible impact on the lives of these girls. They were tested, and we had to wait some time for the results. It was tormenting. When the results finally came through, they were all negative. I've never felt more relieved, and the girls instantly started singing and dancing and jumping. Was it the right thing to do, to test them? I still don't know, but we are both grateful that it turned out the way it did."

22
BANKRUPTCY LOOMS

In the meantime, life at Wartburg remained difficult. In the farming community there remained scant sympathy for what Heather and Patrick were doing. When a local sawmill at Windy Hill decided to stop housing its workforce, the board of God's Golden Acre immediately applied to buy the houses – but the local farmers managed to stop them from doing it. Heather recalls: "The farmers' association decided they didn't want orphans there and that they were going to bulldoze the buildings we could have used. And that's exactly what they did."

The worst instance of racism Heather ever encountered came one day when she was in Pietermaritzburg at a printing company who were doing some free posters for God's Golden Acre. She had gone in to look at the proofs and was talking to the staff about some small adjustments. She noticed there was a man behind her in the queue and from his body language she knew he was becoming impatient. So she turned round and apologized for delaying him. "We're nearly done," she said politely.

"Well, what is it all about anyway?" he asked gruffly, looking at the proofs.

She said: "Oh! It's an exhibition, 'Flowers Through The Home', to raise money for our AIDS Orphans Project."

He hissed: "What do you mean? Black children?"

She replied, startled: "Yes."

"What! You mean you've been keeping me here waiting – and all this to try and save these bloody little black bastards? Look, do me a favour: why don't you stick the whole damn lot of them down a mineshaft. And then do me another favour – make doubly sure that it's sealed, so they can never get out."

She was devastated and shocked: "I'm just so sorry. I don't know what's caused your anger."

He fumed: "Don't feel sorry for me. Be sorry for those little black bastards."

Heather got out of there as fast as she could. "I was devastated at the force and depth of his hatred. It was so overpowering and when I got home I cried and cried. I cried for the man and his anger, and I cried for the children and for all this unnecessary hatred. From that awful incident I wrote a little song and dedicated it to the unknown racist man."

Have you asked the question,
Is life always fair?
Have you asked the question,
And do you really care?
Like a child born today,
They say that she has AIDS,
Victim of the dreaded HIV,
She's condemned at infancy,
A man-made situation,
An infant, the infant had no choice,
Will you ask the question,
Is life always fair?
For you ask the question,
And please, will you care?
And please, will you care?

In fact, the proofs the racist had seen were for a 'Flowers Through The Home' exhibition to raise funds for God's Golden

Acre organized by a close friend of Heather's who had come up with a plan to relocate the charity to an area north of Pietermaritzburg called the Karkloof. Heather remembers: "One day a dear friend of ours, Yvonne Shaw, who lived in a beautiful and wealthy farming and plantation area called the Karkloof, 60 miles from Wartburg, came to see us to look at Patrick's work, because she was interested in buying a sculpture. She saw some of the children and was impressed. I told her about my vision, and she went back to the Karkloof and spoke to her son William. He agreed to give us a piece of land, which was marvellous because we did not have much money at that time, and it would have meant all we had to do was raise enough money to put up some buildings and get things started. We were going to do a little craft village, and a gallery for Patrick's sculptures. At the back there would be a few dormitories for the children. It wasn't going to be anything too big but it would have catered for our needs at the time, and we would own it.

"Yvonne did the 'Flowers Through The Home' exhibition, which was very successful and a lot of people came. But somehow people had got to hear that William had offered us this land before he had actually spoken to the farmers himself. I got a phone call from a man who said that people wanted to know what was going on. He knew that we were to be given land – and he and his neighbours wanted some answers. So I agreed to set up a meeting and told them I was very willing to answer any questions that people would like to ask me. I did not ask Yvonne or William to come, because I did not want to involve them in any nastiness. They had been kind enough to offer us the land and I felt I was quite capable of answering the questions.

"The meeting was set up for the country club up in the Karkloof and I went there. I knew I was going to be facing some angry farmers because of what was happening at Wartburg. I asked the chairman to keep control and not allow anyone to get out of order because I didn't want to face being lynched. He assured me he'd keep order. Well, my goodness, did they have a go at me? Yes, they did – with everything. I had no chance. It was a lynch mob. I have never been so humiliated. I turned to the chairman and said, 'You are supposed to be keeping order.'

"Then I turned round and looked at the farmers and I said, 'You know, gentlemen, even if you offered to build me that place on that land, I wouldn't want to bring my children amongst the likes of you. I wouldn't actually like to bring my children up in this area. I think we're better off where we are.' I walked out. The meeting was adjourned and they invited me to go and have a drink, which I accepted, and some people came round who felt bad about the way they had behaved. Once again I had come across aggression because I was trying to help little black children. They did not want us in their area. So we abandoned the idea of moving there and remained at Wartburg – for the time being."

Meanwhile another much more serious dilemma presented itself. Heather had to manage the growing community at Wartburg, yet the crisis in the valley was escalating and she was needed to go there more often. There were no spare hours to go to the pottery. Soon, the pottery was in serious decline. Although Heather tried to delegate the creative work to the most experienced women, when she wasn't in the pottery keeping a direct eye on the process, quality control would quickly fall apart.

When they lost one of their biggest contracts because too many bonsai pots were sub-standard, Heather realized she was going to have to choose between the pottery and God's Golden Acre. She must revive the pottery and run it properly, or else close it down, put her faith in God, and run God's Golden Acre full-time. "It was a very hard decision to make – because if we abandoned the pottery, we risked going bankrupt. We were grinding along with 41 children, many of them sick. But the needs of the children, and the plight of those in the valley, had priority on my time – and so we prepared to take a desperate gamble by closing the pottery."

23
THE STREET PROTEST

Heather and Patrick decided to apply to the Nelson Mandela Children's Fund for financial assistance. "I had the organization structured as best I could," she says. "We had a management board and a constitution, and I believed that we were now eligible for funding. We applied to the Fund thinking that what they had said about raising money to help underprivileged children would apply to our orphans. I was now living, waiting daily, for this funding proposal to come back. I saw it as a lifeline with the pottery closed. Then Patrick got sick with hepatitis and both Brendan and I had to have expensive hospital operations. I began to feel that God was throwing everything at us. Then came a further disaster – our vehicle was stolen and so we had no wheels except when the local Lutheran pastor, Hugo Fulter, was able to lend us his car.

"There were friends who tried to discourage us from going on. Among these was Dave Beyers, a bank manager, who shared our love of bonsai tree cultivation and had worked with us at Deep Valley many years before, building and staging a number of fantastic exhibitions.

" 'Look, Heather, you can't save the world,' he would tell us over and over again. 'You can't let yourself go bankrupt. You have neglected the pottery, and you have neglected your bonsai. It's not good business. You can't do that…'

"Meanwhile we were heading for real trouble. One day when we met Dave at a convention for bonsai growers he said, 'I'm sorry, Heather, I don't even want to sit and talk tonight, because you are crazy – you can't save the whole bloody world! Get that into your head.'

"Very shortly after that I told him, 'Dave, I need .you as treasurer. You are a bank manager, and you would give us credibility because we want to register as an NGO. So I'm asking you, calling in a favour, since I shared with you all my knowledge of bonsai.' He was surprised at my request.

" 'You know I don't believe in this whole thing,' he said, 'because I don't believe in something that is going to bankrupt you. It doesn't make sense to me.'

"I was pleading now: 'Please, Dave. There's hardly any money, and it won't take up much of your time. I just need to have a treasurer and I need to have a small bank account – if people do donate funds to God's Golden Acre, everything must be properly handled... because up till now it has all been our own money.' Dave reluctantly agreed. It gave me a sense of some security to have him around, despite his doubts."

The stress was now getting to Heather... no money, no wheels and no support. Around this time, some close friends from the Lutheran church decorated a large basket with ribbons and put it in the local supermarket with information about God's Golden Acre, what it was trying to do, and asking for donations of food items. The result was a disaster and illustrated clearly what the local community thought of God's Golden Acre. As she recalls: "In six months we were given one loaf of bread and a few cents. Some of the richest farmers in South Africa lived around Wartburg, and the best they could do was one loaf of bread and a few cents. We agreed there was no point in keeping the basket there. There was deep anger within me when I got home that afternoon – but worse was to come. A letter delivered that day told us we had been rejected by the Nelson Mandela Children's Fund. They said sorry but they couldn't help us. It was such a disappointment and I was very angry.

"'What the heck is this Nelson Mandela Children's Fund about?' I raged. 'Here we've got children who have been orphaned and abandoned. We are helping the vulnerable children in our community, supporting many of them in their extended families… What other criteria do we have to meet to be able to get this money?' I could not understand what else we would have to do to meet their requirements. I believed there could not be any organization in greater need than ours.

"I was devastated, angry, tired and at the end of my tether. I was near to my breaking point. Life was becoming impossible without a vehicle. Things were hectic. I had so much to do! I had to keep finding a car to borrow for this, and borrow a car for that, and it was driving me crazy. I picked up the phone and rang the office of the Nelson Mandela Children's Fund. A man answered the phone and I blasted him from all sides. I said, 'How can you reject this proposal? How is it possible that an organization that is caring for the most vulnerable children in its community does not qualify for your support? I just want to tell you something – don't you ever forget the name God's Golden Acre and don't you ever forget my name, Heather Reynolds.' I was furious and slammed the phone down."

"Some years after this," Heather admits, "things would be patched up and we did get funding, and the children got to meet Nelson Mandela – but that comes later…

"Next I phoned up the police station, the local commandant, and all my frustrations came pouring out in a strident torrent: 'Look, I'm just going to tell you that I'm going to stage a peaceful parade through town tomorrow. We're going to do a march. I want to walk around the streets and say: "Here I am with my children, these are the children orphaned because of AIDS-related diseases and violence. They exist and we love them." There won't be anything violent or anything but I want it so that no one will be able to say they don't know about God's Golden Acre, who we are, and for whom we are caring. I want them to understand that there are whites who love black people and who love black children too, and that you white people can hold children who have the HIV virus, and you won't catch it because it's not contagious. I want all this to be seen, and I want it heard too at a public meeting afterwards in the church hall.'

"So I took out with me a lot of little blackboards and I wrote all over them – slogans about caring about children, appropriate verses from the Bible, and so forth. I sent out word to the choir and others in the valley to come up to the taxi rank and prepare to sing.

" 'What's it all about, Gogo?' they asked.

" 'Just come up,' I said. 'I want people to know that God's Golden Acre exists, that we are providing a useful service to the community.'

"So I went into the town, with all the children. I parked the truck and put all the placards out. The choir from the valley arrived, and other supporters too, and I said, 'Sing, guys, sing... ' They looked at me sheepishly and I said again, 'Come on, let's sing!' And they did – right there in the taxi rank. Then we marched around the small area. Lots of people saw us and read the slogans on the blackboards. The evening came and a mystified Dr Ter Haar arrived to chair the meeting. I told him confidently, 'Oh, we're just letting the local people know about us.'

"We slipped over the road to the church hall for the meeting, and our friends attended – as did a number of local white people. I stood up and welcomed everybody and explained our difficulties in trying to do our work, in particular our lack of transport. I told them about the AIDS pandemic, and its impact, and how it was going to affect everybody and that we needed to take action and support each other – and they

needed to support us because we were actually doing something responsible which would benefit the community in the
years to come... I read in some people's eyes that I had lost
them; they had shut me out. I hadn't reached them. Then suddenly I got angry.

"I said, 'It would be better for us to leave this area – we are
never going to get this community to support us.'

"Suddenly a hand went up at the back of the hall and a man
stood up. We had never met him before. He was Ron Kusel, a
highly respected member of the local community, who came
from the nearby village of Harburg. He said: 'I think I could
take care of your transport problems.' There was a stunned
silence. I could hardly believe my ears. He added: 'I've got a
relatively new Toyota truck, and I think we could help.'

"Dr Ter Haar stood up and diplomatically took over where
I'd left off, thanking Ron and the rest of the audience for their
help. At the end of that meeting it was arranged that Ron
would deliver the vehicle to us in the morning. The Toyota
provided us many years of excellent service. It was the lifeline
we needed. Ron's act of generosity came at a very crucial time
when I was at breaking point. This act of kindness gave me the
courage to go on. Subsequently Ron was to help us in many
other ways with resources, like wood from his sawmill to
build our hospice and accommodation for our volunteers."

The desperate measures Heather had taken to win partial
support from the white community around Wartburg had met
with success. However, it wasn't only the white community
who failed to show compassion. Many black people resented
Heather. It became, for example, a humiliating experience for
her to get sell-by-date food from the supermarkets in
Pietermaritzburg.

"A large chain store nearby kindly agreed to give us the
daily sell-by-date foods. However, the young black assistants
employed there were the first generation to work in a South
Africa not ruled by whites. I would spend hours waiting in the

delivery section, waiting — sometimes with Brendan or Patrick — for the shop assistants to bring out the trolleys. They would be quite rude and shove the trolleys out so hard that they would tip over, and there would be cream cakes and doughnuts everywhere, all over the tarred surface. After clearing the trolleys, we had to clean up the mess. Can you imagine what it was like to have to go there and fetch this food, night after night, for nearly two years?

"We had to sit there from six o'clock and wait for the hatch doors to open, sometimes as late as nine o'clock. It was dark — there was no lighting. We were tired. We had children to go to who needed us. We were exhausted from the night before. Rats and cockroaches were everywhere.

The moment the hatch opened, and the food was pushed out on trolleys, the cockroaches rushed, like an advancing black shadow, for the food. We were competing with these repulsive creatures. I did not want to take them home with me and start an infestation there. We would salvage what we could, and then we had to scrape the cream off the tarmac. At any one moment I could have said: 'I'm not going to close the pottery. I'll just place the children in an institution, and go back to my normal life.' I didn't have to be there, kneeling on the tarmac in the dark with cockroaches all around me, scraping cream off the ground. There was nothing forcing me to do this. The only thing making me do it was that I knew our sick babies and children would probably starve to death back where they came from, so we had to push on.

"I knew that at any point I could give up. I could still salvage the pottery, turn things around, get old contracts back, and abandon God's Golden Acre. I could return to the art of growing bonsai trees, and to my painting. I could still change my mind! Perhaps Dave Beyers was right after all. There was no money coming in; the children needed clothing, medical care and schooling. My own children were being neglected. I could let it all go, and return to normality. As I scrabbled among the dirt outside the food store, night after night, can you imagine my dilemma?"

A volunteer, Susan Balfour, who worked at God's Golden Acre in the later years, expressed Heather's dilemma in her journals:

There *are* moments of doubt, pain and discouragement for her. Resistance to the work has been enormous at times, some intensely painful instances of rejection by friends and family. The cruelty of strangers can be equally devastating. That is what I have seen in my time with her, and believe me, it cuts deep. Sometimes, when things have really built up, Heather has expressed thoughts that she would like to disappear, go back to her art and her bonsai. But somewhere in that pain, comes the realization that if she were gone, there would be no one to care for the children. You can see this awareness come upon her. It sends a shiver through her sometimes, and then she goes about the work just as she did before and as fiercely! This is human frailty. Although there *is* an almost superhuman quality in Heather's endurance, she is still human, and vulnerable.

The arrival of Vibeke and Marianne shortened the waiting time for food at night because the young assistants realized two beautiful European girls were hanging around outside. It aroused sufficient interest for the store assistants to open up earlier – but the two Norwegians nevertheless found the food run a repulsive experience. Marianne wrote:

The worst part was the bread. Most of it was all right, but some of it was disgusting, all green with mould, and smelly. And they wouldn't let us throw it in the big container; for some reason we had to take "all or nothing", so we couldn't protest. A lot of it was unhealthy stuff, cakes and buns, not very suitable for bringing up children. I couldn't understand why we didn't get fresher stuff. In order to give us green mouldy bread, they must have stored it for weeks to rot. I still don't understand what they were thinking."

Heather had also managed to get a contract with another food chain, to have the store's leftovers for free. This time there were none of the squalid goings-on, with food being literally thrown out of garage doors. Heather, Brendan, or one of the volunteers, would have to be there about 3.30pm. They would press a bell at the warehouse, go in, and be given what was available. It improved things a lot. They were supplied with some really classy food and lots of good meat and chicken, but never knew in advance what they were going to get, so it made meal planning a virtually impossible task. Sometimes the remnants consisted of all the same thing – on more than one occasion the menu at God's Golden Acre had a rather eccentric appearance. Marianne remembers the night of fish pâté: "We sat in the lounge and ate loads of really fine trout pâté. We had to eat it before the wonderful food turned into a major health risk."

However, it was the expense of the powdered milk, special foods, preparations for the sick babies, and the cost of disposable nappies that blew one of the biggest holes in the God's Golden Acre budget. They managed to find a Muslim company that supplied them with nappies when they had them. Nestlé supplied them with powdered milk. So for the moment there was enough for everybody – just. Heather's sister-in-law was working for a pharmaceutical company and they gave God's Golden Acre boxes and boxes of vitamins. It meant all the children could now have a proper baby formula, and even the older ones, who had been malnourished, benefited from that aid project.

The day came, however, when even the small change in coins had gone. Unfortunately, it was a date that coincided with a visit from deputy chairman Dr Gerrit Ter Haar. Heather was desperately anxious that he should not find out how bad things were. She did not want to scare him. Before he arrived she said, kneeling in a quiet prayer by her bedside: "God, now we stand absolutely alone, and only you can help us."

Halfway through the meeting an African girl who was helping to do the cooking came to Heather. "What are we cooking, for tonight, Gogo?" she asked.

Heather replied in an exaggerated tone of unconcern: "Oh. Don't worry about that. We'll deal with that later."

The look on the Zulu girl's face was one of total bewilderment, because she knew that Heather knew the kitchen staff needed to get started with the cooking – if everything was to be ready in time for the evening meal at 6pm. Heather tried to conceal the look of fear upon her face, and turned back to Gerrit to continue their discussions, but privately she was thinking, "What am I going to do, what am I going to do? I must not let on that the situation is so bad."

As in so many other moments in Heather's life, there appeared to be divine intervention. The next moment the phone rang and it was a young man, Sarel van der Merwe, from Family Favourites products. His boss in Johannesburg had read an article about God's Golden Acre in a magazine and decided to help with food supplies. Heather explains: "His company had decided to place 2,000 Rand each month on account at Metro, and we could buy food from there to that value, on the basis that most of it would be his branded foods. The account had been opened and we could start purchasing right away. We rushed out that afternoon to get food and came home with everything we would need for the month. God had provided."

Heather casually told the unsuspecting Dr Ter Haar: "Oh. Wonderful news. We've had someone give us 2,000 Rand of food every month!"

However, the act of generosity was only a temporary respite from the ongoing financial crisis – and just around the corner loomed what appeared at the time to be a disaster from which there could be no recovery. It came from an unexpected quarter.

Patrick was now planning to turn out exquisite saleable bronzes, and he was preparing to send them off to the 1998 annual exhibition in Pietermaritzburg. It would be the first group of bronzes, just as all those years before they had worked to create the first group of sculptures in wood. Patrick collected the waxes and took them to the foundry. Then came terrible news. They had a call from Dave Falconer: "I'm sorry, they haven't come out. We had a bad run with the metal and they all failed."

The men at the foundry poured them again, recast them, and cleaned them, but the foundry couldn't get them finished in time. It had failed to produce the bronzes in time for the exhibition. The collection was brought to Wartburg two days after the exhibition had started. There they were, all finished, sparkling and beautiful, and sitting on the lounge table when they should have been in Pietermaritzburg, being seen by thousands of people. Heather recalls: "Can you imagine? We were devastated. We had nowhere to sell them. This was our next year's income. We were in big trouble. That week we did not have enough money for food again because our credit card was taken away. I have never been a person to have much debt, but we depended upon the bank overdraft and credit facility. However, things were now out of my control. I owed money on the credit card. The First National Bank promised to give me until the 18th of the month to pay. Then a representative from the bank arrived at Wartburg the week before that date, and demanded my card. I had to give it to him."

Heather was exhausted. She would have to give up her babies and her children. The alternative was bankruptcy. One of the first people who would need to know this was her treasurer, Dave Beyers, and she went to his office to break the news. She spoke almost in a whisper.

"Dave, you know what? You were right. You were right. I should never have started this. Never done it. God hasn't offered anything. We've lost the credit card, and we've run ourselves into the ground. I'm just thinking now what I'm going to tell the committee."

Dave stood up with an angry look on his face. Heather could see he was really cross. "What's this?" he said. "I've just come to believe in you! I believe in you now! How can you tell me you've achieved nothing! You told me yourself that if you asked any one of those children what difference it's made to them they'd tell me... I believe in it now. I've seen those kids. We are not disbanding anything!"

At this moment Heather's life switched itself on again. She felt a surge of excitement, and her strength came flooding back. "I was so excited that Dave Beyers had made this whole turnaround in believing in us, and believing in God's Golden Acre. I walked out of that office with my troubles temporarily forgotten. I felt as if I'd won a million dollars!"

24
HEATHER'S DESPERATE GAMBLE

When Heather got home triumphantly from the meeting with Dave Beyers she discovered that they'd sold one sculpture for 2,500 Rand – which was now all they had in the world. Suddenly, as she stood looking at the pieces in the lounge, her eye fell upon an arts magazine that had been left on a chair. Patrick had picked it up at the exhibition. She flicked through the magazine out of curiosity, and saw an advert listed: " 'Royal Birmingham Society of Artists international competition and exhibition. Prizes to be won for painting and sculpture.' The closing date for entry was that very day. The day I was reading the advert."

She thought to herself that with the 2,500 Rand, if she could get a ticket for about 2,200, she could fly to England and submit the artwork to the selection panel. Heather wondered: "Is this God?" She'd never sold Patrick's work in England but rushed out of the room and told him about it. She warned him they might not get the pieces into the competition because the selection panel could reject them – but maybe they should have a try anyway; they could just afford it!

Around that time, Harry Tomlinson from Greenwood Nursery in Nottingham, England had been out to South Africa as a guest speaker to the Bonsai Society and had stayed at Wartburg. Heather knew she could save on hotel bills by staying with him if she flew to England. Patrick, with his total faith in his extraordinary wife, said: "It's up to you – it's our last money."

Heather had made her mind up: "I phoned Birmingham, said what we had got, and the person replied: 'Sure, just fax us through the titles and give us a bank draft for the entry fee, and be here on the right day to hand the sculptures in – and then we will let you know whether you have made it.' Well, I did it. I sent in the bank draft, and phoned up the travel agent who found a ticket for me two weeks later – which was the time when I had to deposit the bronzes with the Society. I took the two sculptures we were entering, and other bronzes we hoped to sell, and packed them into my suitcase with my clothes in it, and the smaller ones into my shoulder bag.

"The luggage was very heavy and I was in despair at the airport at both ends – but my real problems began at New Street Station in Birmingham because I didn't have enough money for a taxi. I had no choice but to drag my suitcase and shoulder bag, both loaded with bronzes, up the hill to the art gallery. I also had a trolley with small wheels, upon which I had strapped the two biggest bronzes, *The Curled Up Nude* and *The Chairgirl*. The street outside was cobbled, and every few yards the heavy bronzes kept slipping off the wheels. I was under pressure because I knew I had to get up to the gallery before it closed, as this was the final day for exhibits to be entered. I had to make it up this hill before closing time.

"Now I reached breaking point. I just started crying. I couldn't go on. Then somebody put his arm around my shoulder and whispered, 'I'm so sorry.' I dried up my tears, bucked up my ideas, and just carried on. Somehow I managed to get up the hill to the gallery. I arrived dishevelled and out of breath and a young man helped me to get the bronzes up the top flight of steps. The pieces were all wrapped up in towels and paper etc. and once they were opened, they caused an immediate stir of interest because they were so beautiful. I left them there and headed over to the National Exhibition Centre."

There was a gardening exhibition going on at the NEC and Harry Tomlinson was exhibiting on a stand. So he and Heather spent part of the evening on the stand and then he drove her to his home in Nottingham. Next day they had to wait for the reply to find out if Patrick's work had been accepted. It was nerve-racking and soul-destroying. Heather could not bear thinking about it too much, yet she could think of nothing else. The future of God's Golden Acre depended upon the decision of a panel of strangers about Patrick's bronze sculptures!

When the letter came she could not open it – because if they had not made it, the consequences seemed unimaginable. Harry opened the envelope and smiled. Hurrah! Both of the entries had been accepted!

"We went to the opening of the exhibition and found even more wonderful news awaiting us. One of the pieces, a curled up nude, had won the Bryan Hyde Prize, and had been sold for £2,000! That was a huge amount of money in Rand."

The following day, Sir David Shepherd, the well-known artist, also bought a piece for over £1,000, and so did Harry Tomlinson. More commissions followed from people who had been impressed by Patrick's work at the exhibition. That night Heather prayed and thanked God for rescuing them. God's Golden Acre would stay in business.

The following week she flew back to South Africa, feeling happier than she could remember. Now they could carry on and develop God's Golden Acre in the way that they had always hoped. They had real, real money! They were able to deposit around £5,000 in their fund. The partnership between Patrick Reynolds and Dave Falconer of Birdman Foundry at Nottingham Road had at last paid wonderful dividends, bringing success and recognition to both men.

Dave Falconer recalls: "I just think it is amazing because in those very early days when we began to turn out good bronzes, all Patrick's money was going to support the orphans and I think it is marvellous that eventually the whole situation came round a full circle for him. He now has a tremendous market through the people he has contacts with in Europe and it is a fitting reward for a job well done. Patrick is now probably one of South Africa's leading sculptors in the human form, and the 'big five' animals *Elephant, Buffalo, Rhino, Lion And Leopard*, done for Coca-Cola in Johannesburg, reveal his extraordinary talent in creating the spirit of creatures too. Patrick is the only sculptor I have ever worked with who has always paid tribute to the foundry. Most people don't do that – they just forget the foundry and concentrate on their own egos – but Patrick at every opportunity mentions the foundry and makes us feel good."

2 5
HATRED AND
RESENTMENT GROWS

In 1998 the farmland on the estate was sold to a near neighbour, and this neighbour's white foreman, who hated and resented Africans, began to behave in a way that threatened the lives of the children. At the time, some of the older orphans were using the roads because they were doing a running programme. If the foreman saw the orphans he would try to run them down in his truck. He was prepared to wipe out children he considered were on a par with wild game. After a couple of serious incidents, Heather contacted the new owner to express her disgust at his foreman's behaviour. She explained that the children had only escaped by running into the sugar cane.

"Please, the kids have just got the first decent clothes they've ever had, thanks to our friends in Norway. The clothes are now torn because the orphans ran into the sugar cane, some of them have been cut, and the others hurt their ankles. Please tell your foreman to stop doing this," she pleaded. It had little effect.

As 1999 approached, Heather and Patrick realized they would have to get out of Wartburg and find a new place. Dr Ter Haar was also becoming increasingly worried about the sanitation and hygiene at Wartburg. God's Golden Acre was close to saturation point with 41 children, and a further fifteen adults. He also realized that God's Golden Acre could only raise funds properly if it was registered as an NGO and that was the next step that had to be taken. Then there was more depressing news when the Chairman, Professor Ron Nicholson, resigned because of new commitments in the academic field. His departure meant they would go through the transitional period of any coming move without anyone at the helm.

The Reynolds became even more distressed when Cats and Trisca Nelemans, with whom they had been so close at Umgeni Waterfall Care and Rehabilitation Centre in Howick, passed away. However, their son Roland, who inherited the estate, gave God's Golden Acre 10,000 Rand, in an act of unsolicited generosity. At least they could now use this as a deposit and look for somewhere rundown, a derelict small-holding perhaps, that no one else wanted. Heather wrote later:

> We found several suitable sites but they all seemed to be just beyond our price range and we never seemed to have quite enough deposit. Finally, when at last we found a property we felt we could afford, the bank would not help us with the loan. We had the deposit, but nothing for surety. It meant we had to pull out of the deal, and this was deeply humiliating because I felt guilty about letting down the vendors at the last moment. The whole business had depressed me deeply, and I told the board: "Look, for the moment, let's stop searching, getting excited, going through the hoop, and then being disappointed. Let's wait for God."

Heather was at home at Wartburg when Mary Van der Leeuw phoned to say she had seen an advert in a local newspaper for a little place that was going cheaply, 30 miles from Durban. Heather replied: "Mary, I really don't want to look at a place right now. I just don't feel like going through the whole business again with banks failing to support us."

Mary continued: "Heather, it's at a place at Cato Ridge and it's got some sort of resort on it." Bells suddenly started ringing in Heather's head. Right at the early stages, when she came back from Uganda, the Reynolds had been friendly with a young architectural engineer, Didier d'Hotman de Villiers, from Mauritius, whose wife Michelle had been the second secretary at God's Golden Acre. When Heather and Patrick were planning the future God's Golden Acre, Didier did a drawing of how it should look.

Heather had said at that time: "I'd like a little place at the back of the property where our choir could sing and perform. From what I have learned from exhibitions where Patrick's work is displayed, many adults are driven by their youngsters, who within minutes of arriving are pulling on their parents' arms shouting, 'Come on, Mum, or come on, Granny, let's go, let's go!' The problem with places grown-ups want to visit is that usually there is nothing for the children to do while the adults look round."

A new Water World had recently been opened just outside Durban, and every kid in Natal wanted to go there. "I felt we needed a place with a waterslide, or something like that, as an attraction for the children. Either they would encourage their parents or their grandparents to come to spend a day here, or else when they got here, they would be shooting off to play in the water while the adults looked round the galleries, or listened to singing etc. and hopefully became involved with our children and provided a donation."

That whole concept had gathered dust, years had gone by, and the Reynolds had more or less forgotten about it. Their budget, by this time, had also made it a pipe dream. Now Heather followed up the lead in the local paper. She phoned the number, but the man at the other end was extremely unforthcoming. She could hardly get anything out of him – there were no ancillary buildings and what there were had fallen down, he said. The man seemed very wary and unenthusiastic about telling Heather anything about the property, McPherson Farm, a former dairy and pig farm, at Cato Ridge. He was putting her off rather than trying to sell.

Finally, Heather said to him: "What is this resort? What do you have, what is it all about?"

He said: "Oh, we've got a waterslide."

There was a pause as Heather's thoughts were racing. She was excited, thinking to herself: *This place is in the middle of nowhere, four miles off the highway, with a waterslide, and water features!*

The man added: "Em... and there are also two swimming pools and another little paddling pool."

Trying to contain her excitement, Heather said: "I'd like to come and have a look at the place."

26
BUYING
MCPHERSON FARM

As Heather stood on the summit of the hill her memory stirred and returned to Mtubatuba in KwaZulu-Natal, and Madada in the Transkei, the settlements of her childhood more than 40 years before. Both had overlooked the rolling veldt and bush. There was a feeling within her that at last her journey with God had been defined. The wheel had turned a full circle.

McPherson Farm was a derelict, rusty, rundown place but in a wondrous position. The settlement, with its single-storey farmhouse, overlooked two valleys. This was rural Africa at its most magnificent. On the northern horizon lay the Valley of a Thousand Hills, and they could see the summits from the farm. The main house, about a hundred years old, was surrounded by gum trees and bougainvillea, and was an elegant wood-and-iron building – but in an advanced state of disrepair. Close to it was a wild fig tree, with branches sweeping in every direction. The iron roof was laid out in a pleasant design in several shapes, to enable the rainwater to run off effectively, and there were verandas on three sides of the house. The main front room, the dining room, had a large fireplace and high ceilings, but there were several leaks. When it rained, water poured into the room through the corrugated iron roof. The Reynolds knew it had the potential to be just what they required as their principal building – but the challenge would be in finding the funds to restore it properly.

As well as the large farmhouse, there were several small outbuildings, including an old dairy with milking bays. On the scrubland there was a gum tree plantation, and this, with its timber, would later provide a vital component for the God's Golden Acre building programme. Next to the farm was the resort, which although shabby, was landscaped, terraced and in working order.

On the downside, there were snakes: deadly green and black mambas, cobras, and worst of all, puff adders, which are small and aggressive. The Reynolds knew they would have to remove as many of the snakes as they could, and keep them under control, because the creatures would be a considerable threat to the smaller children. The snakes had moved in over the years, as human occupation had declined.

The owner, an engineer, had inherited the dairy and pig farm from his father, but had lost interest in the agricultural side and tried to convert it into a resort. He had funded the waterslide, swimming pools, trampolines and other landscaped features, including several reservoirs, before running out of money. He was now under tremendous pressure to sell up from his wife, who hated living in a semi-derelict property. His lack of enthusiasm on the telephone had been due to the fact that he didn't want to sell and was still hoping to find a backer or partner for the resort project.

When Heather stood on the waterslide, she knew. It was a defining moment. This was the place. There was no question about it in her mind – although there were, she correctly anticipated, going to be plenty of misgivings from the board about such a risky project. The charity had limited money, barely enough to pay the deposit, let alone carry out the vast amount of corrugated roofing repair work that was required. Some of the outbuildings had no roof and the others were like lacework. You looked through the holes at the sky. She knew her board would say: "Heather, it doesn't add up. We know you've got the deposit, but you'll need lots more money to do what's necessary here, and where are you going to get it from?"

Nevertheless, it would have to be a board decision because of the constitution. So, nervously, Heather called a meeting of the board at Cato Ridge, and they all stood under the 100-year-old fig tree by the main residence. As she had expected, half the members thought she was crazy. All they saw was a derelict heap. They looked at her as if she had totally lost her mind. Patrick, Mary and Carl, on the other hand, who understood her walk with God, were behind her. Mary said: "Heather, it's your vision. If you feel this is right, since we have come along this far, we'll go with what you want. We'll stand by you."

With Heather's vote, it was four against four. The others, who voted against, said they were sorry, but they wouldn't even dream of saying yes to something like that. It was now all down to the deputy chairman, Dr Gerrit Ter Haar, who was also acting as chairman, and so had two votes. Heather thought to herself: *He is a meticulous and precise man and I know he is going to be against it. There is no way this man is going to say yes to such a mess.* She looked at him frowning and said quietly to God: "This is your vision. I can't persuade this man. You know how difficult he is. You need to persuade him, because you know this is right."

Then she said to the acting chairman, quietly: "Gerrit, this is the place. I'll tell you the story of the waterslide another day. But you have got to trust me. This is the place. It might look dreadful and filthy and whatever, but this is it, Gerrit. I don't know how we are going to put a roof on the main house so the kids can be safe, warm and dry, but we have got to buy it."

He looked at her and after a pause said: "Well, I am just going to try one thing. If it works I can give the OK."

So the board agreed to take an option on the property for one week, and Dr Ter Haar went off to do what he said he had to do. Heather had no idea what he had got in his mind, or what he was working around. In fact she hadn't quite read her deputy chairman correctly. He had more faith in her judgement and intuition than she realized, but the canny doctor took good care not to tell her that.

Gerrit Ter Haar said long afterwards: "For six months we had looked around Pietermaritzburg to find a suitable place, and once, when we had nearly made a deal, Heather confided her bad gut feeling about the place, although the owners were committed Christians and were willing to meet us financially. She was right. It proved to be a false lead. A shebeen was hidden in the entrance, selling liquor and stolen goods. I have come to respect Heather's gut feelings."

Later that week the phone rang in Heather's office. She picked it up and found Gerrit on the other end, very excited. "You won't believe what's happened, Heather! I e-mailed a couple of my friends," he said. "Do you remember you met a Dutch couple a few years ago at Wartburg called Gerrit and Anneke Mons? They provided some money for a lawnmower and washing machine and then the wife, Anneke, came back again with her brother and they provided more support for the children?"

"Yes," she said, "I remember all three of them clearly."

He continued: "Well, the Mons went today to mortgage their house in Holland, and they are sending you all the money so that you can use it as a surety for the bank."

Heather and Patrick were astonished. She said to her husband: "How many people that anybody has met just twice in their life would mortgage their house so that some strange woman could go on helping kids in the middle of Africa? No, it doesn't happen in real life. This is fairytale stuff!" The Mons had mortgaged their house and deposited the money into the God's Golden Acre bank account without Heather and Patrick even having to sign a single piece of paper. There was nothing in writing that stipulated the charity had to repay the money at a certain time; there was no time limit on the loan.

Dr Ter Haar explained that his e-mail had informed the Mons that Heather had found the property she wanted for God's Golden Acre and that he believed in her judgement, but God's Golden Acre did not have any way of securing the property because it lacked fixed assets. The quick and astonishing response of this couple showed the sort of trust and Christian action that had kept Heather in her faith over the years. The Dutch couple were strangers; they didn't know her, apart from meeting her again one afternoon, when Gerrit and Anneke Mons had visited the Reynolds a couple of years later. That was the sum total of their knowledge of Heather, who she was, and the work of God's Golden Acre.

The Dutch couple's courageous generosity was also seen as final confirmation to Gerrit Ter Haar that God believed McPherson Farm at Cato Ridge was the correct home for God's Golden Acre. Far from being opposed to the concept of buying and converting the farm and resort, Gerrit had decided when he sent out the e-mails that if anyone responded with help, in answer to his questions, then he would say "yes" to Heather's plans. That's what he did. Within the week, the money was put into fixed deposit at the bank. The Reynolds bought McPherson Farm in August 1999.

Gerrit and Anneke Mons were not wealthy people – which made their intervention to help Heather and Dr Ter Haar even more astonishing. He had been a policeman based in Arnhem, and later a public relations executive. Anneke had been involved for many years with the Red Cross. They were an ordinary Dutch couple – members of the Baptist Church – with five children and twelve grandchildren. They met Dr Gerrit Ter Haar through their son Marcel who had done voluntary work at a hospital in Rietvlei, where the doctor was the director. The Mons went to South Africa to visit Marcel and soon became close friends with Gerrit Ter Haar. It was on a subsequent visit in 1997 that they met Heather.

They recall: "We saw a woman with a heart and a love as big as the whole of Africa, with a way of believing we had never encountered before. While the children were playing, she told us her life story, spoke about her dreams for God's Golden Acre, and her belief in the Lord. We are not people who give money away, because we are not rich. But after a final phone call from Gerrit Ter Haar about the situation, we asked ourselves: 'Shall we lend them what they need?' Anneke immediately said yes, so we mortgaged our house. When we mailed Gerrit about our decision, we got a reply saying that this was an answer to many prayers. We now go to Cato Ridge every year and every time we discover more children, new buildings, more staff, more volunteers, more help, more love and care – and more Heather!

"We go with the children to the shops, to the beach, to Shakaland, to Hluhluwe, and the children call us *Oupa* and *Ouma*, Grandfather and Grandmother, and we love them so much that sometimes we can hardly speak. To go with Heather to the valleys is a shocking experience. We think everybody should see the poverty, sickness, hunger, and the broken huts. We believe Heather's mission stands above disputes between tribes and politics. It is close to God. She can lose her temper, and sometimes she is so tired that she cannot argue, only shout. Then you had better get out of her way. She is not a saint, but a wonderful woman."

27

A MAN SHE COULD DO BUSINESS WITH

When a challenge or difficulty presents itself, Heather goes into overdrive to get a positive result – alone if necessary – when those close to her fear it may be impossible. Negative outcomes are not an option. She draws strength from her total trust in God. Dr Ter Haar says: "I think any record of her life should focus primarily not on her achievements but on the blind trust she has in God. He gave her a vision and empowered her to make it happen."

There are certainly no doubts in Heather's mind about the guiding hand of God in her life. She sees herself as an ordinary woman, and has never been quite sure why she was chosen for the task of saving thousands of lives in Africa. All she knows is that she does have that mission, and everything and everyone in her life must be subjugated to it.

People who meet Heather for the first time are struck by her softness of nature, good humour and concern for other people. She is easily moved to tears. Tell her a sad story, or of a personal tragedy or disaster, then this mother figure will weep in distress. On the other hand, she can flare up easily, and can be so stubborn that she sometimes fails to see the logic in an argument that appears to contradict her point of view. There is also a tough streak which some at first mistake for selfishness.

One of her greatest admirers, Hugh Evans, Young Australian of the Year 2004, summed it up succinctly: "She is a doer and great visionary and her whole life is in response to it. Every person she meets, she has to find some way that he or she can fit into the plan. It's not possible for her to meet someone and for that person not to be able to contribute something. Everybody has something to offer as far as Heather is concerned – and she has an innate ability to find out what that is. Then in a very short time she has the inspirational and persuasive ability to fire that person up. Sometimes, like many great visionaries, she can be erratic, and even make decisions that don't seem sensible. But this is partly because she is pushing herself so hard. She is always out there extending the territory."

Bronwen Reynolds wrote this moving testimony to her mother:

Many people ask me what it's like to be Heather's daughter. I know they're asking because of the impact she's had on their own lives, and I have wondered what it would be like to be like the volunteers or visitors she meets, to encounter this phenomenal woman it is so easy to admire.

I have come to realise that, as much as they do admire her, they'll never have more admiration than her own family, who know her – and her shortcomings. We can vouch for her human frailty, and because of that we stand in astonished wonder in the face of all she has accomplished through her faith.

My mum has become to me the definition of the word "capable". Nothing seems too much for her, no matter how impossible it may appear. She has this way of making things happen, and pulling them together in the last minute, just when the rest of us are losing the last shred of hope we may ever have had. I'll never forget the afternoon of my 21st birthday. We'd hired a large tent and I'd spent the day trying to get the decorations done, while still working in the office. With half an hour to go, and the tent far from finished, I was not dressed, and had hit absolute panic mode.

Mum arrived back from the valley, and as I sobbed my frustrations, she took control and sent me off to get ready. I remember thinking that even Mum couldn't fix this one, as guests would be arriving in the next 30 minutes.

Emerging from the house at the time we were supposed to start, I stood in the driveway, staring with unbelieving eyes at a perfectly decorated tent, with flower arrangements hanging that half an hour before had been bunches of blooms in buckets on the ground, hundreds of candles glowing a calm welcome, and everything in its place. A million-and-one stories like that are testimony to her uncanny ability to "make things happen".

Linked to her "nothing is too much" approach to life is her incredible empathy and boundless love for humanity at large. As far back as I can remember, Mum would stop the car along the road to pick up perfect strangers who did not have transport. Odd characters coloured my childhood as she reached out to anyone in need. As much as I resisted this impulse of hers, sometimes very vocally, as I entered my teenage years – not being able to bear being late for my activities as a result of unnecessary detours to take extra passengers to their destinations – I think it was because deep down I knew she was right, and admirable, in refusing to push those impulses aside like many of us do, as we justify our refusals to become involved.

When making the decision to work for my mum at God's Golden Acre in 2001, I remember a friend telling me that it would be a good decision, as I'd get to see a side of my mum I'd otherwise never know. He was right. In that year, I saw another aspect to her capability – as a good businesswoman, and having the strength of character to make difficult decisions and stick by them in the face of sometimes very hot-blooded opposition.

The blend of love and strength that characterises my mum has been a fascinating revelation to me, as I've realised that they are often the same thing. It is because of her love that she finds the strength to do the awe-inspiring things she does. Add to that the immense power of her faith, and you might begin to understand how she has come this far. But I doubt that anyone could ever understand.

My mum is by far the most inspirational person I have ever known or heard of. I have grown accustomed to the miraculous, as the unbelievable becomes fleshed out in daily life, through her unwavering faith in a living God who most certainly still answers prayer. I am grateful for this opportunity to let her know now, just how much she has changed and shaped my life in the most remarkable way, and how grateful I am to know her as a mother. There isn't a daughter alive as blessed as I am, and none loves her mum more than me."

On a slightly less endearing note, Heather is also a perfectionist who finds compromise difficult – which can make her hard to work with. That was certainly the case in finding a new chairman for God's Golden Acre in 1999. Following the widely anticipated failure of Heather to find anyone measuring up to her requirements, Dr Gerrit Ter Haar had set himself the challenge of seeking out a dynamic chairman for the charity. The board agreed a capable person was required, and he or she would need to be someone who could lead the charity into the next stage of its development. Heather knew the kind of person she wanted, but this did not always conform to what Dr Ter Haar, and some members of the board, thought would be the ideal choice.

Gerrit said to her: "Heather, you say you want this particular, fantastic person, who can guide us and support you in your faith and be a shrewd business person. You haven't found him, and so I'm going to look for a chairman. We can't run this organization without one. Apart from anything else, it doesn't read well on a funding proposal if we haven't got a respected chairman."

That night she prayed: "God, why don't you send me the

right man? You know that God's Golden Acre is a special organization. I need someone incredibly special to be able to head up the board of management." Nobody came, despite her prayers. No great man walked through the door. She wanted someone she felt would listen to Gerrit and her, whenever they met head-on, and give them a clear direction.

Finally, one day Gerrit walked into the office at God's Golden Acre, looking like the cat that had stolen all the cream. He said quietly: "I've found the right chairman."

Heather's heart sank. "I was worried that he might have found a wealthy businessman with lots of influence. But I wanted somebody who also knew about God and about stepping out in faith – about not always doing things according to the book. Jesus didn't do everything by the book, either. I needed somebody who would understand that sometimes you have to break, or bend, the rules."

Gerrit interrupted her thoughts: "Don't look so apprehensive, Heather!"

"I'm not looking apprehensive, Gerrit," she said. "Who is it?"

He said: "It's Mr Alan McCarthy."

She felt herself going ice cold, and said: "Gerrit, who did you say?"

"Mr Alan McCarthy," he repeated. Then he raised his voice defensively: "Heather, please don't get on your high horse! This man is a Christian, and he is chairman of this and chairman of that... "

She said quietly: "Gerrit, sit down. I have a long story to tell you." He looked puzzled and sat down opposite her. "Gerrit, 22 years ago I was driving down a hill and my brakes failed. A car hit me, nearly killing my son, and the man who drove that car and prayed at my side was Alan McCarthy."

The man who had changed her life 22 years before was about to come back into it to be her mentor, and God's Golden Acre's chairman. She had completely lost touch with him. However, when she had given her life to God one night at Deep Valley, she had phoned him the next day and said: "I just want you to know that I am the woman who crashed into you all those years ago, and I want to tell you that it was your Christian behaviour that turned me again to God."

Gerrit had been attending an African Enterprise Seminar, and Alan McCarthy was a speaker. The vice chairman was very impressed by his abilities as a speaker, his business credentials, and above all by his Christian faith. Knowing nothing of Alan McCarthy's shared experience with Heather, Gerrit had approached him about God's Golden Acre. He found he really didn't have to do a lot of persuading to get him to agree, in principle, to join God's Golden Acre. Alan McCarthy recalls: "My initial reaction was that I was exceedingly busy at that stage and that being such a small outfit it didn't really need a big support group. So I asked Gerrit to give me a couple of days while I prayed about this. I seemed to get a strong connection that I should do it."

Once again, Heather believed God had answered her prayers in an unexpected way. A meeting was arranged at Gerrit's house, and she was apprehensive about that because it had been a long time since she had met Alan McCarthy. She knew they would both have changed a lot in 20 years. So she went in, and there he was. She didn't recognize him. "Even at the time of the accident I wasn't really looking at his features, so now his face was not familiar. I just remembered he was a tall man. It was like meeting for the first time, and yet he was someone who had changed my life. It gave me an uncanny feeling."

They all sat down, and didn't have much to say. Both of them looked at each other like strangers. It was quite formal. He was reserved because he didn't know much about Heather. But it was a meeting he had wanted before he made up his mind about her.

Heather said later: "At least it was businesslike, and we

were able to explain about the work of God's Golden Acre, its finances, constitution and administration. When we had discussed everything on the agenda, he said he would go away and pray again, and talk to God. We waited for several days in a state of apprehension, and about a week later he told us he would accept the chairmanship. Shortly afterwards we had our first board meeting with Alan McCarthy in the chair, and now he was relaxed."

Alan McCarthy had been extremely impressed by that first meeting: "There was Heather, a capable, lovely lady, battling in rented premises, and the farmer wanted them out. Her love and care, even taking sick kids into bed with her, so they might die being loved and cared for, was amazing. She was and is a very capable woman with tremendous energy, foresight, and vision. If you added to that Dr Ter Haar's background and experience in founding and running hospitals it was clear God had put together an incredibly good team. My major function was to smooth the path between two very strong personalities, and keep the peace."

They all discovered they were on the same wavelength. That, according to Heather, has never changed. There is mutual trust.

28
MORE MIRACLES FOLLOW

The staff and children started moving to the farm at Cato Ridge with the Reynolds in late August 1999, and christened it Khayelihle which is Zulu for "beautiful home". Superhuman fundraising efforts would be needed to restore the settlement. Some of the older Zulu lads, who were part of the choir, and whom the Reynolds had helped to bring up, worked as labourers. They formed the backbone of the do-it-yourself team in the absence of funding to pay for professional builders. The young men worked with Patrick, Brendan and Heather on the removal operation from Wartburg, and began tidying up the new place, which was extremely overgrown. They took away loads of rotting corrugated iron, rusty wire and broken farm implements. Heather even hired a digger to bury some of the rubbish.

In the farmhouse there were cobwebs and choking dust everywhere, and many of the floorboards were rotten, so the boys had to lay makeshift planks across some of the rooms. The house appeared to be sinking into its own foundations. When they walked in, they felt they were going downhill. Nevertheless, out of necessity, Heather and the caregivers had taken 25 children with them to Cato Ridge, while friends looked after the fifteen tiniest babies until she was ready for them. This process took about four weeks.

"We had a bed in the middle of our bedroom," says Heather,

"and the rain poured in all around it, except on one dry spot. Five little children slept on the dry bed. We managed to find spaces out of the rain in other rooms too, so that all 25 children could sleep soundly. The pantry – also dry – became the clinic. It was touching at night to see the children lying there, not lengthwise, but in a line across the beds like little sausages. Nearly three years later, when we built the foster homes, each child had his or her own bed. They all got quite confused and tried to climb in sideways."

For the first few months there was no place to eat, and the entire community, which now numbered in the region of 70 people, ate their meals outside on the veranda. The Reynolds had a bedroom in the farmhouse and there was only one kitchen, bathroom and single toilet for the whole community. The lounge was a communal meeting room where the choir would sing, and it would double as a large family room for TV, and prayers in the colder evenings.

It was clear the first job should be to get what they had in the way of outbuildings fixed up. It was easier said than done – most of the buildings had no corrugated iron roof, or just the remains of one. Heather and Patrick were particularly worried that visitors might find their circumstances too shocking. Rather than provide them with donations, they might decide the charity was not fit to look after the children, and try to get God's Golden Acre closed down. To add to the problems when they arrived, Heather and Patrick had to meet the commitments – made by the former owner of the resort – to nine schools who had booked up to spend a day at the resort in September. It was up and running and the equipment was working, but some of the picnic shelters were derelict and required thatching, and the whole grassed area needed cutting to keep the snakes at bay. In the early days Patrick and Heather ran the resort. Later, the work was shared around, but at the beginning the Reynolds had to be everywhere.

As Christmas 1999 approached Heather found herself

facing a new dilemma. "The white Toyota that Ron Kuzel had given us and that had served us so faithfully started to boil on the long uphill stretches in the valley. It was so bad that by November I found I could no longer go to the valley because I was scared of seizing up the engine. We could only use it to take the children to and from hospital in Pietermaritzburg and to pick up supplies, and so forth. I did my last drop-off for food in the valley in the old truck in October, and November came without my being able to get there again. I was at my wits' end. Dr Ter Haar had sent away funding proposals to some organizations that he knew in Holland who might help us. He told them about our difficulties with delivering food to the valley.

"November went past, we were into December, and still I hadn't heard anything and there was no car. I hadn't been able to deliver any parcels. I felt terrible because I knew these people were getting desperate. I could just imagine how they would look up the road expecting me every day, and praying that I would come down it with the food parcels. I didn't know how they were surviving and I felt terrible. I was actually getting quite ill, and people started worrying about my health. It was the first time I had had real pains across the chest and all sorts of things were happening due to overwork and the consequences of not having had a break for so many years."

It was now the beginning of December and Heather went into town to get supplies. Everybody was rushing around doing Christmas shopping. She went into one of the supermarkets in Hayfields and saw dozens of loaded trolleys and people getting into the Christmas frenzy.

"All those trolleys, and so much food. It was almost as if there was going to be some famine or something, or the shops were going to be shut for a month. It was sheer greed and it upset me so much. All I could think about were the children in the valley a few miles away who were going hungry – or worse – and what was happening as these rich people stockpiled food. I went home angry and was physically sick with despair. I couldn't comprehend how this could happen in a civilized society."

Then Dr Ter Haar arrived at God's Golden Acre and brought with him some medicines with expired sell-by dates. Heather said to him: "Gerrit, I need a vehicle. I have got to get food to the people. They haven't had food parcels for two months."

He replied: "Heather, I know. I've done what I can. I have sent off the funding proposals."

He got up to leave and suddenly she again felt this anger shoot right through her and she thought: *No, it's not good enough. I can't go on with all those people buying that food, and me eating three meals a day, and all the money in the world, and the injustice of it...* She said: "You know what, Gerrit, people in the valley are starving. I'm not going to eat. I'm going to fast until I get a vehicle. I'll fast until God provides a vehicle."

Gerrit turned round and was really cross. "Don't be stupid. You'll ruin your health and you're really not well anyway."

Heather was adamant: "Gerrit, I tell you now I'm just not going to eat. How can I, when these people are starving and haven't got any food?"

So Dr Ter Haar walked back to the table. He realized Heather was absolutely serious. "I think we'd better pray about this, Heather." He sat down across the dining room table and put his hand over Heather's, and they prayed together: "God, you see the need, that Heather really needs a vehicle. God we urgently, urgently, urgently need a car. God, I put this in your hands. Amen." Then he left.

Half an hour later, when he had got back to his home in Pietermaritzburg, he phoned her. "Heather, you won't believe this! You are just not going to believe this – as I got home the phone was ringing while I was opening my front door. I got to it just in time and answered it, and Metter Daad, from Holland, was on the line saying they have approved the funds and issued a deposit today so we can go out and look for a vehicle."

Within a week, and well before Christmas Eve, Heather was back in the valley in her new vehicle, a second-hand Isuzu truck. Once again God had provided in her hour of need, and the desperate families were provided for. "We worked right into Christmas Day getting the sacks of food, and the donated presents for the children out to the valley. They were over-joyed to see us, so grateful and so relieved, and it was won-derful to watch the happiness on the faces of the children. They just glowed. That's what Christmas is all about – giving joy and happiness to the poor people."

Shortly after Christmas, in the New Year, a British team from the Soul Survivor Church in Watford, who had been working on a Durban street children's project, arrived virtu-ally unannounced at God's Golden Acre. The young Christians did a thorough job in clearing much of the site over their four-day visit, helping the Zulu lads to remove old corrugated iron roofing and rotted timber beams. They returned a week later to clear the final roofing, and presented Heather with a gen-erous donation from a collection they had made.

Meanwhile, another miracle solved the roofing problem, and came in the form of an elderly missionary doctor from America called Dr Hales. He was a Mormon from Salt Lake City, in Utah, and he was in Africa with his wife to carry out various medical projects. He had arrived at God's Golden Acre, Wartburg, earlier in 1999, and now visited the new headquarters for the first time with his wife to treat Nondeka, the little girl who had been shot through the spine by her step-father. Her leg was numb and she still had a nasty sore on her left foot. Dr Hales had a brace that he hoped might straighten the knee. Two operations had already helped to straighten Nondeka's leg, but more work was required. Dr Hales looked around the settlement, and exclaimed: "This is too awful; you can't live here like this! The roofs are collapsing!"

He contacted church friends in America and within a few months raised 70,000 Rand. On his last visit, before returning to the USA, he told Heather: "I want to see a proper new roof on all the old buildings when I return. I know you're going to use everything."The building supplies for the restoration work arrived, and the African lads got to work on the repairs at the beginning of winter 2000. Within a few months all of God's Golden Acre's collection of tumbledown buildings had a new corrugated iron roof.

Later that year, a team of Dutch volunteers, led by Ralph and Heidi Hekman from the charity Livingstone, were diverted from another project to Cato Ridge to do a month's work, much to Heather's delight. "It was just what we needed when there was so much work to be done, and they brought with them project money, but it was also a bit of a predicament for me because the children were really cramped in Mons House. So we juggled things around and then worked hard for a month refurbishing the farmhouse, sanding down, and repainting the iron cladding on the walls and cleaning the wooden beams. We repainted it white, and the place just looked so different.

"We also used the project money to put in a better bathroom in Mons House. The Dutch worked tirelessly, fingers to the bone, and when the work was all finished we decided to officially christen it Mons House, at a special ceremony in honour of Gerrit and Anneke Mons. They were there for the opening on Christmas night 2000."

Gerrit Mons recalls: "They kept it from us to make it a huge surprise. They tricked us into leaving the family's evening dinner. As we walked in, the orphans stood there with burning candles in the dark and sang for us. It was one of the very few times in my life that I've had tears in my eyes."

Dr Hales came back to visit God's Golden Acre two years later and could not believe his eyes at the incredible progress that the charity had made with all its building work, much of it done by the Zulu lads.

29
MORE VOLUNTEERS ARRIVE

Since their arrival at Cato Ridge, Patrick had been growing very concerned about the crippling workload upon Heather – the stress of it had already made her unwell late in 1999. The community was now nearly 80 strong and she was directing every aspect of its life, nursing the babies, organizing food and supplies, managing the fundraising, educating the orphans, and then finding time every day to make her journeys into the valley. She was often up during the night, awake by dawn, and sometimes did not return from the valley until long after dusk. The Zulu caregivers provided solid support with nursing, housekeeping and cooking, but Heather desperately needed specialized help, such as that provided the previous year by her Norwegians, Vibeke Blaker and Marianne Jenum. Once again, fate intervened. In January 2000 Heather received a call from Project Trust in England. They wanted to place two female volunteers with God's Golden Acre who had been working at Durban Boys' Town. The organizer of Project Trust said: "Could you use two volunteers for a year?"

"Oh, that would be marvellous!" Heather replied.

One of the new volunteers was Lucy Foster from Warwickshire, England, and the other Sarah Rodin from North London. Heather's life was immediately made easier by the arrival of the two British teenage girls. She told Patrick:

"They literally put down their suitcases and started work tonight changing nappies, feeding the babies, lifting toddlers out of the mud, and making sure they had something to eat at mealtimes."

In the following years hundreds of young people from many countries were to become volunteers at God's Golden Acre and most of them have remained ambassadors for it, raising funds and raising its profile in the world. Their presence enabled Heather to establish a hospice, a crèche, an infants' school, and various project teams for building and maintenance work. At any one time there may be more than 40 volunteers working at God's Golden Acre.

Shortly after the arrival of Lucy and Sarah, Project Trust contacted Heather again to say a young man, Sam, and another girl, Helen, were not happy at their placement in Swaziland. Would she have them too? So the two additional volunteers arrived at God's Golden Acre the following week.

Sarah Rodin took special care of Millie. This little girl was both disturbed and mentally challenged when she arrived at God's Golden Acre, at the age of twelve. She had severe learning difficulties and was aggressive towards the other children. A charity worker had found Millie wandering by the road in December 1999 and discovered that her mother was a prostitute and when her mum couldn't work she'd send Millie to "fetch water". The little girl would be taken away and sexually abused by men. The first thing Millie said to Heather, upon arrival at God's Golden Acre, was: "Please don't send me to fetch water for anyone." The charity worker had taken Millie round to several children's homes but none would have her because she was so retarded and disturbed that she needed one-on-one care. She pleaded with Heather: "Please take Millie, because if you don't, I'm going to have to take her back home to where I found her. No one else will take her on."

Heather took her in and at first, until Sarah arrived, she did not know how to cope with Millie. She did not play with the other children, was aggressive, swearing in Zulu, and would shuffle around mumbling and shaking. If Heather paid Millie any attention she would grab and squeeze her, and often bite. It was Millie's way of showing affection, but easily misunderstood. Sarah took on the job of calming Millie, gaining her trust, and working with her for two or three hours a day.

Heather wrote: "Sarah gradually turned her around, and she went from not being able to concentrate on anything, to becoming a pupil at a special school where she is learning maths and English. Millie is now tidily dressed, she can take care of herself, and gets along with the other children. They don't push her away any more."

Eighteen-year-old Susan Balfour, from Stirling in Scotland, arrived shortly after Sarah and Lucy. Susan soon started to focus on one of the sickest and weakest babies, Thulani, a blind HIV-positive baby, by caring for and cuddling him for hours. Thulani's was a shocking case that appalled other Zulus because it involved the betrayal of two daughters by a father — from whom they should have expected to receive protection. He raped Thulani's thirteen-year-old mother, who was his younger daughter. He was prosecuted for this offence, released on bail, and then returned home and turned his attentions to his older daughter — whom he also raped. It is a sickening fact that many African men believe the myth that they can be cured of AIDS by having sex with a virgin. The nearest virgin is usually a young female relative, and so there are many cases of sex abuse like that of Thulani's mother and her sister.

In the months after she arrived, Susan Balfour made sure that Thulani's last days, as AIDS gradually killed him, were spent in being loved and cared for. The following are extracts from her journals.

6th February 2000. My third day in Khayelihle. Starting tomorrow I have been assigned to work with the nursery children aged birth to six years. I am to establish a preschool class for the three-year-olds and Heather has also asked me to work one-on-one with one of the babies. His name is Thulani, he is eleven months old and he has full-blown AIDS and hydrocephalus, a build up of fluid on his brain. Because of this, he is blind and disabled.

"He just looks so lonely," Heather told me with a troubled countenance.

So at about 7:30 this evening, after the children had eaten and been bathed, I went into the nursery to spend some time with the little ones.

Absolute madness! There are children everywhere; sprawled across the beds, rolling all over the floor, on top of the wardrobe...

"Down from there *right now*," I shout across a din of squeals and shouts and laughter as a little body darts out in front of me from under a bed. And in the thick of it all, lying in a pram in the middle of the room – Thulani.

I bent over him. "Hello my little man," I crooned, "I'm Susan." Thulani's appearance is heartbreaking. Huge milky eyes deviated downward in a bulging skull. Thulani is obviously completely blind – his gaze is darting and completely unfocussed: quite spooky. He is tiny – more like eleven weeks than eleven months and there isn't a single ounce of flesh or muscle on his bony frame. He has twig limbs, I can trace every rib, his stomach is caved in and the skin around his knees is loose and wrinkled. He looks like a famine victim, like he is hanging on in this world by a thread.

There was a bottle in the pram beside him. He looked like he cold do with a good feed, so I picked him up. His skin was hot and dry to my touch and Thulani screeched as I lifted him into my arms. He was prostrate and burning.

Meningitis, the doctor told Heather over the phone. The hospital wouldn't treat this in a terminally ill child. Keep him at home and keep him comfortable, was the advice. These were difficult words to hear. My processing mechanisms slowed the path to realization, and I struggled to come to terms with this cruel aberration of nature. The death of a baby – surely not.

We gave Thulani paracetamol syrup and were sponging him with tepid water when Heather returned from the storeroom, clutching a medicine bottle in her hands.

"I don't know if this little one will make it through the night," she sighed quietly, "But he deserves a fighting chance." Heather explained that children with compromised immune systems were vulnerable to a rare form of meningitis caused by a fungus and that this extremely expensive antibiotic was effective against it.

Hope!

Thulani was too weak to suck from his bottle. Heather showed me how to feed him with a syringe. "Take it slowly," she instructed. "You'll have to feed him every hour. Give him as much as he will take."

Six international volunteers, Thulani and I were with Heather in her sitting room that night. Those of us who believed prayed. It was a beautiful time of fellowship. Thulani was surrounded by love.

7th February 2000. My Thulani did not die last night! He took two full bottles of his milk today, and two small servings of baby porridge. He is tired and lethargic, but he is here! He seems a little realer today: just a little more "here". God, what a victory! I am surprised that I have the courage to love a fatally ill child. I suppose at first I clutched the drop of hope Heather offered. Now I know Thulani is my little fighter. I'll fight with him.

24th February 2000. We celebrated Thulani's first birthday today!

I am so, so proud! Less than three weeks ago, we would never have dared to dream about this day. Now it has come! For the first fortnight, Thulani got better, then sicker, then better and then sicker again. I can't remember the day the fever broke for good, but at some point, Thulani moved from better, *to even* better. The last week or so just seems to have been up and up, and up again! I am still holding my breath! Is it my imagination or is this baby filling out? Is that a double chin? Is there flesh on those thighs? – Wishful thinking perhaps?

Maybe, but Andrea, German volunteer, says Thulani is definitely looking fatter and yesterday he smiled when I said "Good morning" to him. *I know* that was real! Then later, as I was outside doing preschool with my little boys in the yard, Lucy came out of the nursery.

"Your baby is very lively today!" she commented. I went in to find him cooing and babbling in his cot! So then I stroked him under the chin, kissed him, blew a raspberry on his tummy and Thulani laughed! Wow, so many firsts in one day! Here is my little man doing all this "proper baby stuff," and I feel so warm and fuzzy inside! I swear, I never knew what joy was until that moment!

And that's not the best of it – I have three small witnesses to all of this! Khethiwe, Zinhle and Mlu saw Thulani's response. They began to take turns entertaining him, and encouraged by his smiles and giggles, continued with this until someone rang the school bell out in the resort to signal the end of break time. Pure magic! Thulani has emerged from that cold dark place called despair. Gone is the little skeleton child. Thulani is all soft and sweet – too cute!

27th February 2000. It's official – Thulani's transformation is nothing short of miraculous – Heather says so! She has just recently returned from a trip in the Drakensberg mountains. I was cleaning Thulani up in the bathroom, feeling a little low as he had just projectile vomited his entire feed! Heather was with a guest in the living room. She asked to hold him and marvelled over how heavy he was, saying she had heard how bubbly he had become.

"See, Susan my girl," she told me, "God sent you across the

ocean to make a difference in the life of a child!" I turned red, but of course, I was very flattered. Heather continued to talk about how this transformation was all down to my gentle way with him, my care and attention. Of course, her praise is totally unwarranted, but her words meant so much to me. I have felt quite despondent at times. Heather has boosted my confidence today. She has achieved such a lot and she has a huge vision, and it's *amazing* to be noticed by her! I find that I'm really pondering her words on the impact basic care and tender loving care on Thulani's spirit. Was it really that simple? Is it really so easy? Surely there must be more to it? Yet Heather absolutely maintains there is not! If she's right, this miracle can be replicated and one person really can make a huge difference, step by step, one child at a time. And if this is what one person can do, imagine what we can do if we all get in on it!

30

THE DEATH OF THULANI AND THE INSPIRATION OF ELLIE

Lucy Foster and Sarah Rodin were still only teenagers, but the English girls were so well organized that in April 2000 Heather felt confident in leaving them in charge of the children and the eight senior caregivers while she was out of the country on a trip to Zambia. The other senior male staff, Pieter Nel, George and her son Brendan, were there to give them support. Heather has always put a priority on making sure her volunteers and visitors get the chance to experience the real Southern African wilderness and introducing them to a variety of countries.

Sadly one night while the party was out of the country, Thulani passed away and the two English girls who had been left to run Khayelihle had to take charge. They laid Thulani out, placed him in the coffin, and organized the funeral. Lucy Foster recalls: "His death was a big, fast lesson, and the most important thing that had happened to me while I was there. Sarah and I were woken very early one morning by one of the carers who was sleeping with Thulani, who said that he had passed away. We went into the nursery and found that he had gone. We checked him over, laid him out, and somehow coped with it, sort of going into autopilot. We phoned Dr Ter Haar as Heather had instructed we should do if we needed him, and he helped us get the death certificate and all the legal side of things sorted out. Thulani's body was taken to the mortuary.

"We just coped. We got things arranged, ordered the coffin. At the funeral Sarah and I were the only white people, and everyone stood in a circle around the grave. They had dug the grave in preparation, placed in the coffin, covered it with earth, and then built a mound of rocks over it.

"The Zulus took it in turns to start a song and then other mourners joined in. When each song ended there was a pause and you wondered what would happen next. Then someone else would start another song. It was very spontaneous and there was singing for the whole funeral really, lasting perhaps 40 minutes."

Susan Balfour went on to care for Ellie, who at the time was two-and-a-half years old and a victim of the HIV virus. The struggle to keep Ellie alive was eventually to succeed. Lucy Foster and Susan Balfour spent many hours each day pouring love and care into Ellie. They tried everything they could think of to make her smile and eventually came up with the answer. The Teletubbies! They would sit with her and watch the big beam of happiness appear on her face. Heather says: "It was wonderful to see. So, thank you, Teletubbies!" The nurses at God's Golden Acre placed Ellie on expensive vitamins and good nutrition, and she responded well. In time, Ellie grew into a healthy little girl and went on to attend preschool, where she became an excellent singer.

31

VOLUNTEERS AND VISITORS IN THE VALLEY

If life at God's Golden Acre, a sanctuary for the orphans, was witness to occasional tragedies like the death of Thulani, interspersed with joyful news like the recovery of Ellie, then new volunteers soon became aware that real horrors were to be found in the valley. Sophie Wong, a 25-year-old British volunteer worker at God's Golden Acre for several months, wrote on the Internet of her experience in the valley:

We went to Swayimane today, which is one of the valleys where God's Golden Acre delivers food parcels. We drove to the drop-off point where there were already quite a few people waiting. We spent some time with the children, who sang and danced to us. Heather gave a short talk and pointed out to us a couple of children who were the heads of their families, and looked after their younger brothers and sisters. One of these girls was perhaps 16 years old, and she cried when she was pointed out to us.

At first she did not want to speak to anyone who tried to comfort her. We found a Zulu speaker and asked her if we could pray for her. She agreed and a few of us just gathered around her, and her brothers and sisters. For a brief moment whilst we were praying, God gave me an insight into how she was feeling.

My heart ached with how she was hurting, how she felt so lost and in despair. I could not stop the tears from rolling down my cheeks. How could we in our comfortable lives imagine for a moment what she goes through every single day that she lives?

Just as we were packing up and ready to go I went over to say goodbye to her. We had a photo taken together and she smiled and gave me a hug. I was so touched how she had allowed us, complete strangers, to comfort her and to pray with her in the space of a few hours. While we were there, we obtained some profiles for the child sponsorship programme that is being set up. Some of the children had written that their happiest moments had been the day that Heather had brought them food. Their most difficult moments were when their mother died or when their parents "left and never came back".

I saw these children today and they were so friendly and loving. Not once did I hear any of them complain and they were so grateful for the food and clothes that they received. Being there today has been the most special day of my trip so far. I can only try to imagine how they all must feel – and pray that God will guide, help and protect all of them every day that they live, and remind us that we can do our bit to help, and together make a difference.

Volunteers like Sophie Wong who come to work at God's Golden Acre soon discover that things are run in a highly unusual manner. Heather is so swept up in the tidal wave of unplanned events that the only workable way of operating is to prioritize them as they happen. The casualties of this method of working are that important, long-term or strategic matters get shelved, appointments are missed, and even important people kept waiting.

Heather regrets this but is unrepentant because she believes the important things that need doing first usually concern a child's life. "I sometimes have to stand people up; when there is an emergency call I have to go. I am answering a call to a situation where a mother may be dying and I must reach the children to bond with them before she dies. I get in my Land

Rover and I shoot down to the valley. The ones I go to are usually those who have no family support. So I know it is going to be somebody passing on, and in need of help for the children. You can never be sure how bad the children are. The sufferers will always be incredibly thin, wasted and in terrible pain. It is very important for me to be able to make a bond with the children because these are such incredibly sad situations."

She e-mailed to a close circle of friends one night:

I have had a most dreadful, trying day and evening and feel so very upset. I was doing my rounds in the rural valleys, taking poverty relief parcels to the grannies, or child-headed households, and as we were approaching our last port of call – it was already getting quite dark by this time – we were stopped, and an old woman begged us to come to help her friend.

We turned around and went along the most appalling road that finally petered out, and so we parked the vehicle and took the last poverty food parcel and our first-aid kit. We walked the remaining kilometre down a mountain in the dark with a miserable flashlight. When we arrived at the little hovel it was in total darkness, with only a small portion still with any roof covering at all. We always put candles and matches into our food parcels, so we lit a candle and entered the tiny room.

There on the small bed lay a young woman, approximately 26 years old. As we entered, rats took off across the bed: they had been eating her feet. There were three little children aged 18 months to seven years. The dying woman was clinging to her babies, and by her sunken face and shrivelled body was obviously HIV-positive which was now full-blown AIDS.

There was not a single crumb of food or any medication. The children were in tatters and so cold and hungry. I spent a few hours sorting things out and I will arrange a small support team but this has really shaken me. I should be used to it, but I still find myself so emotionally involved.

It is so awful – how many other people are lying helplessly in the same way? I just wanted to share this with you all. It is 3am and I find sleep impossible.

Heather added later: "The people in the valley know I do not have endless money, but every dying mother wants me to take care of her children because she knows they will survive. I have often wondered how it must feel to be that dying woman, praying that I will come to her hut. For her, my arrival may be a miracle."

Ann Smith, treasurer of God's Golden Acre in the United Kingdom, who also heads the child sponsorship programme there, arrived for her first visit to Cato Ridge. On her first morning she was packed into the Land Rover, with other visitors, to distribute food and supplies to the valley. She wrote:

News comes that a girl of ten has suddenly died. She was at school the day before and seemingly well. The little girl had the "voice of an angel" and a promising future. The cause of death is probably meningitis. The parents would not be familiar with its symptoms or how to deal with it.

Our group makes its way to the mud hut where the body lies on a mattress. The mother and grandmother are there. The women mourners sit on one side of the door, and the men on the other. Gentle songs are sung in harmony, led by Heather. The grandmother is shattered. The child's mother sits silently, grief-stricken.

Our group moves on. Heather says she will now go to another hut to say prayers for a mother who has just lost her second son, just 18 years old, to AIDS-related diseases. We climb to the home and sit indoors while Heather prays with the family. Two mounds in the garden are the only remaining symbols of the existence of the mother's sons on Earth.

The girlfriend of the latest victim is 16 and banished to a tiny hut further up the hill where she will die alone without care. We walk quietly into the darkness where the girl lies; not a single candle burns. At first there is no sign of anything in the bed, but soon our eyes become accustomed to the darkness; the girl is so emaciated that there is not much left to see. Heather prays for the teenager. It is evident she will not need to visit again.

One more family is calling for Heather today. There are fifteen of them and they have no food. The Land Rover climbs higher and higher in the fog and drizzle until we get to a tiny path where we get out and walk to a hut. Darkness falls in a matter of minutes and there is no light. Inside, the father makes a fire in the middle of the floor – burning sprigs of wood and plastic bags. The smoke is overpowering, and we realize this family has no choice but to breathe these fumes every day. The family is touchingly grateful for the supplies of rice, beans, candles and tea. Only one candle is lit at any time. They are stockpiled in case Heather is unable to get through next time.

Susan Balfour wrote in her journals on her first visit to the valley, of her horror at observing the potential for child abuse in these rural areas:

We go to see a thirteen-year-old girl, Thandiwe, who tends to four younger children. These are her eight-year-old sister, a six-year-old nephew, a four-year-old girl, and her own baby. Thandiwe has headed this little household since their mother abandoned them two years ago. The children all have different fathers. Maybe the men are dead, maybe not, but they certainly are not here.

Thandiwe greets us at the gate with the warmest smile. She asks politely, in broken English, to please wait a few minutes before coming inside – she wants to wash the children first. Home is a cold and dark stick-and-clay hut with a dirt floor, no electricity or running water, a set of lopsided shelves and a bed. A campfire burns dimly in the centre and the acrid aroma of the smoke hangs in the air. I am gripped by an acute sense of gloom.

We have all seen the pictures of gaunt adults, the sick and dying, naked pot-bellied children with twig legs. Now reality.

As the sun rises every morning Thandiwe and her sisters set off on a walk of two-and-a-half miles to the river with empty plastic containers. They fill them there, and then return to the hut, with the containers balanced on their head. They sweep the dirt floor inside.

There will be no breakfast. They never eat in the mornings – the sacks of rice and mealie-meal and beans must be used sparingly if they are to last. Thandiwe unties the baby from her back and the oldest children make their way to school with empty stomachs. Four-year-old Nomosa is now in charge of the baby until the children come home. They will go to collect firewood, cook supper and then, off to bed. The children are beautiful but frail, and their thin arms are bare, even though it's winter. The baby scratches at a scaly rash on her bare buttocks.

Some of the orphans from God's Golden Acre are with us. "Last year," an eleven-year-old girl whispers, "I visited Thandiwe here." She describes how the children had run out of food and how, after scraping the burned starch from the bottom of the rice pot and eating it, they had lain down on the bed and cried as hunger pains racked their empty stomachs.

All the children join us outside the hut to sing with her. A drunken man in a blue boiler suit saunters up to the group, leering at a young girl, who is no older than twelve. I prickle with a new awareness. These children are open to abuse. They were born out of wedlock, and in the Zulu culture that means they are not recognized by their extended family, and there is no protection within its traditional patriarchal structure. Child rape is rife here, and in this hut there are five children alone, with no way of securing their home at night. Anger inflates inside my chest. I have a lump in my throat. Visualize it as a rock in my hand... On the way back up the dirt road out of the valley, I simmer with rage. Orphans lose their childhood – and the breath of innocence around them disappears. Sickness, death, malnutrition, ostracism and rape… it is a shock that this reality exists for tens of thousands of children in the Valley of a Thousand Hills.

Many other volunteers ventured into the valley in the early years of God's Golden Acre – some reluctantly. The Norwegian girls Marianne Jenum and Vibeke Blaker travelled to the valley against their better judgement. Marianne recalls: "I remember Vibeke and I actually made the decision never to go to the valley. Heather told us horrific stories before we got a chance to go there – especially about white people being killed. The worst story was about a white nun who was raped and then got her throat cut. For me, the rape and murder of a nun symbolizes the dangers of the valley. Of course, Heather talked us into it. And as long as I was with her, I only experienced short moments of fear.

"But there have been other times when I've been very afraid. Heather always stressed how dangerous the highways were, how the breakdown of the car could lead to robbery, and sometimes death. In short – African men walking along the roads at night could be very dangerous. Then, one late evening we were driving home. It was pitch-dark and misty. There was a tall Zulu man walking along the road. And suddenly Heather stopped the car! She rolled down the window and asked him if he wanted a ride. I just froze as he climbed in. Nothing happened, but it was a very scary ride. Her explanation for picking him up, despite her own warnings, was simple: 'He needed a lift.'

"Heather always rushes to get out of the valley before dark. But sometimes there was too much work, and it got dark and misty before we could leave. It freaked me out when I noticed that Heather looked worried. One night we experienced the worst storm on the way back. I was sitting in the back of the 'bakkie', with no canopy, when the rain came pouring down. It was impossible to see more than one metre ahead, and there was lightning every five seconds. Trees were falling over the road. I've never experienced the violence of nature like that. Heather drove the first car, and she drove very fast to get back. I was sitting in the second car, and I was terrified that we would lose her, because we didn't know the route back. And if we'd been trapped by a big tree, or if the car had broken down, we'd have been all alone in the dark valley. So – as long as Heather was there and was in control – everything was fine. When she looked worried, the rest of us freaked out... "

3 2
PRACTICAL HANDS
ARRIVE... AND MORE
MIRACLES

With the arrival of the first volunteers, the workload in terms of nursing, and managing the community and its needs on a day-to-day basis, was shared around. However, there were serious problems of an entirely different nature to resolve at God's Golden Acre. The Reynolds remained desperately short of practical help. There were no electricians, mechanics, plumbers or carpenters within their little community. There was no one to take a lead with the Zulu lads and teach them how to develop their building skills.

One afternoon a car arrived at Cato Ridge and 20-year-old Orin Wilson stepped out. He had been a close friend of Bronwen for some years. Orin had a good job with an engineering company but told Heather he was fed up with the corporate world. Heather said they would be happy to have him there, especially since he spoke English and Zulu. She recalls: "Orin was brilliant for us, as was his cousin Taffy Lloyd who went on to become our driver. Orin wired Mons House and put up poles with lights around the pool and the yard to improve our security. He did many other practical things like tiling, plumbing, laying floors and keeping the equipment in the resort maintained."

Then the Reynolds came to an agreement with Les Young, an experienced local builder, who had been very generous to them by donating reject concrete blocks for the various building projects. Les owned a neighbouring farm and could also speak Zulu. He agreed to become head of works, and organized training. The African lads mixed cement, pushed wheelbarrows and gradually learned skills such as bricklaying and plastering.

Around this time Patrick felt that he and Heather needed some privacy away from the main house. He wanted to move into one of the barns that were being converted by the building team. Unfortunately, the building materials were running out fast and there was no budget to fund continuing construction work. There was no cash at all to buy building sand, and despite two badgering phone calls by Heather to a local building supplies company for a free load, none was forthcoming. One day a German volunteer, Ove Spreckelsen, who was an atheist, and impatient to get on with the work, challenged Heather: "We need the sand to do the floor, so why don't you ask your God to provide the sand if you have no money to buy some? We need a miracle," he said.

"I was so cross at that moment," Heather recalls. "I said to him, 'Please don't make jokes.'

" 'I'm not joking,' he replied. 'You're always telling me about this God of yours.'

" 'Just go,' I said."

After Ove went, Heather sat down and said to herself: "God, this young man is quite right. Why don't you answer our prayers? Why don't you? What is it, Lord? God, if you really want me to beg, I will make a third call to these guys." She swallowed her pride, picked up the telephone, and rang the local building supply company again, asking for a load of sand as a donation.

The girl on the other end of the phone was both curt and unsympathetic. She went to consult with her boss. A moment later she was back and said impatiently. "The manager says, please, please don't phone him again, please. He is not going to give any more sand and that's that." (He hadn't actually given God's Golden Acre any before.)

Heather now prayed quietly: "God, what more can I do?"

She continued with her work in the office but after about half an hour was disturbed by loud laughter coming from outside. Volunteers Orin Wilson and Ove Spreckelsen were hooting with laughter.

"What's all this about?" asked Heather.

"It's your miracle," Ove told her. "You see that man walking through the gate over there? He's the driver of a ten-ton truck of sand, and he has just broken down at our driveway. He has asked our permission to tip all this sand so his company can tow the truck away – apparently the gearbox is broken!"

In fact the contractor offloaded half of the sand and tried to tow the truck away, but only got about 100 metres. The remaining load was then dumped by the side of the road. Ironically, it was the same company from which Heather had just asked for some sand.

Meanwhile, the Reynolds continued to lurch from one financial crisis to the next. The problem was that although God's Golden Acre was a registered charity and an NGO with a board and a proper constitution, it remained financially largely a one-man band, with Patrick's sculptures funding everything except for various small cash gifts, and donations of food, clothes and medical supplies. All through 2000, and for most of 2001, the familiar spectre of bankruptcy continued to present itself again and again. What were they going to do? The community was bulging at its "seams", and there were thousands more children out there in the valley, in desperate need of help, yet God's Golden Acre was chronically underfunded.

A new crisis emerged suddenly when there was no money to purchase powdered milk for the babies. Heather summoned a group of God's Golden Acre staff and volunteers for prayers. She explains: "What I do in a moment like this is say,

'Let us pray, and put it before the Lord.' Most people don't make a fuss or argue, and if they happen not to be a Christian, they just come and join in. I don't worry if someone is a Christian or not; they are there and people just stand around while I pray. On this occasion they stood and listened to me in prayer on the veranda of Mons House: 'Our dear heavenly Father, we thank you for this day, we thank you for our blessings, Lord. Father, right now we just come before you. You know the problem that we are having, Lord, you know the crisis, know what we are facing, Father. In your name, Lord, we will pray now that you may help us with this crisis. Give us a solution Father, if this is your will. We pray now that we need a miracle, and that you will answer this prayer, so, Jesus, we just thank you that you have brought us into your Kingdom, that we may know you, and that we may turn to you in a moment like this, Father. Dear Jesus, we love you and trust in you, and we ask this in your name. Amen.' "

Divine intervention came just a few days later as it had with the sand. This time it came in the form of a broken-down truck three miles away. The truck, laden with powdered milk, broke down on the highway just off the turning to Cato Ridge. It could not be towed away with a full load and so the transport company needed to get rid of the powdered milk. As soon as she heard about this, Heather thanked God, then she made a call to the manager of the company. He said: "You're welcome to it, but you'll have to get it off the truck yourself."

Again, Heather's little army came out with the small truck. It took a lot of work to bring in – but the powdered milk kept them in supplies for three months! Heather says: "I've had proof of the power of prayer – that it works when it is done unselfishly. We just can't be blasé about this."

33

THE YOUNG ZULU WARRIORS TOUR THE UK

Dance Link emerged out of the blue at God's Golden Acre. Some say it was another miracle. Dance Link is a forum of about twelve dance companies, directed by a woman called Lynne Maree. It decided to give free dance classes to underprivileged children, selected a charity, and arranged to send professional dance coaches to them every Saturday. Luckily for God's Golden Acre, the agreement with that charity fell through.

Lynne heard about Heather's charity from an article she'd read, and offered her the chance to get involved with Dance Link. She rang Heather: "Would you be interested in having some of your children trained in dance?"

"Oh! We'd love that, it would be absolutely wonderful," Heather replied. So every Saturday, Lynne Maree sent over a dance teacher, and the children started to receive professional training.

South Africa was chosen to host the World AIDS Conference in 2000 at the International Conference Centre in Durban, and the children of God's Golden Acre were invited to perform on the main stage. Thanks to Lynne, they were brilliant and full of confidence. They performed in front of former President Nelson Mandela, Madiba, and afterwards he asked the children to meet him. He waited for them as they came off the stage. Heather recalls: "It was a wonderful moment to go and meet

him and shake his hand. I told him: 'Madiba, these are my children. I am not just their choirmaster, or choreographer."

When the Nelson Mandela Hospital was opened in Durban,
he asked for the God's Golden Acre Children's Choir again.
They sang at the opening ceremony. "He has a wonderful sense
of humour," says Heather, "because when we met again on that
occasion I stepped up and said, 'Hello, how are you, Madiba?'

"He replied: 'How wonderful that you remember me!' We
both laughed."

Heather met Nelson Mandela on several further occasions
but was unable to attend his 85th birthday celebrations in
2003 because of family commitments. She remains extremely
impressed by his humility.

The tour to England of the Young Zulu Warriors was the
idea of Howick Rotarian, John Tungay, who rang Heather just
before she was due to be a speaker at a World AIDS Conference
in Durban. They knew one another because Rotary has been
supportive of God's Golden Acre on rural outreach projects.
John said on the phone: "Rotary has done a lot for God's
Golden Acre. There's a group here of young Rotarians from
Britain; can I show them God's Golden Acre?"

Heather replied: "Sure, but if it's tomorrow we'll have to
get someone else to show you round because I am a speaker
at the conference in Durban."

He asked: "When do you speak?"

"I am due on at two o'clock," said Heather.

John responded: "How about we make the tour during the
morning?"

Feeling pressured, Heather replied: "I am already in Durban
at the conference." Somehow she felt that was not going to be
accepted as an excuse. "OK, I'll come back if you want me to be
there. I will drive all the way back to Cato Ridge, meet you, and
then go back in time for my speech," she heard herself saying!

What a cheek! she thought to herself. She had reserved time
to be in Durban because she wanted to hear all the main

speakers. There was still so much to learn. Now she would miss two speakers. That evening she drove back to God's Golden Acre and told the children that they would be needed next day to perform in front of the visitors. "Let's do our best," she said.

She met the party the next day and showed them around, giving it her best shot. Then, just before the English party left, she decided on impulse that they ought to hear the whole works and said: "Would you like to hear our full choir?" The Zulu lads overheard this and were really angry because they had just mixed up cement, were covered in dirt and in their overalls. A quarter of an hour later, however, the choir appeared. The party from England listened in awe to the singing, and when the choir stopped there was silence.

John said: "Wow! This choir is really very good. Would you like to take them abroad?"

It had always been in Heather's mind to travel overseas with them and she jumped at it. "Yes! Yes! We'd love to tour," she exclaimed.

"OK, leave it with me then," he said.

Heather didn't hear one word from him again for three months. As the weeks went by she thought to herself: *Yes, a great idea, but talk is cheap!*

Suddenly in December John Tungay was on the telephone to God's Golden Acre: "Well, I've got Rotary on board and it all seems like it is going to be happening – and so have you got all your passports in order?"

Heather shouted down the phone: "What? Don't give me a heart attack! Most of them don't even have birth certificates, let alone a passport!"

John replied nonchalantly: "Then you'd better get on with it, hadn't you?"

The moral of the story for Heather is that it pays to walk the extra mile, to go to that extra bit of trouble for people, as she did in making herself available on that day.

For the next few months the team worked hard to create

the show. She was choreographer – a first time for her – and they got it together as the story of God's Golden Acre in song and dance. It was a challenge to integrate the talents of everybody in the group and come up with a blend that would work. The younger ones were now trained to dance and move on stage; the older ones could sing well, but had not been trained to professional standards in movement and stagecraft. Gradually they achieved a remarkable standard. Together, they told the story of the early days of violence, and the children being affected by that. Then followed the death and the dying, and finally God's Golden Acre creating hope for the future.

However, while the youngsters were literally "getting their act together" creatively, the tour organizers faced a nightmare with officialdom in getting the relevant papers in order to allow the party to leave the country. First there was the problem of the birth certificates, which they eventually managed to assemble, then there were the individual identity documents and finally the travel documents, or passports. The God's Golden Acre office worked night and day for over three months and just when they believed they had all the papers in order, and the permissions signed from guardians and foster parents … a bombshell. The Home Affairs Office in Pietermaritzburg advised God's Golden Acre that a computer had gone down, and all the files containing the IDs were lost.

The party would not be able to get passports without the documentation being recreated and signed. The horrified organizers of the tour realized they had less than 24 hours to do all the paperwork that had previously taken several weeks. Mandy de Vos and Kath Simms rushed down to the Home Affairs Office with a small team from the God's Golden Acre office. Plane tickets had been bought by now, concert venues and accommodation arranged in England. Financial disaster loomed on the horizon. Heather recounts: "I got a desperate phone call from Mandy late in the afternoon saying that all the necessary permissions were signed except for a handful from

Baba Jila, who lived in the Swayimane and was legal guardian to a small group of our leading performers. We would not give a credible performance on stage without them. Mandy pleaded with me: 'We have got to reach him and get him down to the office straightaway. Heather, you've got to go and find him.' I was an hour away from Swayimane. Even if I'd found Baba Jila immediately in the valley I would not get him to the office before it closed for the day.

"I said: 'Look, Mandy, there's no way I can get Baba Jila to you in time. It will take two hours and the office closes in an hour's time. We have got to put this in the hands of God. We must pray for a miracle. You pray where you are, and I will pray here.' So I got down on my knees and prayed for God to help us, to inter-vene in some way. I spoke on the telephone to Dr Gerrit Ter Haar, God's Golden Acre's deputy chairman, who was in bed. He had just had a serious back operation. We agreed that we needed a miracle. He said he would pray all afternoon. I then got on with a backlog of work and the next thing I remembered was Mandy walking through the door back at God's Golden Acre.

"She said: 'Oh, Heather, it's amazing – something extra-ordinary happened. Just as you said you would pray for a miracle and you put the phone down, I looked towards the doorway and, guess what? Baba Jila was standing there in the Home Affairs Office in Pietermaritzburg! We grabbed him and he signed all the guardian permissions. So it's OK.'

"We never found out how or why Baba Jila, who lives miles and miles away in a rural valley area, happened to be in Pietermaritzburg on that day, and why he appeared at the Home Affairs Office right at the moment we started to pray. Maybe we should just let it remain a mystery. The other extraordinary thing about it was that while all the fuss was going on about Baba Jila turning up, the cashier was being robbed in front of Mandy and Kath by an armed gang who stole all the money from the till. They were so excited they didn't even notice the robbery and couldn't give any descriptions to the police afterwards."

Each person on the tour, in which over £30,000 was raised, was sponsored by a different Rotary Club in England – hence the 30 performances and venues. The group travelled around on an English single-decker school bus that was given to them. The last night of the UK tour, staged in the Temple speech room at Rugby School, was its highlight and many former volunteers at God's Golden Acre came to see this show. There was a fantastic party atmosphere. Susan Balfour was in the audience, and the performance evoked both memories and emotions for her. She wrote:

The hall seats 600 and is bursting at the seams. The atmosphere sizzles as my little ones give a spectacular performance: an effortlessly professional, stunningly choreographed blend of drama, music, songs and dance. Among them is a ten-year-old girl who sat on my lap almost three years ago and revealed a long-guarded and terrible secret. One night a man that she regarded as a brother took what wasn't his to take – he raped her. My little one wept bitterly as she recalled the events of that night in graphic detail, releasing a dam of emotion, and a cleansing balm of tears.

Now she performs. She is far from broken. She looks out boldly, rejects the shackles of fear, dares to trust, to love and be loved. She is sweet and affectionate and her steps are full of energy and grace; she is one of our most accomplished dancers. I watch her with pride as she plays her part in the performance … traditional Zulu harmonies and contemporary township dances alike, pulsating with pure African rhythm; the resonant drumbeat throbbing in her veins and through the dancers' perfectly synchronised, exuberant steps.

A powerful display of resilience; the children rise against a past rooted in the wastelands of humanity. The audience is enraptured as their performance reaches its crescendo. It has been vibrant and haunting, with some spicy, mischievous twists. The applause is exhilarating; they receive a standing ovation.

Now I know that these children are the true stars in my life. Little ones, born in humble mud shacks, are rising from the wastes of human depravity and broken dreams, shining bright with a message of hope, a living expression of God's compassion, power and grace.

Heather had similar feelings by the end of the tour:

It was the last weekend and we were all attending a barbecue at the home of friends in Rugby, and I found myself sitting on a chair, watching my many children in incredulous wonder. It seemed for a moment that time had stopped, as I surveyed the scene before me in a kind of frozen clarity. The older members of the choir sat comfortably chatting with past volunteers who had formed friendships with them after many experiences together. The younger children ran with arms linked with those of their new British playmates, their giggling fervour heightening at the prospect of a second helping of ice cream.

It seemed to me that the days on which I had witnessed each child's arrival at God's Golden Acre were somewhere far in a distant past lifetime, out of reach of the happiness and restoration I saw before me now. It was difficult to reconcile the two pictures: children, formerly abused, broken and abandoned, now confident and happy, assuming their rightful place in society with seemingly effortless ability.

I knew the truth: I could tell you each and every tragic story behind the smiling faces I now gazed upon. Heartbreak, fear, desperation and hopelessness had coloured the features of faces too young to have to deal with such trials. But meet and overcome them they did, and I could only pour out the thankfulness that swelled in my heart, silently heavenward. Overwhelming pride for all they had accomplished, and gratitude for the opportunity to witness the second chances each of them had received and embraced, made me realize how truly blessed I am to be a part of what God is doing.

34

OPRAH WINFREY COMES TO GOD'S GOLDEN ACRE

The phone rang in the office at God's Golden Acre. It was someone working for one of the world's most respected television personalities, Oprah Winfrey. Heather was told the famous talk show host was planning to visit South Africa to build an academy for girls and to launch ChristmasKindness South Africa 2002, an initiative to create one day in the lives of underprivileged children that they could remember as a happy one. Oprah's team would organize 12 massive Christmas parties as well as local orphanage parties – in total involving 63 rural schools and three orphanages, reaching 50,000 children. Could one of these be held at God's Golden Acre?

"Yes, of course! We will welcome Oprah's help and attention, and feel deeply privileged by it," Heather told the Americans.

Later, Oprah sent out her researchers to Cato Ridge and they also travelled to the valley, where the rural outreach programme is active. Heather soon found herself closely involved with one of the ChristmasKindness South Africa 2002 orphanage parties. She went to Chicago with Hugh Evans of The Oak Tree Foundation and they spent several days with Oprah's organization, talking through the project, and agreeing Oprah's producers should film at God's Golden Acre later that year.

Oprah, accompanied by her team, which included a camera crew, arrived in South Africa before Christmas to host the pre-planned parties. Then came the day of Oprah's party at God's Golden Acre in a festively decorated marquee. Two hundred children, the orphans at God's Golden Acre and more than 100 youngsters from the valley, enjoyed the biggest party anyone locally had ever seen. "I have never witnessed such happiness and gratitude," said Heather. It was also part of an experience that changed Oprah Winfrey's life, and she wrote a moving account that was published on Oprah.com.

The miracle workers from HOPE*worldwide* and God's Golden Acre orphanage helped us gather some of the neediest children affected by AIDS – children with no food, no family, no home. It was a day of Christmas celebration that the children could always remember as happy. The children we were blessed to meet, and the people who care for them, changed our lives.

At each orphanage party, children whose lives had been devastated by AIDS were gathered together for a day of Christmas celebration. They were children who often had nothing, and no one. No school... no food... no family. Some did not even have a home. Many had to borrow clothes or shoes, just to be able to come.

As soon as I began to meet them, I knew, these were my children.

Children like 14-year-old Thanda, whose parents were dead and who, with her 8-year-old sister, lived at the mercy of a drunken uncle. When I asked Thanda what gift she wanted more than any other in the world, she asked not for a toy or clothes, but for a school uniform, so she could attend school, become a doctor, and return to care for her village. I promised her the future she dreamed of.

Children like Esona, whose only wish was to share her Christmas joy with her 29-year-old mother who lay dying in a nearby hospital. Esona hadn't seen her mother in two weeks. I took her to her mother that day. Their courage overwhelmed me.

We wanted to create a Christmas wonderland that would live in their memories forever. Games, jesters, lights, fairies, silver bubbles floating in the air, gifts piled high, shoes to fit each child, small and large, and all the food they could eat!

The children began to play, to laugh and sing, to feel a moment of connection. I watched as their eyes lit up, and their burdens seemed to melt away. Then it was time to gather around the Christmas tree. I called each child by name and handed each boy and girl a gift, individually chosen, wrapped and labelled just for him or her. I wanted each of them to know that on this day they were thought of and beloved.

They waited – so incredibly patiently – to open their gifts. Not even a whimper from the tiniest tot. I cannot describe the moment. "On the count of three you can all open your gifts together – ONE. TWO. THREE…OPEN YOUR GIFTS!". Many girls had never even seen a black baby doll. Now they each had one to love. One little one couldn't unwrap her doll fast enough, and furiously kissed it through the plastic! Trucks, soccer balls, solar-powered radios, and a big box of brand-new clothes for each child!

"Can I keep this?" one child innocently asked.

I know it wasn't the gifts that made these parties so huge. Even more than the gifts was the IDEA that someone thought of you, that someone wanted to make sure *you* were happy, even for one day. If you feel that, you can feel hope. You can imagine a possibility, a dream beyond this moment. *That* is a gift that will live longer than the toys, the clothes, and the shoes.

"I feel like flying," said a boy to my best friend Gayle, "but I don't have wings."

As we left the party, another little boy took my hand and wished me: "Go well." That was it for me.

"Mother Oprah," said a letter from a 12-year-old girl, "Thank you for making me feel human again. I am convinced that God provides." I am convinced that God provides, too. And the joy I felt from those children was a pure Christmas miracle.

Heather, deeply moved by the scenes from Oprah's day at God's Golden Acre, wrote:

> Imagine what impact that day must have had on the children — most of whom would have come from a falling-down hut with barely anything inside it, probably not running water, or electricity, and maybe not even enough food to go round the siblings.
> All were orphans. I would just love to have known what was going on inside their minds! They were so grateful and happy for what was happening to them.

During Oprah's time at God's Golden Acre, Heather suggested that in order to understand more about the lives of the children who had been at the party, Oprah should go to the valley herself to see how the people live. She recounts: "Now I could take the chance to get to know Oprah better. She is an admirable woman, highly intelligent, and well informed, good humoured, and with a sense of mission that she can help to make the world a better place, especially for children, and with girls a priority.

"She was already well aware that the magnificent Valley of a Thousand Hills was the setting of one of the world's worst black spots in the AIDS pandemic. But if you haven't experienced it, then of course you cannot really grasp the awful implications. I explained to Oprah that although we were hard at work with the rural outreach project in a few valleys, the overwhelming majority of them had not even been reached. Thousands of children were out there starving and dying — little kids abandoned and alone who hadn't asked to be in such a helpless situation. There was nobody out there to care, to hear the cries of children who have nobody to turn to.

"An entire orphan generation would be lost, I told her. The

evidence was all there for Oprah to see. This affected her profoundly. She saw mud huts that were falling apart because
there were no adults to repair them, untended and unculti-
vated land, long since abandoned and overgrown with weeds,
and the absence of farm animals to provide milk, or meat, or
poultry for eggs. I told her that in the vast valley areas that we
had not reached with our rural outreach project, there were
thousands of sick, weak children. On another visit we showed
Oprah the results of our work in those parts of the valley that
the rural outreach project reached and she met community
health workers who lived in the valley. Oprah was visibly
moved."

Oprah Winfrey's understanding was soon translated into
action and she subsequently helped to fund a very significant
increase in the number of families getting a monthly food parcel in one rural outreach project, sustaining hundreds of families in the valley of Sankontshe for twelve months – solely
from the resources of her private foundation.

Heather said: "These orphans owe so much to her. It hum-
bles me to think that what we do every day touches such a
famous and important person. We have made a significant
impact upon one of the most important communicators in
America and she publicly vowed in front of millions of
Americans to devote a large part of her life to the AIDS
orphans."

BBC correspondent Bill Hamilton, a distinguished international television journalist, arrived at God's Golden Acre a
few months later. Hamilton was on an assignment to make a
TV documentary called *Children of the Epidemic*. A Christian,
with long first-hand experience of acute human crisis,
Hamilton was curious to meet Heather and discover the
woman behind the legend:

I had read that her response to the AIDS orphans crisis was fired
by her religious beliefs, having experienced a dramatic conver-

sion to the Christian faith. Like the Apostle Paul, Heather's came whilst on the road – not to Damascus – but after her brakes failed at a stop sign and she ran straight into a brand new Jaguar sports car. Instead of berating her, the owner offered up a prayer with her. A clear sign, she thought, that there must be a God.

God's Golden Acre… sounds like heaven on earth… so would there be a Peter-type figure on the gate?

No, instead a young man called Andrew – the name of Saint Peter's brother – signals us inside the compound. Andrew is a volunteer worker from Toronto in Canada… one of many young people who'd heard through the grapevine what was going on in this remote part of the world and decided he had something to offer to the cause.

No sooner have we pulled our vehicle to a halt than we are surrounded by an excitable pack of dogs leaping at the open doors and licking our bare hands in an obvious show of affection. I guess they are probably from broken homes too.

Andrew leads us to the office where Heather is busily trying to sort out the latest problem to hit her desk… the refusal by the authorities to let one of the boys in her charge sit his school exams because he isn't able to pay. I have two contrasting visions in my head of Heather. One is of a resolute and assertive head-mistress whom you would cross at your peril. The other – totally the opposite – is a cherubic-type figure dressed in long, flowing robes whose posture and charm would melt the ice off even the most resolute opponent. I am completely wrong.

Here is a larger than life character, intensely loquacious and voluble with beaming face and an obvious capacity to cope with the multiplicity of challenges and quandaries that come to the fore here at almost every minute of every day. Her desk is piled high with papers and lists of important contacts with whom she must get in touch. The computer is playing up… the sweat pouring from her brow. She breaks off a hundred and one other conversations with volunteers, *gogos*, and helpers all clamouring for attention, to welcome us and hand over the keys to a house in the grounds that has been prepared for our needs, including a pot of chicken and rice placed on top of the oven.

Behind the office, her living room... a double bed is barely visible beneath a myriad of books, lamps, curtains, clothes, toys and every conceivable gadget and novelty necessary to look after the needs of 97 children for whom God's Golden Acre has become home.

She glances up at my blazer curious to know the origins of the badge that adorns my buttonhole. I explain that, like thousands of others, I have been a member of The Boys' Brigade that has been around for more than 110 years, and is part of the boyhood experience of many adults.

The Boys' Brigade is a Christian youth organization with over half a million members worldwide. It offers a wide range of activities, including games, crafts, sports, Christian teaching, music and holiday camps. It also embraces the Global Fellowship of Christian Youth whose object is the advancement of Christ's Kingdom, the promotion of education and the relief of poverty among the youth of the world.

It seems to me that the movement Sir William Alexander Smith founded in Glasgow all those years ago is just what Heather needs to help catch the energy and enthusiasm of youth and to channel it purposefully. She readily agrees.

When it comes to interviewing Heather for our BBC World documentary *Children of the Epidemic*, I find her oddly shy and diffident. It is as if the experience holds a terror for her. She understands the needs of the media but has been tricked in the past and now delivers her message in a way that leaves no room for misinterpretation.

Her relationships with Government – both national and regional – are nothing if not fiery. At first, it seems Pretoria took a dim view of her "cluster foster" experiment because it did not fit readily with their idea of *ubuntu* or care in the community. Indeed, some in authority went as far as accusing her of uprooting orphaned children from their own areas and engineering new families. But now they're softening their line... at first grudgingly and now enthusiastically supporting her idea of placing orphans in the care of foster mothers, many of them grandmothers.

The grants she receives, though, fall well short of what is needed to keep God's Golden Acre afloat. Some call Heather a maverick but then she willingly courts controversy in defence of her aims. She's also a great believer in chasing money from the private sector to ensure survival. Contrast the rather Spartan surroundings, where children spend much of their time, to the Zulu Theatre that is now rising from the dust where dignitaries, businessmen and celebrities will be lured to watch her local dance troupes perform.

There's method in this seeming madness... for these are the very people she wants to sponsor her cluster fostering project and they cannot fail to notice it.

Heather's relationship with the Zulu people in the villages that straddle the Valley of a Thousand Hills is perhaps the best indicator of her success. Traditional leaders, witchdoctors, ministers and countless families salute her missionary zeal. She speaks Zulu fluently and is accepted as one of their own. The Outreach Program she runs from God's Golden Acre supports 300 families and 4,500 children in the valley. Desperate that so many AIDS orphans here should not end up as a generation of street children, sucked in, through desperation, to a life of crime, desolation and abuse, she has started a local football league and is organizing educational and sporting challenges to engender team spirit and promote habits of obedience, discipline and self-respect.

Her relationship with her husband Patrick is an intriguing one. He has his own studio where he sculpts exotic and interesting pieces of art. Some attract notable buyers, and money helps to keep the Reynolds afloat and provide much-needed income for God's Golden Acre too. My visit is for but a couple of days... but it is long enough to get a feel of the place and of the people who run it. Chaotic, eccentric, vibrant and God-driven. My only concern would be whether it could function without her. Well, she has four project organizers now and things are moving forward apace. Whenever Heather feels low, she turns to read the slogans she's plastered across her office wall. One best encapsulates her single-minded determination: "Obstacles are those frightful things you see when you take your eyes off the goal."

OK, Heather, I've got the message. Come to think of it... so too, at last, have the Government.

35
THE CHILDREN OF
GOD'S GOLDEN ACRE

Visitors to God's Golden Acre at Cato Ridge never forget sunrise and sunset. At the back of the farm there are tall gum trees, and below them a sheer descent into the valley, with stunning views. The sun, a huge ball of fire, drops swiftly into the trees and slides straight down below the horizon, enveloping everything around it with a crimson and golden sheen. The magnitude of the fireball, which people feel they can almost touch, is nothing but an optical illusion of course. The human eye and brain are fooled by the seeming proximity of the falling sun through the familiar perspective of the near horizon.

They are in rural Africa, their senses and intuitions sharpened by the air, the light, the sounds of the greatest continent on earth, and perhaps 50 metres away the throbbing drumbeat of the boys and girls at God's Golden Acre in rehearsal for a concert. Are they dreaming? Why, no! It's real! It's part of the magic, mystique, and perhaps, the sheer witchcraft of Africa. They feel more alive, more aware, more excited, and perhaps closer to God than anywhere else. The falling sun at dusk, and its rise at dawn, is a moment all the arriving volunteers and visitors at God's Golden Acre long to experience, and one they remember for ever.

The musical enchantment of God's Golden Acre also manifests itself time and again in the recollections of the young people who have been volunteers there. The Zulu orphans express themselves poignantly in their songs. They seem to know the words from four or five years of age. Long after a tour of duty, the sounds of God's Golden Acre – the beating drums, the harmonies, and the melodious lilting tones of singing voices inspired by faith and love – dwell in the subconscious. Among those who have experienced this breath of rural Africa is a young Australian volunteer called Hugh Evans.

The Oak Tree Foundation, founded by Hugh Evans when he was 19 years old, is Australia's first entirely youth-run and youth-driven aid and development agency. It is a movement of volunteers – all under the age of 25 – seeking to empower developing communities in South Africa through education. In 2004, at the age of 20, Hugh Evans was voted Young Australian of the Year, and in 2005 Young Person of the World. A tall, slim man with an engaging smile, he is one of many popular figures with the orphans at God's Golden Acre, taking them on field trips, spending time with them at play, and even learning to become a white Zulu dancer!

He says of them: "I think they are the most amazing children in the whole world. They know how to sing, they know how to dance, and they know how to express themselves well. Nowhere do you go in the world and get such a huge hug. Every time I come back to God's Golden Acre I get this nervous feeling in my heart, and I get so excited, like I'm coming back home. They call me by my Zulu name, Echlantabo, ('stone of the mountain') which is from the song I like singing, and when I get there they are shouting it, and rushing up to give me huge hugs. The feeling of joy is indescribable.

"They have an extraordinary level of humility, politeness and grace – qualities that any parent would be delighted to find in their child. Yet they have all – almost without exception – been through appalling times in earlier childhood and we do have to understand that there has been violence in their

lives. One time two of the boys were having a fight and I tried
to break it up. I was in the middle of it and one of the children
pulled a steak knife out of a drawer and faced up to me with
it in his hand. I'm sure he wouldn't have used it but his aggression really shocked me for three or four hours. I was literally
speechless, and could not work out what had happened. Then
I thought to myself – often these children have grown up in
situations where all they have known is abuse, and sexual
abuse, daily, sometimes for years. Violence is a natural
response to threat."

Hugh's friend Esther Perenyi was 17, a pupil at
Melbourne's Carey Baptist Grammar, and on her first visit to
God's Golden Acre. She had never been to a funeral in her
life, but arrived on a day when the children of God's Golden
Acre were saying goodbye to a little boy who had just died in
the hospice – after a brief period in the sanctuary – having
been brought there from the valley by his relations. She
describes the experience: "Because I'd never actually been to
a funeral before – it is a shock. I walk in and the first thing I
see is a tiny white coffin placed on two chairs, and all the little children are seated around the coffin. I am really unsettled
by this because I didn't think there would be any children at
the funeral. I sit down and wait, and suddenly this nine-year-
old girl gets up and starts singing and leads the 95 orphans in
song in a marvellous harmony to send this child off to heaven.
At the end, they open up the coffin and everyone files past,
looking at the child, and paying their last respects.

"I think what gets to me is that these children – who are so
young – have seen this so many times and seem to understand
it so much better than they should. I feel they shouldn't have
to experience all this when they are so young. I didn't really
know what to expect when I arrived at God's Golden Acre,
but I certainly wasn't anticipating going to a funeral. This was
something beyond any of my expectations.

"I shall go back to Australia feeling very different about

things. I want to share my experiences with others, motivate them, and get them involved. Young people in my country need to know and understand about what is happening in South Africa. Children will always be children, no matter where you are in the world, but with these children, in their eyes, you can see an underlying sadness that is very striking. I have played with them a lot and they are very boisterous and outgoing, but they have a constant need for affection – always wanting to hold your hand, and jump on your lap and give you hugs.

"A few days after I came here a little chap arrived and I took a liking to him instantly. Just this morning I went down to the hospice because I couldn't get him out of my mind, and he held my finger as I was sitting next to him. Suddenly his eyes glazed over, and the grip loosened, and I just got the biggest fright. I thought he had died. I know it sounds silly but I started shaking him – and he started screaming. Death has really gotten to me. They took him to a local hospital where he was found to have pneumonia. But he's going to be OK."

Zanele Jila is among the oldest from the first generation at God's Golden Acre, whose arrival there was more due to the poverty caused by the civil war than the later AIDS epidemic. Now, having grown up, she worked at God's Golden Acre as a caregiver, cleaner and teacher of Zulu song and dance, before going to college to train as a teacher and lecturer. At 21 she is still a virgin, has promised Heather not to rush into a relationship, and hopes to go on to study at university where she will prepare for a career in teaching. With her haunting beauty, grace, humility and consideration for the feelings of others, she personifies all the best qualities to be found in the children and young people of God's Golden Acre. She says: "I was eleven years old when I came to God's Golden Acre at Wartburg. If it had not been for Heather I would not have survived because life was really difficult. We came from a very poor family. My mother had seven children and three died.

"Sometimes there was not enough to eat and we went to bed hungry. I would probably have got a boyfriend some time in my early teens and then have become HIV-positive. Heather took me in, became a mother to me, and always warned me about the dangers that I faced. That's why I feel so good about God's Golden Acre – it gave me my childhood back and I was happy as I was growing up. Ten years have gone by and I have not passed away. Had I stayed in the valley I would probably have had three children or more by now, and be facing the risk of death. I have not had relationships with boys. Instead I am proud that I have stayed in control of my life and I have plans for the future.

"I am going through college and want to go to university so I can help my family. I have a mother, a big sister, a brother born in 1985, and Mavu born in 1990, who lives at God's Golden Acre. Mavu would also have died because he had tuberculosis and was really sick when he came here – but Gogo Heather made sure he had hospital treatment and over the years she has brought him back to health. He is OK now.

"When I am qualified I will go back to the valley because I will be able to help people who need it. I want to teach little kids because that is the time to start influencing them to live their lives in the right way. Education is so important to my people – yet so many of them did not have the money to go to school. This is where things must change. If you don't go to school you have no chance of getting a job. Many of the boys grow up with nothing to look forward to – except sex and drugs and joining a gang. They don't think about their lives because no one has taught them to think otherwise.

"As far as AIDS is concerned, a lot of people of my generation don't believe it. Another reason is they are ashamed of it. It is very embarrassing to tell people if you have lost members of your family because of AIDS. You keep it inside you. You don't tell anyone because you feel you will be laughed at and badly treated. My cousin died of AIDS last year. When I saw her she looked like she had AIDS but on the clinic cards they told her she had TB. But I knew the truth but no one wanted to say so. The other girls in my family have learned nothing from my cousin's death because they refuse to believe it was HIV – they think maybe it was just bad luck, or it was God calling her early. One of the things I want to do when I go back to the valley as a teacher is to sit down and talk with the kids, and make sure they know the truth so they will perhaps grow up and have a better life. I'm very proud to be a Zulu, it's very special for me, and I want to protect my people.

"Here at God's Golden Acre I stay in one of the foster homes with 22 girls up to the age of fifteen. I sleep with six of the older girls in one room and we talk a lot about our lives and the future. I tell them, 'Girls, you are really young and you have seen people who are sick in the valley. So don't go to bed with boys and if a boy comes to you and asks you to go to bed with him just say no – otherwise maybe you are going to get HIV, get sick, and are going to die.' They are really afraid about that. They have learned from me.

"I go back to the valley quite often and stay for perhaps three days or more with relatives, my uncles and their kids, but more often I stay with my mother who lives now in Pietermaritzburg with my 18-year-old brother. She is sick and the others look to me as the head of the family. I am strict with my brother and make him save money so that he can become a driver and have a future. I think he is listening to me.

"I believe that the special opportunities that the orphans have here at God's Golden Acre will mean that one day some will become leaders of the Zulu communities in the valley. Although people are sometimes jealous of what we have got, I think our education and Christian beliefs will help us to be people of influence."

36
SYMBOLS OF
RECONCILIATION

One evening as the sun was sliding behind a mountain, Hugh Evans drove a van owned by God's Golden Acre towards KwaNgcolozi, a valley where the Oak Tree Foundation is sponsoring a $100,000 community resource centre that will provide 1,000 students with the opportunity to receive a primary and secondary education, and also tertiary education in fields such as computer training. The road twisted sharply downhill and eventually reached the floor of the valley. The van followed the road for two miles along the shore of a large reservoir. Cattle and goats grazed peacefully on an abundance of bush grass.

"It can be extremely frightening here at the weekends," Hugh explained. "The tracks along the side of the road are full of drunken men, most of them young and aggressive. I get very frightened as a white person travelling alone here on Saturdays, especially the evening, and try to avoid it if I can. The young men drink, of course, because they have nothing else to do. Nowhere to work and nowhere for recreation – the options are drink, drugs, sex and crime. Those who are lucky might have work in Durban, but for most it's a case of scrounging and rooting around for some kind of existence in what they see as a 'no hope' valley. I believe that education is empowerment and so we are helping to finance a pilot project that will be a non-residential community resource centre."

He pointed to a large plot of land. It looked out over a reservoir; grey-green mountains were its magnificent backdrop. "It has been given to us by the local *nkosi* who really believes in our project. And we've got just the right people to run it," he said.

The figures of a tall African, and an attractive white blonde woman in her early forties, appeared at the entrance to the site where clearance and some early construction work had already started. They both waved at the approaching van. Pastor Eric Shezi, of Thandanani Family Church, and his professional partner Debbie Wells, a social worker from Hillcrest (and social worker to God's Golden Acre) are heroic symbols of post-apartheid South Africa. They would be embarrassed to hear themselves described in such a way. However, they symbolize the spirit of reconciliation and selfless dedication that many middle-class people – both black and white – have so far failed to demonstrate in this young country. Eric and Debbie have worked together as a team since 1994, helping poor people whose lives have been shattered by the AIDS epidemic.

At first it was a soup kitchen at Embo, financed by Eric's church, and now they run a rural outreach project supporting 70 families and involving nearly 400 children in KwaNgcolozi, funded by God's Golden Acre. The new multipurpose hall provided by the Oak Tree Foundation will enable them to help people beyond the basic level of food and clothing, and spread a wider net over the community. How did it all begin?

"We were running the soup kitchen for about three or four years and we didn't get involved helping individual people or their families because we didn't have any resources to do that. Then we heard about a child in KwaNgcolozi whose father had died and who was believed to have great potential. He wasn't able to go back to school because there was no one to pay the fees. We came down to see the school, and pay the fees, and we met the headmaster who told us he had a lot more destitute children unable to go to school – could we help any of them? So I said, 'OK. Put their names down and give me a list and we'll see what we can do.' We had a list with the names of 16 children on it. We formed a profile on each one so that we could help in other ways as well. So our project started from that one child, to 16 children, and grew from there."

On the list scrutinized by Eric and Debbie was a child who had been raped by a neighbour in her own home. The man had been charged with the rape by the police but released on a bail – paid for by his family – and he was living at his home again. Meanwhile the girl was going to be summoned to court to give evidence against him. Eric felt her life was in real danger. Heather took in the little girl. Soon afterwards Eric and Debbie's rural outreach programme came under God's Golden Acre's umbrella where it remained until 2004.

Pastor Eric explained: "What usually happens is that far from rejecting Christianity, the adults come closer to Christ. They don't blame him for what has happened to them and what they are going through. Instead they grow closer to God because faith is their only hope. They find prayer a source of great comfort. We are also doing as much as we can to educate adolescents about safer sex. Twice a year we hold a camp and there we teach them a large range of life skills. We are fighting negative apathetic attitudes, however, in many young people, who say they don't care. They know about AIDS, but for some reason they don't seem to think they will be infected by it. Meanwhile, the epidemic spreads like wildfire. I feel this is just the beginning and I am very sorry to say that."

Every Saturday there are many funerals in Eric's parish. Around 150 people belong to his church, but when it comes to funerals he includes the close friends and relatives of his congregation, so he is really responsible for up to 600 people. The dead are nearly always victims of AIDS, in their mid-twenties or much younger. It is the most stressful thing the young pastor has experienced, because the grief is so intense when people die young. He cannot remember the last time he did not have a funeral on a Saturday and is desperate to be with his family so that he can relax – away from the intensive pressure and emotion of his ministry.

All over the country priests like Eric are gradually cracking under the strain. They cannot conduct more than one funeral in a day because Zulu custom dictates that the pastor is an important part of the ritual – which takes many hours. Eric has to assign his lay ministers on Saturdays to conduct funerals. It's a heavy emotional burden and what frightens him is that the scenario is getting worse all the time.

Rosetta Heunis, Cheryl Harris and Alta Collins are also responsible for separate elements of the rural outreach programmes at God's Golden Acre. By 2004, the furthest drop-off point was an hour's drive from Cato Ridge, and in the years to come it is hoped to extend programme boundaries to every corner of the Valley of a Thousand Hills. The God's Golden Acre team constantly witness deprivation and hopelessness in the valley but do what they can to alleviate it within the constraints of the funding available. The white members of the God's Golden Acre team have to be vigilant while working in the valley. Cheryl said: "We're not stupid. We've never been threatened but Zulu people we have worked with warn us that it is unusual we have never been hijacked. The sight of a white woman driving a 'bakkie' alone in the valley presents a target and so whenever possible I avoid that. Sometimes I'll nip down quickly but it would be in the daytime. There are some areas we don't go into. We lost a boy once from God's Golden Acre and Sandra and I went looking for him. We were about to go into one area with one of the *gogos*, and a security guy actually said to us, 'It's not a good idea to go in there because they shoot strangers.' It's a matter of judgement."

Most children who have no parents are redirected into extended families looked after by a granny figure, or older sister, within their own community in the valley. Food supplies, school uniforms, school fees, small livestock, seeds, soap and sapling fruit trees enable each family unit to be self-sustaining. Cheryl personally feels pity for many of the *gogos*. "You just look at their life and think, *It's so hard*. At a time when they should be sitting back and relaxing, they've now got their kids' kids to look after because their own kids have died – yet when they talk to you they have courage, spirit and a sense of duty that seems to be ingrained in them."

Getting the children back to school and providing them with school uniforms is recognized as a most effective way to help them regain their self-confidence; and it brings back a sense of order into their lives. Alta Collins is responsible for the stationery, uniforms and clothing for the children on the outreach projects. "The orphans would rather go without food than go to school looking shabby. Their appearance is everything and in actual fact I would say that the sad thing is that while most of the children who go to school in the valley are well dressed, some of them have not even had a cup of tea or slice of bread before going to school. I think it's a pride issue, because even as children the Zulus are very proud people. For instance when they attend any kind of function, they will put on their best clothes. They are always smiling, and so grateful and excited when we take the uniforms to them. They rush off and put them on – often over their old clothes! It's a fantastic feeling to be able to help them."

Cheryl continued: "The African women gather at the drop points and bring their wheelbarrows. We unload the right number of food parcels at each drop point. Once the food is unloaded, the community health workers get the women to line up behind their food and when that is done we take their card and click it, mark them off, and hand it back. It works really, really well. The people stay there, they are patient, and are extremely grateful for what we are doing. To miss a family by mistake could mean people going hungry.

"The women stroll off to their hut with the sacks and boxes

perched on their head. They are the lucky ones. A mile or so down the valley others may be hungry or even starving, but for the moment, they cannot be helped because of lack of funds. It seems cruel, and it can create tension, but most people appear to understand that God's Golden Acre cannot help everyone."

Some analysts in organizations like the United Nations believe that rural outreach projects – such as the one pioneered by God's Golden Acre in stricken areas of the valley – are capable of bringing back a measure of normality and are likely to be the most effective self-sustaining approach to take, in recreating family life in the wake of the AIDS pandemic in rural areas. It frustrates Heather to know that much of the infrastructure is now in place that could drive a massive expansion programme, not only in the field of rural outreach, but also in the provision of community resource centres. These would have a huge impact throughout the Valley of a Thousand Hills. Painstakingly, she has worked out all the statistics, the logistics and the final amounts of money that would be required to launch the rural outreach project there.

Heather explains: "We have the methodology – the process model as they call it – and could organize projects on a massive scale. We know how to get the food there; we've got the wholesalers who would be only too happy to be able to provide the food and deliver it – it's good business for them. We can employ more people to be rural outreach coordinators and service the areas – that would mean more employment.

"We also need to create self-sustaining craft industries with links to markets outside the valley. Training in craft skills is vitally important because adults who are skilled in them may die before they can hand on their expertise to the next generation. So we have got to set up the programmes to get craft education into the school curriculum. It means the children, as they grow up, will have a basic form of employment within their own community. As the pandemic begins to peak we are discovering that the stricken communities are not able to absorb the loss of loved ones and everywhere the impact of that is having devastating effects.

"There might be a self-sustaining extended family where perhaps a number of brothers and sisters are working. They have all got children, and a granny, and at this level it all works out. Then one will die, perhaps a sister leaving three children, then another sister will die leaving now her three children, that's six children, and so now a brother has to support his own, let's say, four children, plus those other six. Then he dies after a year. Suddenly Granny is faced with ten children. What does she do? Maybe she's too young to get a pension – because African women often have children at 16 or 17 – so she could be a grandmother by the time she's 40 years old. But she can't leave to go to work because she's now got at least three children who are under the age of three. She's got to cook and wash and try and help to keep this family together and get them off to school, and then after a certain period of time she's begging and borrowing from neighbours… so how does this granny survive with no income and ten children?

"One day I went with Councillor Shabalala – a councillor from Sankontshe – to look at a 'worst case' scenario. There was a community in his ward at Georgedale based around a working textile mill where people had moved to find work. He wanted to get me involved in that area. We were taken to see a granny and she came out in a very tatty dress; one breast was almost completely exposed because of the tears in it. She explained to us that she had had to farm her grandchildren out because there was no way she could keep them together because they were starving. I thought, *How amazing she is*. She stood there with all her dignity in this dress that revealed so much of her tired body – and she was so poor. But it took nothing away from her, and I felt so incredibly sorry for her.

"It's an amazing quality the Zulus, and other Africans, have. No matter how much sorrow, and how much pain, and how much poverty, and the things they have to bear, when you go down into the valley and you say in Zulu, *sawbona khungani*, 'Hello, how are you?', a big smile will always greet you and the person will nearly always reply, 'Oh, I'm fine, thank you.'

"In KwaXimba, there are 42 community health workers but their dedicated work falls far short of what is needed. There just are not enough of them to look after the 62,000 people who live there, 52 percent of whom are HIV-positive. KwaXimba is a spectacular setting. Sometimes the summits are above the line of the clouds, and the African sunlight illuminates the valleys in a myriad of changing shades. The birds are singing, tropical plants bloom, and there is tranquillity. Yet for many Zulus who live in its 26 traditional rural districts it is hell on earth. Families beyond our reach are starving to death.

"One day a group of the local councillors came to me and pleaded for help. It was hard for me to witness these grown men in such a state of despair. I had to tell them it would cost about two million Rand (£200,000) a year to launch an effective rural outreach project in KwaXimba, and we did not currently have that kind of money at our disposal. However, I promised them that when I went to Europe I would represent their cause, provided they were able to fulfil certain conditions to help me. I needed facts, figures and statistics from them. Nkosi Mlaba had sent the group of councillors to see me. However, I was still worried by the security problem. 'Your area is so big it is going to be a nightmare for me to try and roll out any programme, you are going to have to guarantee our security, and do this, that, and this...' I warned.

"The next day I received a phone call from Councillor Ngubane just as I was about to set off from God's Golden Acre to fly to England and he said: 'Heather, you've got to come down here now!'

" 'I can't, I'm flying today,' I replied.

" 'You've got to, you must,' he insisted.

"I was exhausted and tired from having been working seven days a week, and I hadn't even packed for my long journey to Europe, but I rushed down to KwaXimba knowing it was something that was very important to them. I discovered they had fulfilled every requirement that I had stipulated to the last letter at our previous meeting. All the names, the locations, the families, the amount of people who were HIV-positive, and the number of children who needed help to go to school etc. were listed. It was just as I'd asked. 'We wanted you to have this before you went overseas, so you can really go and fight for our area,' the community development officer Mr Mapunga told me.

"I was very heartened by what Nkosi Mlaba had done because it was the first manifestation of a return to the rule of law, and respect for the law, in a very large area of the valley. I felt like a jet of energy had been pumped into me. My exhaustion was replaced by a feeling of elation. KwaXimba was an area I had long wanted to get into – but had been put off by the enormity of the place and the scale of the problems I knew we would encounter. Now it would become a priority area for action. Perhaps unexpectedly, the first major project we would undertake there was to establish a football league for boys, through another miracle with the help of some of the top men in British professional football.

37
"I FEEL LIKE CRYING TILL I DIE..."

The community health worker's voice was tense with urgency over the phone line. She was adamant that Heather should leave what she was doing at the time and come to the valley. She gave Heather a brief outline of the little family she had identified in Sankontshe. It was to be a day Heather would remember for ever – despite the briefing, nothing could have prepared her for the heartbreak she would witness that morning.

"After a hurried descent into the valley, we arrived at the tiny mud hut around midday. Switching off the Land Rover's engine, I steeled myself against the familiar sense of trepidation that rose in my chest as we made our way to the entrance. Each time, I never know just how bad it will be on the other side of the door. As we entered, and our eyes grew accustomed to the dark, we saw a woman lying on a low bed, with her two babies in bundles next to her. Painfully thin, and powerless to move her lower limbs, this proud young Zulu woman could not stand to greet us. Too weak to draw herself up on her elbows, she simply lay on her back, while the community health worker introduced us.

"As I moved closer to her, I was stunned by the exquisite beauty of this dying mother. With high, elegant cheekbones that would have captivated the world of modern fashion, she lay before me, helpless. Her gaze met mine with a strange mix of uncertainty, hopelessness and hope, as I told her I'd heard about her and her triplet babies, and had come to offer my help. Her eyes moved slowly to the bundles beside her as I told her I'd heard that one of the three babies had already died, and that we knew the other two were also sick.

"With the HIV virus attacking her immune system, she had succumbed to one of the common ailments, dysentery, and being so weak, could not even move off the bed to relieve herself. The mattress was sodden and her body had developed sores from lying in her own excrement. Alone with her babies, and shunned by the community around her as the stigma of her disease took effect, she had no help and could only lie powerlessly watching her own body deteriorate and her three babies starve, as her body stopped producing breast milk.

"Now, as I stood before her, as a white woman she'd never met before in her life, she was faced with the most horrific decision a mother should have to make: to entrust her babies to a complete stranger, as their only hope for survival. Deciding at last to take the only chance to save their lives, she agreed to let us take them to hospital. Unwrapping the tiny bundles to change their nappies and give them some of the formula we had brought, I felt overwhelmingly powerless. I could not give this woman her life back; I couldn't tell her for certain that her babies would survive. We had sent for an ambulance to fetch her, but the babies were to be taken to a different hospital – one with the best paediatric facilities.

"The young mother said her goodbyes to her children as we carried them out of the door and rushed them into town. Despite our efforts, Thanda, the little boy, died in hospital after three days. The only remaining triplet, a little girl named Lina, managed to pull through, and we ensured that she had regular visits with her mother at the hospital to which she had been admitted. The beautiful young mother died in hospital, six weeks later. Lina grew up to be a healthy, happy little girl despite her difficult beginnings."

Heather's work at the coalface of the AIDS pandemic in South Africa continues at an unrelenting pace. The pressure upon her – both in the valley and at God's Golden Acre – had by 2004 continued at this relentless pace for nearly a decade. Often, Gogo Beauty, Heather's cook, would prepare three meals in a day, and then discover eight hours later that Heather had not even had time to eat any of them. At times it brought the unhappy Gogo Beauty close to the point of resignation. Living just behind the office for more than three years until 2004 made intrusions upon Heather's privacy even more inevitable. Lucy Foster tried to take some of the strain off in the mornings as early as 2000, but it proved impossible. She wrote:

A day in the life of Heather starts early in the morning, even before she has had the chance to get dressed, wash her face and comb her hair. She will be taking meetings from her bed, still wearing her nightdress. She doesn't have the time to get out of bed, get dressed, and ready for the day before people are knocking on her door. When I first worked for her I'd say, "Right, nobody's going to go into Heather's room until 9am, so she can wake up nicely, talk to her husband, and get dressed." We tried to keep up that regulation, but it lasted about a week! The important phone calls, some from abroad, would be coming in, and because we rely on donations, we just couldn't put people off when they were asking to talk to her."

Heather is held in awe by both her staff and volunteers, who fear her outbursts of anger. Staff and family at God's Golden Acre worry about the stress she faces, and the exhausting workload she places upon herself. In her journal Susan Balfour wrote of her disquiet at the stress Heather's pastoral work was having upon her boss physically, and also of Heather's practice of frequently going without food and warmth herself, so that she could better understand the feelings and pain of those who were deprived of it. Susan wrote the following account in her journals:

"Whosoever will come after me let him deny himself, and take up his cross, and follow me." (Mark 8:34)

A few nights ago, one of the Zulu caregivers knocked on my room door. "Gogo Heather is calling you." I reached for a jersey and my coat and made my way across to her house in the chilly night air. June is one of the coldest months in KwaZulu-Natal. I arrived to find the door and windows of Heather's rooms wide open, and her, in bed in a thin cotton nightdress with only a thin sheet. My eyebrows shot up. Heather caught my look, and went on to explain...

She had visited the Sankontshe valley the week before and found a sick old granny, caring for four grandchildren in a dilapidated mud hut that was almost caved in. They were living in desperate poverty, sleeping on the dirt floor, without a single blanket between them. "When I am cold, I remember that there are thousands of people in the valleys around us shivering in bed with empty stomachs, and it motivates me to work harder and faster," she said. There was a fierce determination in her eyes. I understood the desire but nevertheless, there was a flutter of anxiety below my ribs.

"You'll make yourself sick," I told her pointedly.

She has an unforgiving schedule of outreach visits in the valley, meetings, delivering talks, greeting visitors. She never sleeps for more than four hours per night – Heather is often up until 3am, handling a huge volume of e-mail correspondence or preparing funding proposals. Sometimes, if no one suitably qualified is available, she will care for a sick child around the clock. People often ask how much longer she can keep this up. But for as long as I have known Heather she has possessed a terrific energy and vitality. It persists despite a hectic schedule that precludes any sense of physical well-being.

She is fuelled by an awesome measure of compassion, in a desperate sprint towards a searing vision; "... focused beyond the horizon on a land of rich crops, where justice and peace prevails." (Isaiah 32:15–17)

"I am comprised of atoms," she says, "and atoms don't get sick." Her resolve is unshakeable. She prays, trusts in God, and keeps going. She is quite well.

What the volunteers did not realize, however, was that Heather's mental state of health was indeed deteriorating – but not through the burden of work. Her heart had been broken through physical separation from her babies. After moving to Cato Ridge she made a deliberate and difficult decision not to spend as much time at God's Golden Acre – as she had done for instance in the past at Wartburg – caring for, and nursing, the younger children now living in Mons House. This was something she explained to no one, apart from Patrick, because she was desperately anxious to maintain the equilibrium at God's Golden Acre, and to do nothing to dispel the happiness of the older children, and the high morale of both the volunteers and African staff.

"In the longer term the Lord was telling me that my role in fighting the AIDS pandemic would have to become more strategic. There were going to be millions of children in South Africa that needed my intervention in their lives – and I knew this was where God wanted me to be. Meanwhile, all the babies and children now being brought up at God's Golden Acre would need to be taken right the way through to adulthood, including education. They would each have to bond with a foster mother, a Zulu, who would bring them up in their culture. It meant heartbreak for me personally. I would have to let go of my little babies at God's Golden Acre. I didn't realize how painful it would be until the time came. Thank goodness I didn't know beforehand – because I think that if I had known, I would not have formed the close and very loving relationships with the children that I did."

Heather's first step in this direction came when she and Patrick moved out of the farmhouse and into accommodation at the back of the main office. The nursery-age children like Chummy, Fikile and Marcus had grown up in her bedroom, and the crying, sobbing and deep distress of these infants on the night she walked away will haunt her for the rest of her life. Many children had been abandoned in the valley and now seemed to imagine that it was happening to them all over again. "That first night was the worst, and even now I don't like going back to that memory, because I so very nearly cracked up and gave in. As I walked out of Mons House the toddlers were prevented from following me. They were physically stopped from going with me. They realized I wasn't coming back. Instead of going to my own room in the house with them, I had shut the door and walked out. It was terrible, terrible. I walked away. I felt like a murderer. I couldn't explain to them that I had to do this, why I was leaving them, and sleeping in another house. They didn't understand because they were too small, just two- and three-year-olds. Fikile, Marcus and Chummy, they were the ones who were screaming.

"Marcus had slept in a pram by my bed until he was nearly two years old. How can you explain to a child of not yet three that you are letting go? That it was hurting me more than it was hurting him? I also felt particularly guilty about Fikile, who was adopted soon afterwards, because I will never have the chance to explain it all to her when she grows older. Gogo Beauty, Ida, the aunties and the caregivers – some of the older girls from the choir – they were there for them, but the babies had always been used to me nursing them. I had become their mother. It took months, months. I had to stop going to Mons House at night. I just couldn't stand it any more. I cut it out of my schedule, stopped going. And they didn't understand. I couldn't look at them, but sometimes I could hear their crying. They would scream like wounded animals if they caught sight of me walking to my new house. I would just get in the car and drive out, heartbroken.

"I said to God, 'I couldn't do it again, God. Next time, I'll walk back to those kids, and I won't take care of anything else. I'll just walk straight back to them, and not walk away from them again.'

"Now I threw myself into the valley more than ever to compensate for my misery, and of course found so many terrible and shocking things there that I often could not sleep at night. So I was sleepless because of the terrible things I encountered in the valley – and sleepless because of my feelings of guilt for leaving the babies at God's Golden Acre. It made me very ill. I had an angina attack and people actually thought that I was going to die. It was then that the volunteers became more protective of me. But it was not the workload that was making me ill – it was the pain of separation from my babies. I could only share this with Patrick."

Heather's health had also been affected by her endless problems with the Department of Social Services. It seemed impossible to convince them that God's Golden Acre was not designed to be a residential institution, like an orphanage, but a community where African foster mothers would provide homes for extended families within a larger community providing support, education, and social welfare. The authorities saw God's Golden Acre as a throwback to the institutional orphanage or children's home, where the parental unit had been substituted for something less acceptable. Heather was perceived by many experts to be contravening national policy on orphans, even carrying out social engineering by removing children from their natural family groups and placing them in foster care. Over several years she had to stand up against so-called experts in child welfare, and their prevailing wisdom, to fight her case for the survival of God's Golden Acre. Being white did not make it any easier for her.

"They would not accept that we were not an institution.

They couldn't see that it was developing into a happy and successful community centre, where the children would be taught Zulu as their main language, and have the opportunity concurrently to be part of the community in the valley – going to funerals and weddings and festivals at weekends and holidays. At God's Golden Acre the children live in family units looked after by the African *gogos*, supported by white volunteers. I stand there as the big granny figure, a white *gogo*. What is wrong with that? South Africa is meant to be a multiracial country now, so I didn't see why we could not have a community centre as we envisaged it, with African *gogos* in charge, supported by largely European volunteers. Eventually they gave way, albeit reluctantly, conceding that cluster foster care – as practised at God's Golden Acre – did have an important role to play in bringing up orphaned children. The pandemic still has not peaked yet and I am sure cluster foster care – the vision of people like Dr Neil McKerrow – is going to become an essential response to the huge increase in the number of orphans."

The regulations dictated that the *gogos*, and the aunties, should become responsible as foster parents for a maximum number of six children, and each child had to be registered in the care of a specific adult. It was another strong reason why Heather had to take a step back from the babies. "Two or three years on, it is good to see that my babies have become totally integrated into their foster homes and they are growing up to be strong and healthy children, surrounded by happiness. I am a granny figure to them now, and I don't spend too much time around the smaller ones – because toddlers bond very quickly with me, and frankly it's just too hurtful. I can't go through that again. I spend small amounts of time with them, and then I break it up. I don't want them to get so close in their bonding with me that it then makes the inevitable separation distressing.

"I love those children so much – I think they just respond

to it very easily. It doesn't take long to bond with anybody when there is a mutual love. I feel overwhelming love for them, but if the children grow to sense that in me, it could delay the bonding with their *gogo* in the foster house. Sometimes with all the sadness and tragedy I encounter in the valley, and when I am missing my babies at night, I feel like crying till I die. If I let myself cry, I would just keep crying until I died."

38
A TREAT FOR THE ORPHANS

The white Land Rover was crowded with orphans and towed a battered trailer carrying luggage and food provisions. Heather engaged a low gear and the vehicle began the tortuous ascent of a steep hill with the trailer swaying precariously behind it. The latter performed better since having some air pumped in its tyres at Pietermaritzburg.

The Land Rover was in the foothills of the Drakensberg Mountains on the lonely R617 route, heading towards the small town of Underberg. It was well after midnight – we did not set off until 11pm, but at God's Golden Acre the unusual and the unpredictable are the norm.

It was a Saturday night in rural KwaZulu-Natal and in the moonlight the verges revealed shapes. A few of these had four legs, but most appeared and were gone in a flash – providing the split-second apparition of a man staggering in a drunken lurch along the roadside. This road was not a place to be a stranger and alone in the night on foot. Not a place to break down. Not a sensible time to be travelling with children – but we were. Every half hour Heather rang Patrick at God's Golden Acre from her mobile telephone to give him her location.

"It's best to be careful and stay in regular contact, because vehicle hijackings are not uncommon around here, and I don't

want us to lose this vehicle in such a lonely and remote location – especially with so many young girls on board," said
Heather without a trace of anxiety in her voice. "This is my
special time with the children – a time to be Mum again. This
little team bonded on the UK tour of the Young Zulu
Warriors," she said, pointing her thumb, over her shoulder, at
the youngsters sleeping in the back.

Behind them were another group in the covered rear com-
partment. All the children – Mavu, Goodman, Ruth,
Khetiwe, Majola, Mlungisi, Zinhle and Khanyisile – were aged
between eleven and thirteen, except for six-year-old
Chummy Mthalane and his eight-year-old brother Sizwe.
Their behaviour throughout the entire 48 hours would be
nothing short of exemplary. It was clear they adored their
"granny" but remained formally respectful to her in a manner
rarely seen in Western children. In the back of the vehicle
were Australians Hugh Evans and Alex Bryson of the Oak Tree
Foundation, and 21-year-old Zanele Jila, a caregiver at God's
Golden Acre and one of Heather's original children from long
ago.

The Land Rover headed for the famous Sani Pass in the
Drakensberg Mountains, which offered the only route by road
into Lesotho. The specific destination was a backpackers' hostel, from where the older boys and girls would take a trek
through the mountains with Hugh and Alex. A glorious weekend was in store. The vehicle pulled into a garage at
Underberg to refuel. Heather noticed a rusted blue "combi" at
the pumps with a forlorn man standing next to a teenage girl,
and a boy of about twelve, who was vomiting continuously.
Heather said quietly: "Things don't look right there at all. I'd
better see if they are OK and find out if I can help."

As Heather approached the combi she realized there was a
coffin in the back. The girl was stricken with grief. She discovered an old woman, exhausted and at her wits' end,
hunched in the front seat of the vehicle. Within a few

moments Heather was embracing both the young girl and grandmother and giving them comfort in their native language. Then, as a little group, they came together, holding hands, and prayed with Heather. They sang a Zulu song together. It all happened on a garage forecourt in the middle of the night in the space of a few moments.

She said afterwards: "They are from Durban. The mother has died of AIDS and the father is taking them back to the village for the funeral. The prayers and the song helped them in their grief. The father is sick too, which means the teenage girl will soon have to take over the family. They have nothing, not even enough fuel to reach the village, so I have given them money for diesel and for the funeral."

The following weekend Heather was travelling again. This time north east, along the N2 North Coast toll road towards St Lucia and the Hluhluwe and Umfolozi Game Reserves, for another of Heather's weekends. Now the group comprised younger orphans, all under the age of seven. Three of them were sick. There were nine little girls: Susiwe, Nosipho, Sibongile, Slindile, Noxolo, Thina, Nomvula, Nonjabula and Zinhle, and three boys: Chummy, Khanyisane and Siphamandla. Again the behaviour of the children was exemplary, even for such little ones. The single exception was a lapse from the mischievous Sibongile. She ate someone else's dinner, and left the table without asking. The child was sent to bed – loud sobs of shame wafted down the staircase. Later, Sibongile got an extra cuddle from the white *gogo* before going to sleep.

The next day the African children, the caregivers, and volunteers Gael Tremaux from France, and Peg Judge, a pensioner from England, were absorbed by the experience of seven hours in the drought-stricken Hluhluwe Game Reserve. Groups of baboons, elephants and rhinos strolled past the transit van, a family of warthogs crossed the track ahead, forcing it to halt, and two giraffes pruned the top of a Marula tree in front of them. No lions were visible – but the evidence of their most recent kill, the carcass of an impala, was lying by the side of the track. Vultures were still circling in the sky overhead. Children and adults also watched buffalo, nyala, and zebra grazing within 50 metres of the transit. Throughout the seven hours the children sat absorbed, sometimes squealing with delight, other times singing Zulu songs. It hurt to remember that some of them would never grow up.

Shortly before dusk the party from God's Golden Acre returned to the Tiger Lily Lodge run by Charles and Corrue. While the children staged an impromptu concert for their hosts, Charles spoke of his own concerns about the AIDS epidemic. Fifty-six children had been found the previous month living in the bush some miles from Mtubatuba without any adult supervision, he said. They were aged between two and fourteen and several of them were starving and sick when they were discovered. His own church was trying to provide them with homes. Even more seriously, 200 young people had taken over the Hluhluwe town dump, where they were living off its garbage. They were hostile to any outside approach, and were refusing to have anything to do with social workers. A local pastor, he said, was trying his best to find out if their number included many sick or dying. The story disturbed Heather who made a decision to work with the pastor – even though the district is over 150 miles from Cato Ridge. She wanted to approach the dump early the next morning to see what could be done for the young people – but was advised to speak to the pastor first.

On the return journey Heather was deep in thought about this new challenge, but found time to visit the Mpukenyoni trading station, ten miles from Mtubatuba, where she had spent the first nine years of her life. Some of the Zulu men she met walking near the old trading station appeared to remember her father John McLellan's name. However, as she gazed upon the station, after an absence of more than 40 years, there was sadness in her eyes. It had become semi-derelict and there was no longer any evidence of trading. Windows were broken, doors vandalized, hanging off their hinges, and there was an air of degeneration and decay. Dogs barked and children stared at the uninvited visitors. Heather said sadly: "Mum and Dad kept it beautifully. The window frames and doors were freshly painted and the garden was just a joy to behold – a blaze of colour. Our rooms were immaculate and clean. This brings back no fond memories at all. Now there's nothing but filth, litter, weeds and broken bricks. Thank God they're not here to see this."

39
THE LITTLE BOY
FROM UPPINGTON

Heather was relaxing later that evening, enjoying a few glasses of wine, now the children were asleep. "There is something about the beat and the heart of Africa that is in me," she says. "I feel I must go on searching and discovering the magic of Africa relentlessly. Inevitably God's Golden Acre will follow in my wake – for the AIDS pandemic haunts the entire continent. Although I go to rest, every time I visit another part of Africa I stumble upon a drama – I find people who are starving through drought, or devastated by the AIDS epidemic. God tells me I have to do something for them.

"I love Africa, and its countries. I haven't visited them all, of course, but those that I have been to leave a deep and lasting impression upon me. For example, I am overwhelmed by Namibia for its vastness, and Zambia for its great Zambezi River. Even the moon seems twice as big at night on the Zambezi, and the daytime sky is bigger and wider than any place in the world. It is so quiet and remote, and I go there to camp and gaze upon the stars, to recharge my own emotional batteries, to drink in the aromas, sounds and rhythms of Africa. No one can reach me. Wildlife is all around me in my camp, and there is no thrill in the world greater than the sound of a pride of lions in the bush. One day when we were returning from a trip to Namibia with a party of volunteers, an extraordinary thing happened in the town of Uppington, which I wrote about in my diary:

We stop off to get a burger after a long drive on the dusty roads. As I step down, three street urchins come up asking for food. So I give a volunteer some money and ask her to fetch them bread and fish. I ask the little urchins to look after my car until we come back from the café. Afterwards we start talking to this little boy of about eight who has a cherubic face. There is something pitiful and heart-rending about him. He climbs into my arms and just says: "Please take me with you."

"Look, I can't help you. I can't take you with me. I can't do anything for you. The laws wouldn't allow me to do that. You must stay here. Don't let the older boys teach you to go on drugs and glue and stuff. Just don't do it. Just don't land up on drugs. I can't do anything for you at the moment but I'll be back next year, I promise. Just don't get onto drugs, whatever you do."

The boy starts crying. He is cuddled up in my arms and holding me so very tight. Now I am crying too. All the volunteers with me are crying. All the while the child is pleading: "Take me. Take me with you. Please. Please. Don't leave me here."

"I can't take you. I can't take you. There are laws. I can't just take you, little fellow." I get so cross with God at that moment. Tears pour down my face. "God, what is the point of this whole exercise here if I can do nothing? What can I do? I feel so helpless, so guilty."

I hold this little boy for as long as I can. Finally I take my arms away and leave him – step away from him. I don't talk. None of us speak for at least 20 minutes in the bus. I just cry. *How do I help that child? How do I help these people?*

We drive on a few miles, and arrive at a backpackers' hostel. "I'm going to bed," I say to everybody.

The next morning we get up for breakfast and the manager there, who knows me, says: "You were quiet last night."

"Yes. I wasn't feeling too well. Do you people know that you have a street children problem here?"

"Well, yes, I know. It's dreadful."

"Well, what exactly are you doing about it?"

"What are we doing about it? Well, nothing!"

"Why not? Who's going to do something about it? What are you going to do in 20 years' time when those kids are all 30-year-olds slitting your throats? What are you going to do then? What are you going to do about your children then? You should be doing something about it now!"

That is the mood I am in that morning! The hostel manager looks shocked: "Well, I haven't even thought about it!"

"There are lots of things you people could do at this point because those kids are still innocent children. They might be sniffing glue, but they are not hardened criminals. They are still children. You could organize youth groups, you could organize soccer matches in the afternoons, music nights in church groups – there are seven churches here – and included in that, you could serve soup. Do something now and it won't be dangerous. Just do it for God – instead of asking God to do something for you, which is what most Christians do."

By now the hostel manager is looking startled. "Well, I don't know where we'd start."

"I'll tell you. Get the churches together, call a group together, and I'll come. I'll be happy to talk through any programme that you'd like to start. Any initiative – no matter how small, I'll come – ten hours' drive. No matter. I'll come up and talk you through anything for a weekend if necessary!"

I leave feeling a bit better because, although I have arraigned her, the manager is now committed. She'd like to do something, get people together. She'll give me a ring. So I feel at least some hope for that little boy, and all the others.

We get back home to KwaZulu-Natal, and all the volunteers are feeling a bit empty about the Uppington episode, and the boy there. Everybody feels the pain, a sense of frustration, that first night back at God's Golden Acre.

Shortly afterwards, the Rockefeller Foundation comes through with some money so that God's Golden Acre is able to advertise two posts, one of them for a rural outreach project coordinator. I have somebody earmarked called Rosetta Heunis. Rosetta is somebody I know, but she is running a project.

I ring her and say: "Look, Rosetta, the money has come through – are you still interested in the job?"

"Yes! But I'll have to resign and work out my notice on this project."

So she comes to God's Golden Acre and I am talking to her – and then Rosetta says something extraordinary. "You know, in my home town, Uppington, we've got to do something."

"What?"

"Yes! There's a big street children problem in Uppington."

I put my hand to my heart and shout: "Rosetta! I don't believe this!" Then I tell her the whole story about Uppington and this cherub.

"Well! It's my home town," she says, "and I know everybody, and I'm dying to get my hands onto a project there! I know exactly the right project leaders."

That's how God puts things together. I pray the Uppington project will happen.

40

A PROPHET IN
HER OWN LAND

In 2002 Heather attended a conference on AIDS and she was invited as one of the delegates to a reception afterwards in the premier's office in Pietermaritzburg. As she returned to her car in the car park and switched on her lights she noticed something lying on the road. She got out and picked it up and thought at first that it was her First National Bank chequebook. When she opened it, however, she found it wasn't hers – it belonged to a Mr T Blose, and had a telephone number in it.

"I was on my way to go and pick up a sick child that I had left in town," says Heather, "and when I got there I called the number. A man answered.

" 'Mr Blose, I've got your chequebook. You are obviously going to the conference tomorrow so I can return it. I'm one of the delegates, Heather Reynolds, from God's Golden Acre,' I said.

" 'Oh, thank you so much. Yes, I know all about you,' he replied.

" 'OK, I'll see you at the conference. I've got your chequebook; don't worry about it,' I told him."

The next day Heather had completely forgotten about the chequebook because she was there at the conference to look for new funding organizations, and in particular the Nelson Mandela Children's Fund, because now the board of God's

Golden Acre felt ready to send another submission. "We still needed money from them, and we were now more structured than before. The next thing, I saw this big chest in front of me, and I looked at the badge to see whose it was – and it said T Blose.

" 'Oh, it's you,' I said. 'Where are you from?'

" 'Oh, the Nelson Mandela Children's Fund,' he replied.

" 'You mean to say I've had the Nelson Mandela chequebook all night?' I joked.

"Neil McKerrow had overheard what I said and came up afterwards with a smile on his face: 'You mean you gave him back his chequebook?' Well, we had a good laugh about it at the conference and when I got home I mentioned it to Patrick.

" 'What did you say his name was?' asked Patrick.

" 'T Blose,' I said.

" 'Well, you do realize, don't you, that that was the very man whom you tore a strip off a couple or more years ago when they turned down your application?' So again we roared with laughter!

"In fact we did get funding some time later from the Nelson Mandela Children's Fund and we are extremely grateful that they continue to support us. Temba Blose also came to know us better in the course of his important work in KwaZulu-Natal for CINDI and was a respected figure there. I always remember him advising me about my refusal to back down on the controversial issue of cluster foster care: 'Heather, if people challenge your ideas, and make it more difficult for you – then go out there and prove them wrong!' I like to tell people he was absolutely right and I followed his advice."

Heather's model for cluster foster care has now been copied elsewhere. By 2003 there were fewer people in government and in voluntary organizations who disputed her vision. Heather has turned out to be correct in both her judgement and her faith. Cluster foster care is now being seen as an effective way to bring up orphaned children right the way through their childhood and education, without losing touch with their culture and communities.

Furthermore, the South African government, inspired by Nelson Mandela himself, has now accepted the link between HIV and AIDS, and has implemented a new programme making highly active anti-retroviral therapy (HAART) available to millions of South Africans. Some of the orphans at God's Golden Acre are now receiving anti-retroviral medication. The outcome of this treatment will be to slow down and lessen the effects of the illness, in combination with powerful painkilling drugs. The wider recognition of Heather's theories about cluster foster care has enabled God's Golden Acre to attract the sort of funding from international organizations that should underpin its future. After all the hard years of struggle this has come as a welcome relief to the Reynolds.

"However, funding organizations come and go. It will always be important to continue to seek ongoing financial support," Heather reminds us. "Now that we have proper support facilities, thanks to our wonderful benefactors like the Nelson Mandela Children's Fund, Starfish, HopeHIV, and the Rockefeller Brothers Foundation, it seems incredible that we ever managed to cope," she says. "Things have changed such a lot since the days when we were trying to do everything on our own, and had just about enough food to eat. Our dream for God's Golden Acre has become reality.

"It was not until 2002, when we began to become better known in South Africa and overseas, that we started to receive donations on a scale that would enable us to move forward. In fact we will never forget our first large donor, HopeHIV in London. It was the most wonderful feeling suddenly to have something in the bank. There was money now to pay the electricity bills, phone bills, and the many running costs. For a whole year we did not have to worry when utility bills arrived in the post. We felt we were getting there, even though we continued to rely upon finding new funding."

In the early years Marie Godlyman, a senior official from the government's Department of Housing, had arrived unexpectedly on a visit to look round, but not in her official capacity. Later, she told Heather: "I think the Department of Housing could help. These children are orphans, and that is part of our responsibility. The fact that the parents have died shows how calamitous the whole situation is becoming, with all these children having no homes."

She went back to Durban and actually adapted South African government policy to embrace the problem of housing thousands of orphans in need. Eventually, Marie Godlyman orchestrated a 1.2 million Rand scheme for God's Golden Acre that would transfer the orphans into the cluster foster homes that Heather had always envisaged. The project was the catalyst of all change at God's Golden Acre, and the basis upon which everything since has been able to develop. It was, as Sir Winston Churchill once famously said, the end of the beginning.

The Department of Housing brought in Paul Keenan, a consulting engineer, who remained with the charity as a member of the board, to head up the cluster foster homes project – and all this gave the Zulu youngsters a further chance to get an official training in the building trade, because they could use the project as the basis for developing their skills. Four single-storey rectangular houses were eventually built, designed to make them feel to the children like a family home. When the final house was completed, Heather felt the years of sacrifice had been totally vindicated. "The bedrooms are light and airy, there are modern bathrooms, and day rooms for the children to use in the evenings after school. There is also a communal dining room connected to the kitchen. The homes have properly equipped sanitation, modern kitchens, and facilities to wash clothes and bed linen."

A crèche and nursery school provide the first steps in education for the orphans before primary school, and when the purpose-built hospice for the sick babies was completed Heather wrote:

> Today has been a very, very special day. We opened our hospice. Everything went off wonderfully and the place looked beautiful. God has truly blessed us. It was a real team effort and the Dutch volunteers from Livingstone worked like Trojans. The children did several special dance routines and the choir sang. All the children are well and they now also have a beautiful jungle gym to play on. Things are really looking up!

41
OVER THE RAINBOW

In 2004, **Apple Studios** in England gave God's Golden Acre the rights to two songs, "Imagine" and "Let It Be", to use in its choir productions. This enabled Heather to use further the creativity and talent of the young Zulus – proved on their successful tour to England two years earlier – to play a larger role in fundraising for the charity. She wrote:

Rotarians from Rugby Dunsmore, from Warwickshire in the United Kingdom, offered to help us put a CD together and market it, if we could get a good quality recording of our choir singing the songs. In order to do this, we needed recording equipment and a sound engineer. However, after a number of phone calls we realized that purchasing the equipment was certainly beyond our means. Not knowing anyone in the music industry, the time drew nearer for us to have completed the recording. With only a week to go we still had no sign of hope.

While I sat discussing the dilemma with the office staff, a friend of ours, Frank Vurovecz, walked in. He had been installing cupboards in the various new buildings at God's Golden Acre. In desperation I looked up at him and asked: "Frank, you don't by any chance know anyone in the music industry that could help us record a CD?" Frank looked at me and smilingly pointed a finger at himself.

"I have a recording studio," he said.

"What? Since when?" I exclaimed in disbelief.

It turned out he'd always had an interest, and when his son became involved in a band, they had obtained the equipment. "Frank," I said earnestly, "*you* have got to help me. And not only that, you've got to do it for free… I have no money." He agreed.

Don Fardon, a well-known record producer and singer musician, arrived from England to help with the recording, and we rushed to set up the recording equipment in the still-uncompleted Community Theatre building. With the set-up complete, Don and Frank switched it all on, only to discover that one of the amplifiers was not working, and the replacement parts from Japan would take three weeks to arrive. They tried to repair it for the rest of the day, but to no avail. Don told us we'd have no option but to book a recording studio to get the tracks down, as there was no time left. I baulked at the idea of paying between 15,000 and 20,000 Rand for a studio, calculating how many families I could feed in the valley for that amount of money. With no other options presenting themselves, the mood was sombre as we each went off to bed. I spent the night praying, wondering what God was doing, as the provision of the equipment had seemed so miraculous.

The next morning, Don came through to our meeting to say that the equipment was still not working. I turned to the staff around the table and said: "We have to pray. We need a miracle." We joined hands round the table and asked God for a miracle: "Father God, we need a miracle. We need to have that equipment working. We don't need to understand how you do it, but we believe that you can. Jesus, you said that what we ask in your name, it shall be done. So in your name we pray this prayer. If it be your will, then we ask that you repair that equipment, please. You know the situation is desperate and we have no money and we have to do this thing. So in your name we pray this prayer. Amen."

After the prayers some of us walked over to the theatre

building. I was feeling light-hearted somehow, despite the weight of the problem. As we stepped through the door, Don and Frank switched the equipment on again. Suddenly I heard a voice cry, "Whoo-hoo! It's working!" Astonishment registered on the faces of everyone in the recording room. The equipment didn't give one more hitch throughout the entire recording process, and we were able to lay down the tracks for all eight songs in time to be sent off to England for final mixing and production. God had proved himself faithful once more.

The CD album, *Over the Rainbow*, is being sold over the internet and also being marketed via Rotary. Over the coming years the album will provide a substantial revenue source for the charity. It is one of a number of projects – including music albums, concert tours, plays, musicals and TV productions – produced at God's Golden Acre.

On 17th October 2004 Heather achieved another of her long-held dreams. The opening of the Young Zulu Warrior Theatre at God's Golden Acre was an important milestone in the development of the community because it opened up a range of new opportunities, not only for the children of Khayelihle, but also for those in the valley.

At last there was a professional stage to express the enormous range of talent in the field of music and dance that is so vividly expressed in Zulu culture – it was indeed the world's first Zulu theatre and would act as a magnet for talent throughout the Valley of a Thousand Hills... bringing revenue, opportunity and perhaps fame to God's Golden Acre. Talented young Zulus from the valley found themselves presented with exciting opportunities to work alongside professional actors and musicians from the international world of theatre and music.

Lynne Maree of KwaZulu-Natal Dance Link was among the old friends present at the opening night of the theatre and it was an evening when she was able to look back with nostalgia upon a long association with God's Golden Acre and its young dancers. She wrote:

> In March 2000 I was told that the offer that KwaZulu-Natal Dance Link had made, to run weekly dance workshops "somewhere", had been looked on positively by someone called Heather Reynolds who lived out somewhere off the N3 along a dirt track, and that I should visit her.
>
> I drove up past a beautiful tree into a ramshackle parking lot covered in bougainvillea, found an open door that went into a living-room-cum-warehouse full of mattresses and piles of clothes. A quietly spoken man (Patrick) was the only person to appear. He greeted me and suggested that I wait for Heather. That was then.
>
> The warmth and immediacy and rampant readiness to grab opportunities for "her" children took me into her spell, as it does everyone, and four-and-a-half frustrating and incredibly positive years have produced a theatre, a performing arts company of accomplished singers and dancers who did an international tour to the UK, three annual performances of our Dance for Youth production on a specially built theatre in the open air, and a happy relationship between God's Golden Acre and a multitude of teachers and members of KZN Dance Link. Long may it last!"

Bronwen Reynolds was also among the guests and she recorded the poignancy of that memorable day in her diary:

> It's a hot summer afternoon, and as I drive into the parking lot at God's Golden Acre and park in the shade of the enormous fig tree, I sit for a moment and watch the scene before me. Dogs chase each another playfully across the sand, two Zulu dancers in traditional dress carry a pile of chairs into the community dining room, and a group of children deep in conversation suddenly burst into peals of laughter and run off, to where I assume the distant sounds of singing are coming from.

The rhythmic beating of a drum pulsates in the sticky heat as I exit the car and catch sight of my father Patrick coming across the parking lot from his studio.

Entering the coolness of the double-storey thatch building, with its generous roof sloping in graceful curves almost to the ground, we find a seat and observe the final preparations while the crowds who have come for this momentous occasion enjoy a traditional meal in the dining room.

Here in the theatre, Thulabona, the artistic director, fiddles with the spotlights; a young boy carries in a rawhide drum and positions it behind the *inthingos* − stage props made of thin branches roped together. Two men with beads of perspiration on their foreheads carry in extra speakers and begin to connect them, as their companions who stand and watch the process give very vocal, if not entirely helpful, input in Zulu.

Mum arrives, and a cloud of activity trails her as she gives her attention to each of the voices that clamour for her attention, needing decisions and direction for the multitude of tasks that still need to be completed before the ceremony can begin. At last the moment arrives, and the simple, ethnic interior of the theatre is hidden by the 550 bodies who, seated and standing, form a buzz of anticipation, mindless of the summer heat.

Affectionate greetings abounded across the crowded room, as old friends reacquainted themselves, once more gathered in solidarity for the cause of the children touched by God's Golden Acre. Bronwen continues:

The lights are dimmed, and the explosive beating of several traditional drums suddenly resonates through the building, vibrating through the structure and into the very chests of the audience, as a line of Zulu men dressed in traditional animal skins bursts onto the stage in a vibrant and energetic dance. Lifting their shields in unity and moving in fluid solidarity, their bodies hammer out an expression of the passion and pride that resides in the soul of each member of the Zulu nation.

The audience bursts into loud applause and the ceremony begins as Heather welcomes the attending dignitaries, management board members, staff, supporters and old friends. Scrutinizing the faces before her as she attempts to express her gratitude to each one for their involvement in the story of God's Golden Acre, she is overcome, and is stilled for a moment by a wave of tears.

Looking at the faces of the audience, I see several knowing smiles match my own, as together we recognize the Heather we know: strong enough to command an army, yet so full of the emotion that drives her that tears are never far from her and may descend at a moment's notice.

Lynne Maree of Dance Link introduces the premiere of *Thula Sizwe*, the drama production written and produced by Heather that was inspired by her work in the valley. The opening scenes, in which a Zulu king and his wife are killed by a rival tribe, leaving his children orphaned and alone, are emotionally laden and close to the hearts of many present. The powerful performances of the actors and the ever-changing scenes – from deep rural locations to a modern urban setting complete with taxi drivers and gossiping domestic workers, keep the audience riveted until the end.

Emerging from the theatre building, and gathering on the grass outside, we find that the summer heat has been replaced by darkening skies and a cold wind that swiftly ascends the crest of the hill on which we stand. As the storm approaches, and people scurry to their cars, I am reminded that, like the shifting weather, change is inevitable. For all those involved at God's Golden Acre, change has been, and will continue to be, an integral part of the process, and certainly for all the children whose lives have been touched by the work here, it is a change worth welcoming.

Yet behind the scenes of joy, and the chance of progress and consolidation, the fundamental purpose and role of the sanctuary had again been underlined just a few days before the opening of the theatre. Both the staff and children were in mourning for the death of a much-loved infant of God's Golden Acre. The tragedy was recorded by Bronwen Reynolds:

As I sit reading through this manuscript, surrounded by visiting family, and my mother and father sitting on the bed, one of the caregivers, Gogo Elina, comes to let Mum know that four-year-old Sne has just passed away. We'd all known that her time was fast approaching. Now, as Mum gives instructions to have everyone gather together for prayers and songs, she and Gogo Elina begin to sing a hymn of praise for the life that has just ended. Their voices lift together spontaneously until Mum's voice cracks with emotion and she can't sing any more.

The low Zulu voice sings on steadily as Mum's face creases with grief... for a brief moment, the characteristic strength gives way to a threatening flood of sadness. And I wonder how she does it day after day. But then I realize this is *why* she does it. I see in her eyes the peace that comes from knowing that she has fulfilled in some small way the vow she made to her God, to "never let them die all alone". She knows that Sne has passed away surrounded by people who loved her, and that makes it somehow seem worthwhile.

While the staff members go to Cato Ridge to arrange the death certificate, I hear Mum dialling a phone number. She begins to chat, and I realize she's phoned my brother Brendan in Holland. Her voice, a little thin from the crying and singing, warms as she teases him about sleeping late. They talk for a while and Mum starts to sing a funny little song from a movie we'd watched many years ago. I have to smile, and sitting here in a blanket on the armchair, watching my family, I realize that I am truly blessed, and given the chance, I'd not change a thing. The reality of life – and death – reminds us to value the precious arbitrary moments that would otherwise pass us by.

42
THE FOOTBALL
MIRACLE

The world of show business was not the
only one where Heather had ambitions for
young Zulus, and not the only one where miracles would happen in 2004. She believed strongly that organized sport, and
specifically football, could help to instil hope and a sense of
direction in the thousands of youngsters in the valley who had
no outlets for their energy and natural aggression.

Mr Mapanga of the Thandanani Football League was visiting
God's Golden Acre one day when he heard for the first time
that Heather had managed to develop a connection with
Martin Edwards, the president of Manchester United Football
Club, and through him Dave Richards, the chairman of the
Premier League in England. He realized that both Edwards
and Richards were in positions of power and influence and
might be able to help the development of youth football in the
valley beyond people's wildest dreams and imagination. It was
incredible news.

In fact Mr Mapanga's eyes opened so wide it seemed they
would consume his cheeks. He stared out of the window of
the office – his mouth gaping. The mind of the man was obviously racing at the possibilities of a connection between his
humble and largely impoverished organization, and in the first
place, the president of the most famous football club in the
world, and in the second, the world's top football league, the

English Premier League. At length he let out what seemed to be an enormous whistling sound and turned his gaze upon Heather, with a beaming smile upon his face.

It might possibly have been the best and most exciting piece of news that Mr Mapanga had ever received in his life – and yet it was so implausible nobody would have blamed him if he had dismissed it as a joke. Mr Mapanga, head of marketing and publicity of the Thandanani League, had been meeting Heather together with Nkosi Mlaba, honorary president of the God's Golden Acre Junior League Association. They were putting together a memorandum of agreement between the Association and the League. The former would be affiliated to the latter – and the League would organize the administration of, and arrange the fixtures for, the junior games. If ambitions were to be realized, there might be over 100 teams eventually – enabling boys from the age of twelve to 20 to play competitive football on a regular basis.

At the time, Heather still did not know whether her meetings with Martin Edwards and Dave Richards would take place – or if they would help God's Golden Acre. However, she was so excited at the prospect of a meeting with them that she could not resist telling both men about it. The logistics of maintaining and sustaining a successful youth football programme had been worrying Heather for some months. They had three grounds – that the clubs of the Thandanani League shared – and a number of "kick-abouts" for practice. However, there was every prospect that more than the initially agreed 68 Zulu youth teams, at various age levels, would – in fairness to all – have to be extended across the huge rural district of KwaXimba, and beyond into other valley areas.

All her life Heather had followed the English Football League and was a supporter of Manchester United. She felt at this time that she needed top-class outside help and advice, and also a greater level of funding than she could obtain from any local corporate sponsorship. Perhaps, she reasoned, the answer lay in the English Premier League. BBC producer Bill Hamilton, a qualified football referee, had warned her – while filming at God's Golden Acre – that it would be very hard to get direct access to any of Britain's top professional football league clubs. He told Heather they were all besieged by charities looking for financial support or kit sponsorship. The only way in – he advised – was if she could find someone who could be persuaded that the God's Golden Acre Junior League Association deserved priority treatment.

Within weeks, by sheer coincidence, at a meeting at God's Golden Acre she found herself talking about football to a visitor who, it turned out, knew someone very important at Manchester United. By 2004, Martin Edwards had retired from the job of running the club as chairman, and had divested his considerable shareholding. He was enjoying the more honorary position as its president. However, he remained a man of considerable status, importance and influence in European football. Heather was astonished at the unexpected connection her friend was able to offer.

Martin Edwards had been a director of Manchester United since 1970 and succeeded his father Louis as chairman in 1980. The following year he became the club's first chief executive, a position he held for almost 20 years until August 2000. He ran the club during the most successful period in its history. In the more than 30 years that Martin Edwards was a member of the Board of Directors, Manchester United won seven League titles, seven FA Cups, the European Cup, the European Cup-Winners Cup, the League Cup, the UEFA Super Cup, the Inter-Continental Cup, and seven Charity Shields. It was an awesome record – probably unequalled in the history of professional club administration at board level.

The prospect of meeting this very senior man in a world of which she knew nothing made Heather nervous. It was February 2004 when she and Patrick were driven up the M6 motorway in central England to the home of Martin and Sue

Edwards for Heather's first meeting with the couple. The latter had kindly agreed to meet the Reynolds to hear about God's Golden Acre and its proposed Junior Football League. Characteristically, Heather prayed aloud in the back of the car: "Oh dear heavenly Father, I wish to thank you for this day, Lord, and thank you for our many, many blessings. Father, today we ask you to be with us in this meeting. We ask you to guide us with wisdom, Lord, to say and do the things that need to be said and done, Father. We always trust in you, Lord, and your will of what the outcome will be; we shall accept that graciously, Father. So, Father, we ask you to be with Martin and Sue, to open their ears and their heart so they might hear and see the things I shall show to them today. Let them be an instrument of your will, that we may reach and serve these many, many, wonderful disadvantaged children, Father. Amen."

Soon the car was approaching the gates of the Edwards' house in Cheshire and the host himself was at the front door to usher the Reynolds into his home. They remained together for nearly three hours. Heather told Martin Edwards that financial help to kick-start the football league could change the face of the entire valley for the underprivileged children. Any youngster growing up in a normal society – being fed, clothed and educated – and then being put into disciplined sporting activities had a better chance of growing up to become a good citizen within his or her community. Children involved in sport were not so likely to be distracted into a harmful lifestyle.

"You don't find them sitting on the grass verges, forming gangs and using drugs. So it's that important to us. With positive things going on around them, our children can become not only good sportsmen but also hopefully be sent back to school to become the next generation of professionals, and business people – tomorrow's teachers, doctors, plumbers and electricians. It is vitally important that we are able to put them into a disciplined environment like sport, where they can grow up and develop a sense of responsibility. They deserve that chance," she said. Heather came away more than delighted with what the president of Manchester United said to her.

On the journey home she said to Patrick: "The problem is that people like the Edwards are bombarded with requests and pestered continually by people trying to use them. However, the moment Martin stepped out of that doorway I knew he wanted to meet us. His wife Sue was extremely warm and it was clear she is a Christian, and committed to many charities for children. So her heart was in the right place and she put me at ease."

Back in KwaXimba, influential people like Nkosi Mlaba and Mr Mapanga, who knew about the meeting, were praying for it to be successful. It was not every day that someone they knew had an opportunity to meet a person of the calibre and status of the man who has run Manchester United for three decades.

The new friendship with Martin Edwards began to bear fruit for Heather's football ambitions in the Valley of a Thousand Hills within a few months. In November 2004 she was back in England and this time was the president's guest at Old Trafford Stadium where she was thrilled to be conducted round the club's famous museum with its awesome collection of trophies and memorabilia of a hundred years of Manchester United. On this day Heather also met David Daly of Nike, who control the Manchester United kit and equipment brand. He was deeply moved by her presentation of the predicament and social exclusion facing thousands of children in the valley and pledged to help her in whatever way he could by referring her through the organization.

The following week, thanks to Martin Edwards, Heather was able to meet Dave Richards, the chairman of the Premier League and one of the most powerful figures in British football. He turned out to be a man with a compassionate interest in the safety and well-being of children, with strong links to the Football Foundation and also the National Society for the Prevention of Cruelty to Children. Fortunately for Heather he had also spent part of his professional life in South Africa and was well acquainted with the crisis facing the rural parts of the country. He was moved by what Heather had to say and was struck by her sincerity. It was a day he was flying out to Madrid to watch England play Spain but he found time to take her personally in his car to meet David Davies, the executive director of the Football Association; Jane Bateman, head of international relations at the FA; and Alastair Bennett, director of external relations at the Football Foundation. Further meetings followed with senior Nike executives in London and Holland, so that by Christmas 2004 Heather was able to look ahead to the future with confidence for making things happen in her very African world of football.

For her it was yet another miracle. God had once again answered her prayers. She now looks forward to the day – and she believes it will happen – when a steady stream of young men from the valley can establish themselves as international star players, thus feeding the dreams and aspirations of an even younger generation. She believes that with the help of funding from English football through the Premier League and the Football Association, the God's Golden Acre Junior Football Association and its academy can become a benchmark for youth football in the rural areas of southern Africa – laying down an infrastructure for other government-funded projects to follow.

By early 2005 Heather had asked the Premier League and the FA to help fund a project that would include a multi-sports AstroTurf stadium at God's Golden Acre with floodlights and modern changing facilities, and the introduction of FA coaches in KwaZulu-Natal to train African coaches. The stadium, she hopes, would be the home of the football academy for the Valley of a Thousand Hills and the source from which her Junior League would thrive with up to 30 full-size pitches equipped with changing rooms and toilets in the valley itself, plus dozens of kick-abouts for the children to play on – alongside valley schools. She was hoping Nike would also assist in the funding.

If this further miracle happens, then thousands of boys and girls who have previously faced social exclusion will have the chance to play organized sport for the first time.

43

THE PARABLE OF THE
GOOD SAMARITAN

Late one night, Heather was driving one of
the God's Golden Acre vehicles along
National Highway 3, the motorway that acts as the artery link-
ing Durban on the south east coast to the north. National
Highway 3 is imprinted upon the heart of rural South Africa
and continues through Pietermaritzburg, Ladysmith,
Harrismith and then Heidelberg, before reaching
Johannesburg.

It was misty with torrents of rain, driven by high winds,
lashing the front and sides of the vehicle, reducing visibility to
a few yards in the watery haze. There were few cars on the
road. She was travelling after a night out, with a group of volunteers, south from Pietermaritzburg, towards God's Golden
Acre at Cato Ridge. They were sitting in the back, and most
were asleep. At that moment, in the vehicle travelling on the
national highway, came the appropriate ending to a book
about the life of Heather Reynolds. It mirrored the parable of
the Good Samaritan.

Suddenly in the corner of her eye, through lashing rain and
the mist, Heather noticed a man walking on crutches along
the side of the road. It was like an apparition. Many people in
the same circumstances – stormy weather on a dark, wet
night where it is dangerous to stop because of vehicle hijackings – would have driven on, assuming, or hoping, that it was

just a figment of their imagination. Heather, however, made a decision instantly. She called out: "Sorry, guys, I've got to stop. I cannot go on. I think there is a man on crutches walking along the main highway back there."

She stopped the vehicle, gently reversed back in the dark, and suddenly an African in his forties appeared by the side of the passenger seat window. Heather told him quickly: "Come on, jump in." It was not an appropriate thing to say in the circumstances, but she did not want to remain parked on the side of the road for any longer than she had to be.

She said later: "I'll never forget the pain on his face when he tried with his one leg to get in beside us. In a flash I realized he was an amputee. I caught that look, and I was sucked into all the emotions that he was feeling. The pain. The frustration. The anger. The cold winds and the lashing rain. He had endured so much. We helped him into the passenger seat and I asked him where he had come from. He told me he was Mr Zungu and he was a diabetic and had had his leg amputated at Edendale Hospital. I was astonished.

"'The hospital is way on the other side of Pietermaritzsburg – on the other side of town. How long have you been walking on your crutches?'

"'Nine hours,' he replied. 'I was discharged from hospital this afternoon at three o'clock. But I didn't have money to catch a local taxi or bus, so I just started walking.'"

It became clear that Mr Zungu had been sent away with no food, nothing to drink, with nobody to turn to for help. The only way he could get home was to take his crutches and walk. He'd been hobbling along for nine solid hours when she found him. Heather recalls: "It was amazing. My thoughts were racing and it brought me close to tears. Not one single person had stopped to offer him a lift. How many vehicles must have passed him that day? Thousands and thousands of cars and lorries! How could every single person have passed him? What's wrong with us?

"Imagine, you are driving along and you see a man trying to walk with crutches on one leg and you drive by; you do nothing. Surely, somebody could have stopped and picked him up. Even the police patrol cars must have gone along the N3 highway several times during those nine hours.

"I asked him where he was going to and I could not make out the area where he lived from what he told me, but I followed his directions and it turned out to be the main road down to KwaXimba, and of course I knew it well. If he had continued walking on his own it would have been another seven or eight hours before he reached home. I don't think he would have made it. He would have become delirious, either with cold and exhaustion, or sheer weakness. He might have died on that road.

"He sat hunched up beside me and he clearly was at the point of total exhaustion. I put the heater on full blast to warm him and eventually, after 40 minutes, we reached the point on the valley road nearest to his home. He was so grateful he was unable to express himself. I gave him some money, we said some prayers, and we sang a little song together in the vehicle before he left us. Looking back, I could not imagine where Mr Zungu's thoughts must have gone that day. What would have been the most dominant? Would it have been anger, frustration, sadness or despair? All those things must have crossed his feelings during those nine hours on crutches. The poor fellow had only just been amputated. He should have been lying down on his back.

"So were the hundreds, if not thousands of people who passed him by that day on National Highway 3 by definition uncaring or cruel? 'Judge not', the Bible tells us – but one answer to that question could be that it's always easier to find a reason, or excuse, for not doing something, not to help someone. It's easier not to take responsibility for, or not to get involved with, the problems and difficulties of our brothers and sisters.

"Self-justification can start at a personal level, like walking past a beggar on a street corner and turning our head away. It is an attitude of mind that is likely to lead to absence of community spirit, a detachment of responsibility for our obligations towards our fellow human beings. Is this the harvest of the nuclear age – the 'me' generation? The choice is ours. In the same way, if we don't respond to the desperate plight of a generation of children in Africa, and in the other AIDS hotspots in our world, we will be sowing the seeds ultimately of the destruction of those societies that have abandoned them.

"Nearly 5 million people in Africa are HIV-positive and by 2010 there could be up to 4.8 million maternal orphans. Without hope they will turn to crime, drugs and prostitution. Without help and guidance they will not be able to take their rightful place in society. The possibility of a feral society developing within our midst and the implications of that are too awful to contemplate. What would then be the solution to that problem? Shooting young criminals, as has been done in some other parts of the world?

"Are we going to secure the future of the orphans? Future generations will hold us responsible for the world we bequeath to them. Children will look back and ask us uncomprehendingly: 'Why did you not do something? How could you abandon all those children, allow so many to suffer and die?'

"Well, that scenario thankfully hasn't played itself out yet, and we still have enough time to make a difference. As Christians it's so important to remember the two greatest laws: 'Love the Lord your God,' and 'Love your neighbour'. Matthew 25 makes one think very deeply. When you call, 'Lord, Lord', will Jesus say, 'I know you not'? Did you feed him? Did you clothe him? Did you give him something to drink? Did you visit him in prison? This is a clear directive of what Jesus expects from us.

"My journey through life with God, serving him, has taught me the power of prayer, the power of love, and the incredible healing power of compassion and forgiveness. To every one of you who has travelled with me through the pages of this book, I pray that in some way my life has touched yours. Together let us reach out to enrich the lives of millions of little children who would otherwise face a life without hope.

"I truly believe that as brothers and sisters in Christ, humanitarians, people from all races, colour or creeds, we can combine our efforts to change this world into a better place. As a global nation let us take responsibility: what we invest in the future of a child, we invest in the future of our world. God bless."